Edith Tudor-Hart
In the Shadow of Tyranny

HATJE CANTZ
NATIONAL GALLERIES SCOTLAND
WIEN MUSEUM

Edited by Duncan Forbes on behalf of the
National Galleries of Scotland, Edinburgh,
and Wien Museum, Vienna

With essays by Duncan Forbes,
Anton Holzer, and Roberta McGrath

Edith Tudor-Hart
In the Shadow of Tyranny

HATJE CANTZ
NATIONAL GALLERIES SCOTLAND
WIEN MUSEUM

Retrospect

I wanted
to be the flame
of my time
or
part of its flame

I was its shadow
or
part
of its shadow

My time
was the time
of fury—
shadow of fury

My time
was the time
of helplessness—
shadow of helplessness

the time
of tyranny—
shadow of tyranny

I wanted
to be the banner
of my time
or a shred of its banner

Banner
of flame
of fury
of helplessness
of tyranny
or its shred
or part
of its shadow

Erich Fried

Contents

Foreword

Edith Tudor-Hart (née Suschitzky, 1908–1973) is one of the most intriguing photographers of interwar Europe. Born in Vienna, she studied at the Bauhaus before throwing herself wholeheartedly into a life of politics and photography. Pursuing a career as a photojournalist and portrait photographer, Tudor-Hart was recruited by the Comintern in Vienna in the late nineteen-twenties; she continued working as a low-level Soviet agent in London after her marriage to an English doctor in 1933. With intelligence and aesthetic sophistication, her photography provides sharp testimony to an embattled political culture in both Austria and Britain over three turbulent decades.

This exhibition has been curated by the National Galleries of Scotland in collaboration with the Wien Museum and, for the first time, brings together Edith Tudor-Hart's work from collections in Edinburgh, London, and Vienna. In 1951, shortly after the initial interrogation of the Soviet spy Kim Philby, Tudor-Hart destroyed her photographic records, including most of her prints and some negatives. Her negative archive was generously donated by the Suschitzky family to the National Galleries of Scotland in 2004, initiating an exhibition project of detailed investigation and reconstruction. Crucially, this has included the fabrication of new silver-gelatin prints and, latterly, inkjet prints from the photographer's archive. Many of her photographs can now be viewed for the first time.

In retrospect, Edith Tudor-Hart was a Viennese photographer of penetrating insight as she sought to tell a story about a city straining under the push and pull of opposing forces. In Britain, her grounding in the realist dynamic of continental photography lent her work a special charge; British photographers of the thirties appear rather dilettantish by comparison. Tudor-Hart's story is one of political and cultural struggle, certainly, but also one of exchange and continuity.

The exhibition is curated by Duncan Forbes, formerly Senior Curator at the National Galleries of Scotland and now Director/Curator of the Fotomuseum Winterthur. Its organization has only been possible because of the outstanding generosity of individuals and organizations: most especially Wolfgang Suschitzky and, in Edinburgh, the Robert Mapplethorpe Foundation, to whom we are very grateful.

Christopher Baker, Director, Scottish National Portrait Gallery, Edinburgh
Wolfgang Kos, Director, Wien Museum, Vienna

Edith Tudor-Hart
In the Shadow of Tyranny

Duncan Forbes

On a late afternoon in May 1933, a young woman, well dressed, of moderate height and wearing horn-rimmed spectacles, was arrested as she fled in a taxi from the Goethe Bookshop in Vienna's ninth district.[1] This, at least, was the description provided by the police reports, traces of an investigation that appears to have been less than arduous. The prisoner, "Fräulein Braun," revealed herself to be Edith Suschitzky, who confessed that she was a press photographer doing a favor for a man whom she had met in a café some months before and whose name and description she could no longer remember (fig. 1). The sealed letters found in her possession were, she claimed, to be delivered unopened by her to the bookshop in aid of the charitable refugee organization, the Rote Hilfe (Red Aid).[2]

A routine political arrest for the time, perhaps, but one that would have enduring consequences: for the twenty-four-year-old Suschitzky, certainly (she would suffer police surveillance and periodic interrogation for the rest of her life); but also for the history of espionage in Britain; as well as for the evolution of British photography. The essay that follows concentrates rather more on the latter, an effort to provide a fuller picture of Edith Tudor Hart's photography and the political culture that informed it. Versions of this story have been told before, particularly during the nineteen-eighties, but in an atmosphere marked by the silences and repressions of the Cold War. Such silences were pernicious, if understandable, and served to prevent key conjunctions in Tudor-Hart's life from being critically considered. Crucially, these included the conjunctions "Communist" and "photographer," and "German-speaking exile" and "photographer." Here I open these terms out for consideration in relation to Tudor-Hart's biography, above all in examining the transitions in her practice. What happens when a politically sophisticated photographer, trained in techniques of realist reportage connected to an insurgent socialist movement, pitches up in Britain and confronts a proletarian culture with far narrower resources? The results are intriguing and contradictory, at once stultifying and transformative. The conjunctions articulated above remained troubled and unresolved; this accounts in part for the tremendous pressures Tudor-Hart came under. (Whatever one's view of the political nightmare in which she became trapped, it is impossible, I think, to fault her courage.) What follows is by no means definitive: I don't, for example, consider Tudor-Hart's Jewishness, an identity she was resolute in ignoring. Nor am I particularly focused here on her significance as a woman photographer. My interest in Edith Tudor-Hart was initiated when I began to sense that the story told about her in the eighties was just a little too convenient, a little too English. My ambition here is to provoke a more open and dynamic afterlife.

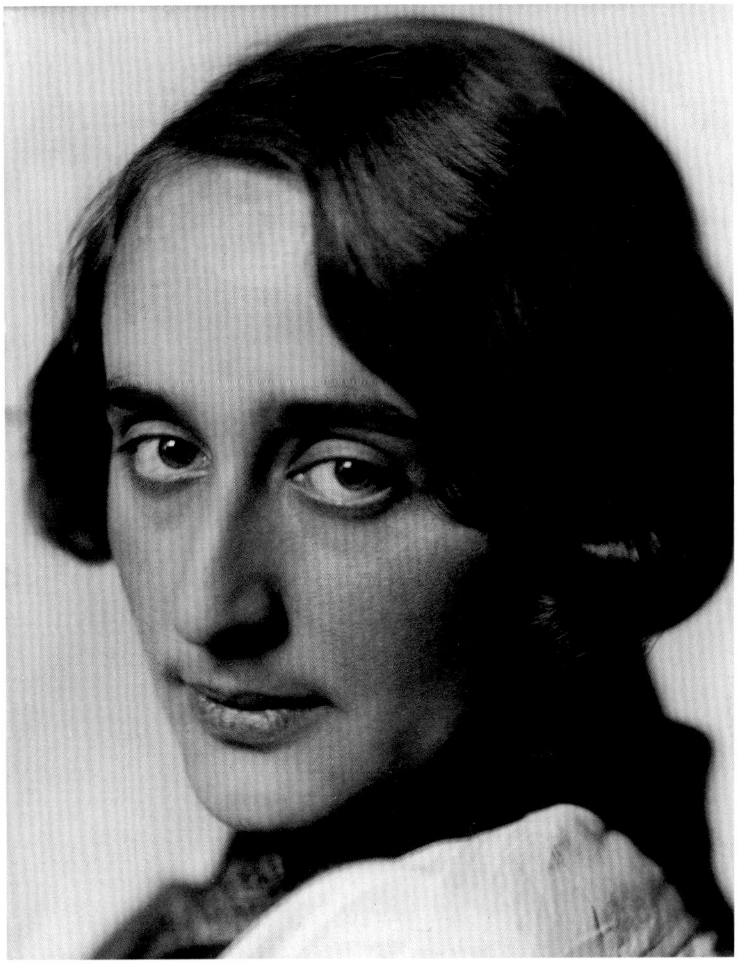

Fig. 1
Rudolf Bauer, *Edith Suschitzky, Vienna*, ca. 1928

Edith Tudor-Hart in Vienna

At the time of her arrest, Edith Suschitzky was, in fact, working as a courier for the Communist Party of Austria (KPÖ) as it countered a dramatic escalation of state repression and prepared for a future of illegality. The Goethe Bookshop was a drop for the Viennese party, and the letters Suschitzky carried contained mimeographed requests to provincial cells for detailed reports of their situation. Inspired by the example of fascist Italy, the Austrian Chancellor, Engelbert Dollfuss, appointed in May 1932, was urgently strengthening his anti-democratic authority. By Spring 1933 the Austrian parliament had been abolished and the constitution abandoned. Dollfuss mounted a massive attack on the courts, introducing extensive press censorship and banning strikes and political demonstrations. With some eight hundred Communists rounded up in the wake of the May Day demonstrations in 1933, the KPÖ's need for reinvigorated communications was urgent.[3] A circular found in Suschitzky's possession called for a "United Front" in support of political prisoners in Austria and Germany and for a campaign to send delegates to the International Anti-Fascist Workers Congress in Copenhagen. It demanded the establishment of opposition groups amongst Social Democratic workers, ordered protests against the banning of the KPÖ, and encouraged an increase in the dissemination of party propaganda. In retrospect this proved to be a crucial turning point in the history of the KPÖ. Its inability to act decisively against the rise of Austro-Fascism—along with the greater failure of the German Communist movement—broke decisively the momentum of the Russian Revolution and helped push the Comintern toward the policy of cross-class collaboration known as the Popular Front.

The police reports suggest that at the time of her arrest Suschitzky was already an experienced Communist courier and activist. Having searched her parents' home—where she lived with her younger brother, Wolfgang—the authorities easily gathered evidence of her complicity. There they found a mimeograph machine; an appeal from the party for increased financial contributions; various political pamphlets, books, and newspapers; letters in English and German (including love letters from her English fiancé, as well as others "with political content"); and a number of translations from English and German, one of which was a biography of Lenin. The police also confiscated a mass of photographic material: negatives ordered alphabetically and a number of prints, including photographs of a recent KPÖ demonstration in Vienna, as well as a portrait of the General Secretary of the Communist Party of Great Britain (CPGB), Harry Pollitt. A letter from a relative in Berlin advised in some detail about how to pursue a professional career, offering guidance as to how to make her photographic essays more commercial. As Suschitzky informed her interrogators, she had recently published photographs in a number of European illustrated journals, including *Der Kuckuck,* the *Arbeiter-Illustrierte-Zeitung,* and *Die Bühne.*

It was Edith Suschitzky's arrest that propelled her into exile. Somehow she reached a deal with her captors, marrying an English doctor, Alexander Tudor-Hart, in Vienna in August 1933, leaving Austria by the following October. She took with her some negatives released by the authorities, but little else (a collection of her belongings, including photographs, was destroyed as the police depots began to overflow in 1938). Her brother, exposed by her arrest, left for Holland soon after and joined her later as a student in London. Her father, overwhelmed by the destruction of the democratic workers' movement, committed suicide in April 1934. Suschitzky's forced departure from Vienna—she would never return—closed a chapter in her young life scarred by personal trauma. But exile is also a political fact and requires us to interrogate what today is highly unusual: a complexly politicized, youthful subjectivity. (The historian, Eric Hobsbawm, who grew up in Vienna, noted that during the interwar period "one acquired political consciousness as naturally as sexual awareness."[4]) To account for Tudor-Hart's photography, we must dig a little deeper.

The first surviving trace of the adult Suschitzky is a blurred snapshot from 1924, showing her alongside the children of a nursery school in Vienna's tenth district, the Haus der Kinder (fig. 2). Suschitzky had recently joined the school as an unpaid teacher, working with a group of young Jewish women as part of a collective under the guidance of a Prague educationalist, Lili Roubiczek.

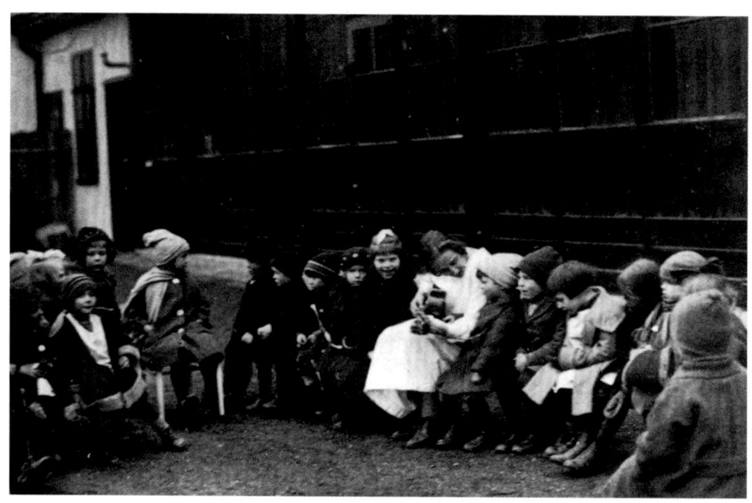

Fig. 2
Photographer unknown, *Edith Suschitzky and the Children of the Haus der Kinder, Vienna,* 1924

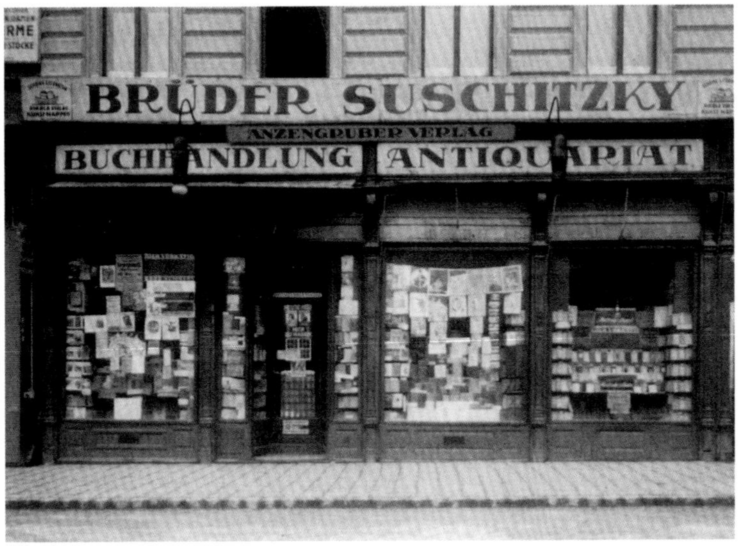

Fig. 3
Photographer unknown, *Bookshop "Brüder Suschitzky," Favoritenstrasse 57, Vienna,* ca. 1925

Inspired by the ideas of Maria Montessori, Suschitzky's engagement with an independent pedagogy was vital.[5] It provided an intellectual resource, a wellspring of political activity and a network of contacts that she would draw on throughout her life. For the apprentices, Roubiczek's communal methods were highly demanding: teachers lived in the school during the week and a year of practical work was accompanied by theoretical training in the evenings, including study in the natural sciences, languages, sociology, psychology, and architecture. Those who coped well were then sent abroad to earn a Montessori diploma, permitting them to teach children of ages three to ten. Suschitzky, still only sixteen, accompanied another student to London for a three-month course in April 1925, her first visit to Britain.

Although by 1930 Montessori teaching had become a core component of the edifice of Social Democratic education in Vienna, its roots in the tenth district were initially a philanthropic response to the acute privation of life in the immediate postwar period. Since the eighteen-sixties, Favoriten had grown to become one of Vienna's largest working-class districts, with its brickworks, heavy industry, and smaller craft business sprawling out across cheap land to the south of the city.[6] Favoriten's streets were a seedbed of Social Democratic radicalism, and the Suschitzky family fought local bureaucracy to open a socialist bookshop and publishing business there in 1901, the first such establishment in a district of over 120,000 residents (fig. 3). Edith Suschitzky's parents were bourgeois socialists in a committed, if somewhat paternalistic, vein: freethinkers, pacifists, temperance workers, promoting working-class emancipation within the lively infrastructure of worker education provided by the Austrian Social Democratic Workers' Party (SDAP). Between 1904 and the liquidation of the business by the Nazis in 1938, the Anzengruber-Verlag published over three hundred texts, mobilizing Enlightenment values to counter Vienna's endemic inequality. Suschitzky had access to a wide variety of reforming literature, from worker poetry and fiction to tracts on the women's movement, sexual emancipation, and pedagogical reform.[7]

Edith Suschitzky's political subjectivity, then, was forged against a backdrop of powerfully formative working-class politics and, in the shadow of the First World War, dramatically telescoped experience.[8] The impact of war in Favoriten was direct and brought the young quickly to organized action. Already by the summer of 1914 half the district schools had been commandeered for war purposes; as the transports of wounded started to arrive, children were mobilized to collect smoking materials for soldiers or to aid women in digging thousands of square meters of vegetable gardens. As the war ended, Favoriten children, weakened by tuberculosis and perpetual hunger, became a focus of concerted philanthropic action—Suschitzky herself was sent to Sweden, returning to Vienna after a few months strengthened and better nourished. Education was a preeminent postwar concern, as socialists and bourgeois philanthropists alike attempted to coral street children into makeshift schools that were little more than soup kitchens. In a period marked by acute awareness of the Russian Revolution, Suschitzky's emerging political sense would have been inflected by an ethic of urgent, practical action.

The politics finding form were Leninist and revolutionary, but it is impossible now to pin down its exact evolution. As histories of the period recall, young intellectuals—men and boys especially—assumed political leadership early as movements of secondary pupils fought against the reinstatement of a postwar school regime according to capitalist priorities.[9] Suschitzky was a few years younger than the leading cohort, but she had close links to them, in part through the activism of the Favoriten schools, but also through her involvement in the circles of creative youth attached to the philanthropist Eugenie Schwarzwald. During the nineteen-twenties, Schwarzwald funded and organized an elaborate series of winter and summer educational colonies for Viennese school children, offering a restorative mix of sport, community, and immersion in nature.[10] Suschitzky visited Grundlsee as a teenager, Schwarzwald's favorite summer retreat, mingling with a progressive fraction of Viennese scholars, artists, and writers (her brother later recalled that she was taught music by the composer Arnold Schönberg). Other colonies and associations—those organized by the

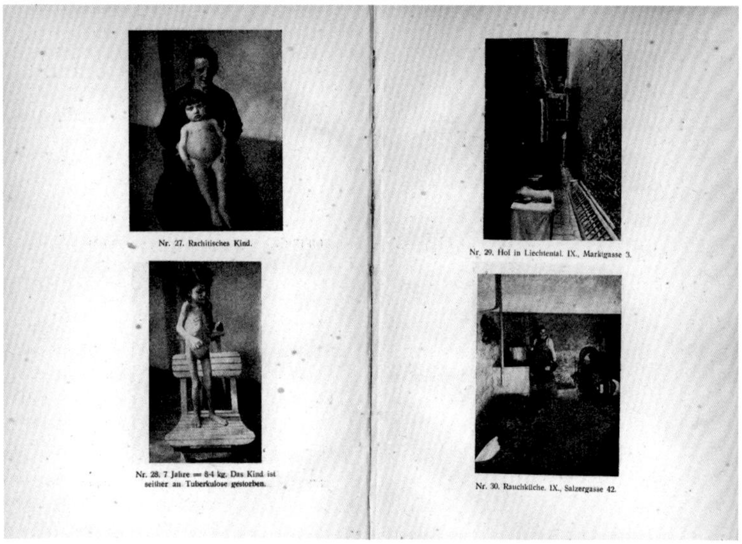

Fig. 4
Anton and Hans Bock in *The Misery of Vienna* by Bruno Frei (Vienna, 1921)

Vereinigung Sozialistischer Mittelschüler (Union of Socialist Secondary Pupils) or the Arbeitsgemeischaft Sozialistsicher Erzieher (Association of Socialist Educators)—were more explicitly politicized, offering a variety of strategies in the struggle for school reform and an anti-authoritarian pedagogy. Although by 1923 the leadership of the school movement had shifted from revolutionary optimism to Social Democratic reformism, Leninist infiltration was commonplace. A common camp joke—reflecting the fluidity of youthful political identification—was that you went to bed a Social Democrat and woke up a Communist.[11]

In her memoir of the period, Genia Quittner describes the transition of a sixteen-year-old girl to Communism: from the Marxist seminars of the student movement, to an understanding of the "opportunism and social treachery" (Lenin's terms) of the Social Democratic leadership; from a spectator of the KPÖ's rallies outside Vienna's Votive Church, to finding her voice as a leftist opponent within the Social Democratic youth movement.[12] Similar moments may have marked Edith Suschitzky's political evolution, complicated by her entanglement in the contradictions of individual freedom and collective action that were central to socialist pedagogy. If one text illuminates the worldview of secular Jewish radicalism that helped shape her, it is Bruno Frei's remarkable work of reportage on the abject conditions in Vienna, *Das Elend Wiens,* published in 1921 and almost certainly for sale in her parents' bookshop. Frei's clear-headed indictment of capitalist inequality, his prophetic emphasis on the dangers of rising nationalism and anti-Semitism, and his commitment to youth as an agent of revolutionary change inform one of the most powerful political tracts of the interwar period. It was also one of the earliest books of the Austrian left to publish photographs to sustain its argument, including several dismal interiors from Favoriten's crowded tenements known as the Zinskasernen (rent barracks). As Frei put it in his foreword, "the images themselves are illustrations for war and revolution" (fig. 4).[13]

It was this complex political awakening that made Edith Suschitzky a Communist Party activist in both Austria and Britain and a willing recruit to the Communist International (or Comintern), the internationalist arm of the Soviet state. When exactly she joined the party remains unclear: she is recorded as working for the CPGB as "Betty Gray" in 1927, and it is likely that she already had links to the tiny, sectarian KPÖ, not least through the Montessori movement which contained a number of prominent Communists. An Austrian agent, Arnold Deutsch, whom Suschitzky first met in Vienna

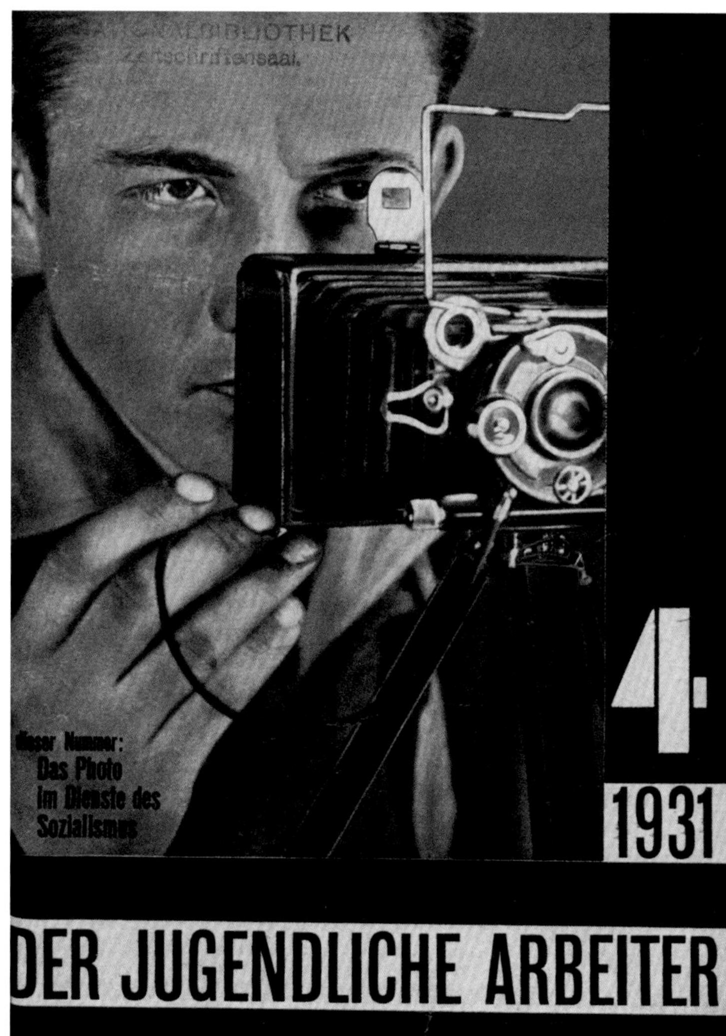

Fig. 5
"The Photo in Service of Socialism," front cover of *Der jugendliche Arbeiter,* April 1931

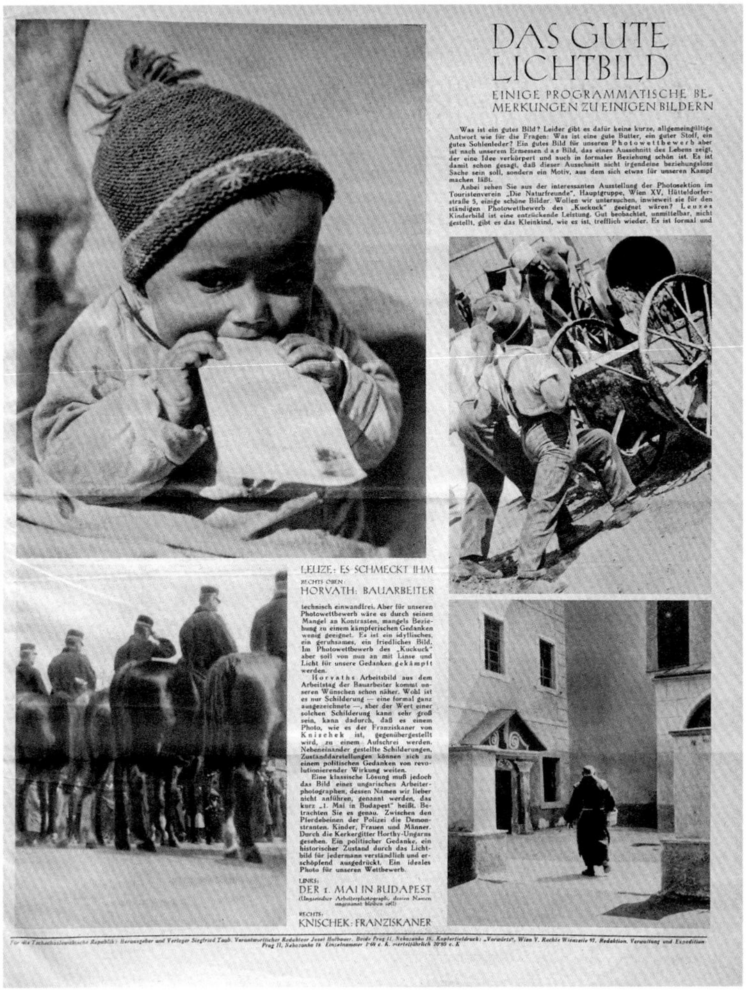

DAS GUTE LICHTBILD

EINIGE PROGRAMMATISCHE BEMERKUNGEN ZU EINIGEN BILDERN

Was ist ein gutes Bild? Leider gibt es dafür keine kurze, allgemeingültige Antwort wie für die Fragen: Was ist eine gute Butter, ein guter Stoff, ein gutes Sohlenleder? Ein gutes Bild für unseren Photowettbewerb aber ist nach unserem Ermessen das Bild, das einen Ausschnitt des Lebens zeigt, der eine Idee verkörpert und auch in formaler Beziehung schön ist. Es ist damit schon gesagt, daß dieser Ausschnitt nicht irgendeine beziehungslose Sache sein soll, sondern ein Motiv, aus dem sich etwas für unseren Kampf machen läßt.

Anbei sehen Sie aus der interessanten Ausstellung der Photosektion im Touristenverein „Die Naturfreunde", Hauptgruppe, Wien XV, Hütteldorferstraße 5, einige schöne Bilder. Wollen wir untersuchen, inwieweit sie für den ständigen Photowettbewerb des „Kuckuck" geeignet wären? Leuzes Kinderbild ist eine entzückende Leistung. Gut beobachtet, unmittelbar, nicht gestellt, gibt es das Kleinkind, wie es ist, trefflich wieder. Es ist formal und technisch einwandfrei. Aber für unseren Photowettbewerb wäre es durch seinen Mangel an Kontrasten, mangels Beziehung zu einem kämpferischen Gedanken wenig geeignet. Es ist ein idyllisches, ein geruhsames, ein friedliches Bild. Im Photowettbewerb des „Kuckuck" aber soll von nun an mit Linse und Licht für unsere Gedanken gekämpft werden.

Horvaths Arbeitsbild aus dem Arbeitstag der Bauarbeiter kommt unseren Wünschen schon näher. Wohl ist es nur Schilderung — eine formal ganz ausgezeichnete —, aber der Wert einer solchen Schilderung kann sehr groß sein, kann dadurch, daß es einem Photo, wie es der Franziskaner von Knischek ist, gegenübergestellt wird, zu einem Aufschrei werden. Nebeneinander gestellte Schilderungen, Zustanddarstellungen können sich zu einem politischen Gedanken von revolutionierender Wirkung weiten.

Eine klassische Lösung muß jedoch das Bild eines ungarischen Arbeiterphotographen, dessen Namen wir lieber nicht anführen, genannt werden, das kurz „1. Mai in Budapest" heißt. Betrachten Sie es genau. Zwischen den Pferdebeinen der Polizei die Demonstranten. Kinder, Frauen und Männer. Durch die Kerkergitter Horthy-Ungarns gesehen. Ein politischer Gedanke, ein historischer Zustand durch das Lichtbild für jedermann verständlich und erschöpfend ausgedrückt. Ein ideales Photo für unseren Wettbewerb.

LEUZE: ES SCHMECKT IHM

RECHTS OBEN:
HORVATH: BAUARBEITER

LINKS:
DER 1. MAI IN BUDAPEST
(Ungarischer Arbeiterphotograph, dessen Namen ungenannt bleiben soll)

RECHTS:
KNISCHEK: FRANZISKANER

Fig. 6
Photographers unknown, "The Good Photograph," *Der Kuckuck* 51, 1932, p. 14

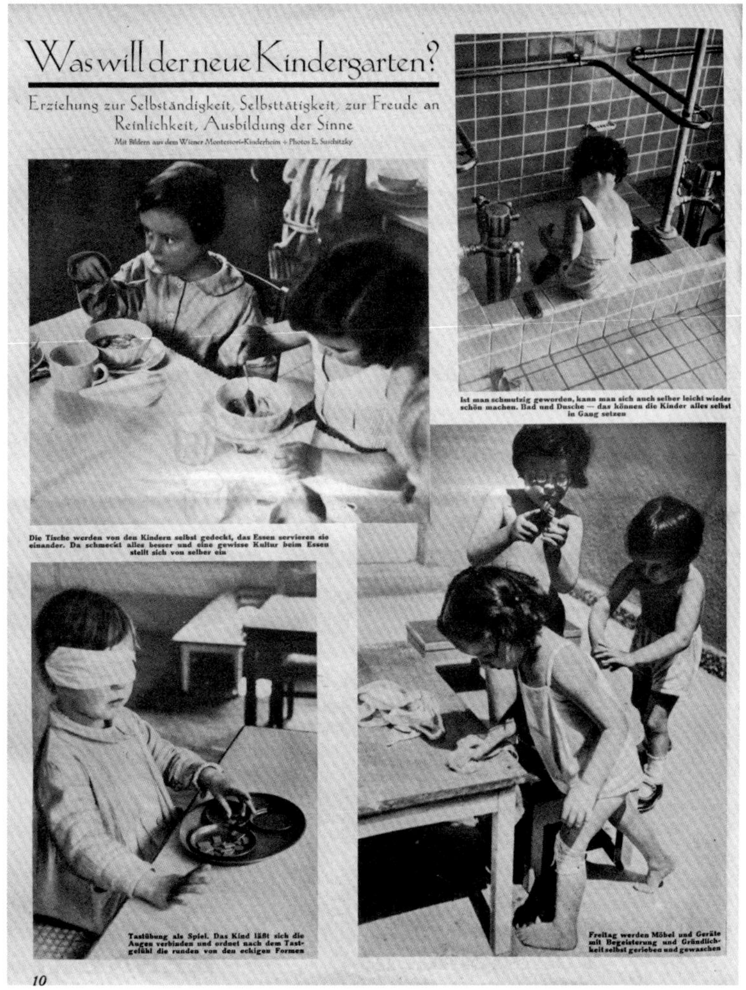

Was will der neue Kindergarten?

Erziehung zur Selbständigkeit, Selbsttätigkeit, zur Freude an Reinlichkeit, Ausbildung der Sinne

Mit Bildern aus dem Wiener Montessori-Kinderheim + Photos E. Suschitzky

Die Tische werden von den Kindern selbst gedeckt, das Essen servieren sie einander. Da schmeckt alles besser und eine gewisse Kultur beim Essen stellt sich von selber ein

Ist man schmutzig geworden, kann man sich auch selber leicht wieder schön machen. Bad und Dusche — das können die Kinder alles selbst in Gang setzen

Tastübung als Spiel. Das Kind läßt sich die Augen verbinden und ordnet nach dem Tastgefühl die runden von den eckigen Formen

Freitag werden Möbel und Geräte mit Begeisterung und Gründlichkeit selbst gerieben und gewaschen

10

Fig. 7
Edith Suschitzky, "Where Is the New Kindergarten Heading?," *Der Kuckuck*, September 27, 1931, p. 10

in 1926, recruited her for Comintern work in London in February 1934, although, as an informant later claimed, she had previously acted under the direction of the OGPU, the Soviet Intelligence Service, whilst still in Vienna.[14] To the concern of her Soviet handlers, Suschitzky mixed legal party work with her undercover activities, a practice she continued throughout the thirties. Britain, still an imperial power, was an important Soviet target and Suschitzky's links with London would have made her particularly useful; one source reports that she completed two undercover missions to Paris and London from Vienna in 1929.[15] Deutsch described her as "modest, diligent and brave," noting that she was "prepared to do anything for us," a willing go-between for a rapidly degenerating and bureaucratized Communist International.[16] This was a compelling life—one of "activity integrated into history," as Victor Serge memorably described it—and Suschitzky's political optimism easily overcame any uncertainty about the twists and turns of Comintern policy.[17] It was from 1925 that she forged a friendship with the Tudor-Hart family, with Beatrix, a progressive educationalist, and her brother, Alexander, training to become a surgeon. Of bohemian upbringing and Communist leanings, they both paid research trips to Vienna during the late twenties.

How in this maelstrom of political activity and ideas did Edith Suschitzky first learn to wield a camera for public ends? Her passage into photography is unclear, although in a city with an evolved studio culture it offered an increasingly accessible professional training for young women.[18] However, this was also a period in which photography as a mass medium was taking on a sharper social purpose, breaking down—through its quality of immediacy and capacity for self-representation—the traditional divisions of culture. During the nineteen-twenties, the enhanced technological capacities of the camera and faster printing processes offered the left new techniques for popular mobilization. By the end of the decade, Vorwärts Verlag, the Social Democrat's publishing house, had initiated

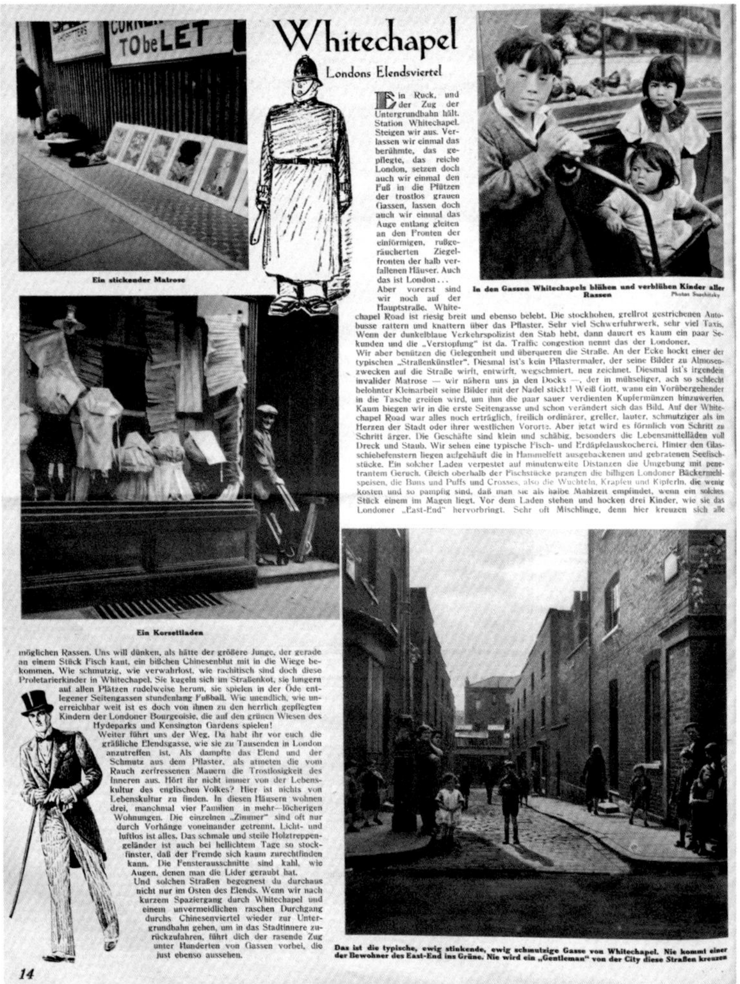

Whitechapel

Londons Elendsviertel

Ein Ruck, und der Zug der Untergrundbahn hält. Station Whitechapel. Steigen wir aus. Verlassen wir einmal das berühmte, das gepflegte, das reiche London, setzen doch auch wir einmal den Fuß in die Pfützen der trostlos grauen Gassen, lassen doch auch wir einmal das Auge entlang gleiten an den Fronten der einförmigen, rußgeräucherten Ziegelfronten der halb verfallenen Häuser. Auch das ist London...

Aber vorerst sind wir noch auf der Hauptstraße. Whitechapel Road ist riesig breit und ebenso belebt. Die stockhohen, grellrot gestrichenen Autobusse rattern und knattern über das Pflaster. Sehr viel Schwerfuhrwerk, sehr viel Taxis. Wenn der dunkelblaue Verkehrspolizist den Stab hebt, dann dauert es kaum ein paar Sekunden und die „Verstopfung" ist da. Traffic congestion nennt das der Londoner.

Wir aber benützen die Gelegenheit und überqueren die Straße. An der Ecke hockt einer der typischen „Straßenkünstler". Diesmal ist's kein Pflastermaler, der seine Bilder zu Almosenzwecken auf die Straße wirft, entwirft, wegschmiert, neu zeichnet. Diesmal ist's irgendein invalider Matrose — wir nähern uns ja den Docks —, der in mühseliger, ach so schlecht belohnter Kleinarbeit seine Bilder mit der Nadel stickt! Weiß Gott, wann ein Vorübergehender in die Tasche greifen wird, um ihm die paar sauer verdienten Kupfermünzen hinzuwerfen. Kaum biegen wir in die erste Seitengasse und schon verändert sich das Bild. Auf der Whitechapel Road war alles noch erträglich, freilich ordinärer, greller, lauter, schmutziger als im Herzen der Stadt oder ihrer westlichen Vororte. Aber jetzt wird es förmlich von Schritt zu Schritt ärger. Die Geschäfte sind klein und schäbig, besonders die Lebensmittelläden voll Dreck und Staub. Wir sehen eine typische Fisch- und Erdäpfelauskocherei. Hinter den Glasschiebefenstern liegen aufgehäuft die in Hammelfett ausgebackenen und gebratenen Seefischstücke. Ein solcher Laden verpestet auf minutenweite Distanzen die Umgebung mit penetrantem Geruch. Gleich oberhalb der Fischstücke prangen die billigen Londoner Bäckermehlspeisen, die Buns und Puffs und Crosses, also die Wuchteln, Krapfen und Kipferln, die wenig kosten und so pampfig sind, daß man sie als halbe Mahlzeit empfindet, wenn ein solches Stück einem im Magen liegt. Vor dem Laden stehen und hocken drei Kinder, wie sie das Londoner „East-End" hervorbringt. Sehr oft Mischlinge, denn hier kreuzen sich alle möglichen Rassen. Uns will dünken, als hätte der größere Junge, der gerade an einem Stück Fisch kaut, ein bißchen Chinesenblut mit in die Wiege bekommen. Wie schmutzig, wie verwahrlost, wie rachitisch sind doch diese Proletarierkinder in Whitechapel. Sie kugeln sich im Straßenkot, sie lungern auf allen Plätzen rudelweise herum, sie spielen in der Öde entlegener Seitengassen stundenlang Fußball. Wie unendlich, wie unerreichbar weit ist es doch von ihnen zu den herrlich gepflegten Kindern der Londoner Bourgeoisie, die auf den grünen Wiesen des Hydeparks und Kensington Gardens spielen!

Weiter führt uns der Weg. Da habt ihr vor euch die gräßliche Elendsgasse, wie sie zu Tausenden in London anzutreffen ist. Als dampfte das Elend und der Schmutz aus dem Pflaster, als atmeten die vom Rauch zerfressenen Mauern die Trostlosigkeit des Inneren aus. Hört ihr nicht immer von der Lebenskultur des englischen Volkes? Hier ist nichts von Lebenskultur zu finden. In diesen Häusern wohnen drei, manchmal vier Familien in mehr—löcherigen Wohnungen. Die einzelnen „Zimmer" sind oft nur durch Vorhänge voneinander getrennt. Licht- und luftlos ist alles. Das schmale und steile Holztreppengeländer ist auch bei hellichtem Tage so stockfinster, daß der Fremde sich kaum zurechtfinden kann. Die Fensterausschnitte sind kahl, wie Augen, denen man die Lider geraubt hat.

Und solchen Straßen begegnest du durchaus nicht nur im Osten des Elends. Wenn wir nach kurzem Spaziergang durch Whitechapel und einem unvermeidlichen raschen Durchgang durchs Chinesenviertel wieder zur Untergrundbahn gehen, um in das Stadtinnere zurückzufahren, führt dich der rasende Zug unter Hunderten von Gassen vorbei, die just ebenso aussehen.

Ein stickender Matrose

In den Gassen Whitechapels blühen und verblühen Kinder aller Rassen
Photos Suschitzky

Ein Korsettladen

Das ist die typische, ewig stinkende, ewig schmutzige Gasse von Whitechapel. Nie kommt einer der Bewohner des East-End ins Grüne. Nie wird ein „Gentleman" von der City diese Straßen kreuzen

14

Fig. 8
Edith Suschitzky, "Whitechapel: London's Slum," *Der Kuckuck,* March 29, 1931, p. 14

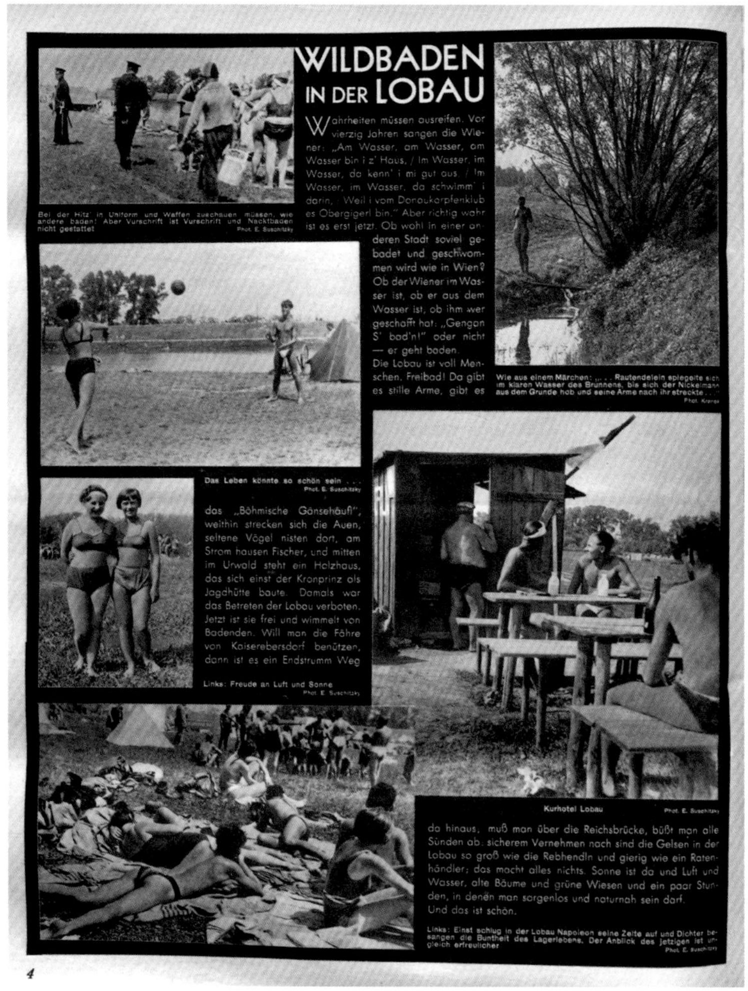

WILDBADEN IN DER LOBAU

Wahrheiten müssen ausreifen. Vor vierzig Jahren sangen die Wiener: „Am Wasser, am Wasser, am Wasser bin i z' Haus, / Im Wasser, im Wasser, da kenn' i mi gut aus, / Im Wasser, im Wasser, da schwimm' i darin, / Weil i vom Donaukarpfenklub es Obergigerl bin." Aber richtig wahr ist es erst jetzt. Ob wohl in einer anderen Stadt soviel gebadet und geschwommen wird wie in Wien? Ob der Wiener im Wasser ist, ob er aus dem Wasser ist, ob ihm wer geschafft hat: „Gengan S' bad'n!" oder nicht — er geht baden.

Die Lobau ist voll Menschen. Freibad! Da gibt es stille Arme, gibt es das „Böhmische Gänsehäufl", weithin strecken sich die Auen, seltene Vögel nisten dort, am Strom hausen Fischer, und mitten im Urwald steht ein Holzhaus, das sich einst der Kronprinz als Jagdhütte baute. Damals war das Betreten der Lobau verboten. Jetzt ist sie frei und wimmelt von Badenden. Will man die Fähre von Kaiserebersdorf benützen, dann ist es ein Endstrumm Weg da hinaus, muß man über die Reichsbrücke, büßt man alle Sünden ab: sicherem Vernehmen nach sind die Gelsen in der Lobau so groß wie die Rebhendln und gierig wie ein Ratenhändler; das macht alles nichts. Sonne ist da und Luft und Wasser, alte Bäume und grüne Wiesen und ein paar Stunden, in denen man sorgenlos und naturnah sein darf.

Und das ist schön.

Bei der Hitz' in Uniform und Waffen zuschauen müssen, wie andere baden! Aber Vurschrift ist Vurschrift und Nacktbaden nicht gestattet
Phot. E. Suschitzky

Wie aus einem Märchen: „. . . Rautendelein spiegelte sich im klaren Wasser des Brunnens, bis sich der Nickelmann aus dem Grunde hob und seine Arme nach ihr streckte . . ."
Phot. Kroner

Das Leben könnte so schön sein . . .
Phot. E. Suschitzky

Links: Freude an Luft und Sonne
Phot. E. Suschitzky

Kurhotel Lobau
Phot. E. Suschitzky

Links: Einst schlug in der Lobau Napoleon seine Zelte auf und Dichter besangen die Buntheit des Lagerlebens. Der Anblick des jetzigen ist ungleich erfreulicher
Phot. E. Suschitzky

4

Fig. 9
Edith Suschitzky, "Free Bathing in the Lobau," *Der Kuckuck,* August 21, 1932, p. 4

an elaborate program to counter the seductions of Austria's bourgeois illustrated press (fig. 5). This included publishing its own illustrated weekly magazine, *Der Kuckuck,* and initiating propaganda training to instruct its members to take photographs so as to make manifest a new proletarian consciousness.[19] Arbeiterfotografie (worker photography), as this movement came to be known, took a diversity of forms and was particularly developed in Germany and the Soviet Union. Here the ideal of a new kind of reporter, the worker correspondent, had been mobilized in order to promote a revolutionary culture of worker self-representation, overturning the image world of imperial reaction. The Austrian Social Democrats, too, adopted similar strategies, training party members in the techniques of the dialectical photograph—techniques that aimed to inform the self-understanding of the proletariat as a class and to foster a recognition of its exploitation within a broader conception of society. As was made plain in the pages of *Der Kuckuck,* its vision of the "good photograph" went far beyond surface appearances. Thus an image of a May Day demonstration, shot by a Hungarian worker through the legs of a rank of police horses, could become a suasive metaphor of authoritarian control (fig. 6).

It was this strategy of realist demystification that was the most powerful weapon in the hands of the worker photographer. It was at once a political tactic, but also, in the writing of the Hungarian philosopher Georg Lukács, a philosophical ideal: it revived the Hegelian notion that self-knowledge is what shapes and directs human emancipation. Whether the young Edith Suschitzky had read Lukács's *History and Class Consciousness* (published in 1923) is beside the point (although the fact that Lukács was working for the Comintern in Vienna at the time raises the intriguing possibility that she knew him).[20] Neither is it possible to force Suschitzky's photography from this period into a political straitjacket: she was subject to a variety of editorial regimes and was working to eke out a living at a time of economic emergency. But the conceptual and practical depth of this context for photography—above all its imbrication in processes of personal and social transformation—is striking and was far richer than anything available in Britain. The Montessori movement, too, made extensive use of photography, as a mechanism to promote its struggle for legitimacy, but also as a means of enhancing its central technique of concentrated pupil observation. Indeed, one of Suschitzky's earliest photo essays, published in *Der Kuckuck* in 1931, used imagery to suggest the intensity of childhood absorption in self-motivated learning under Montessori methods (fig. 7).[21]

The earliest negative material in Edith Tudor-Hart's archive dates from around 1930, suggesting that she only took up photography systematically after a period of study at the Bauhaus, the art and design school in Dessau. Surviving records of her Bauhaus years are sparse: she registered for the famous foundation course in late 1928 and was, unusually, still registered for it in 1930. She is not recorded as a student in Walter Peterhans's photography department (established in 1929), and there is no known surviving imagery from her stay in Dessau.[22] However, it is likely that the Bauhaus years proved important to Suschitzky in aesthetic and political terms. Her time there coincided with its most radical phase under the directorship of the architect Hannes Meyer, and she published a vigorous defense of the school's revolutionary functionalism in an English art journal in 1931.[23] A communist cell had been established in the summer of 1927, comprising around 10 percent of the student body; it became increasingly active outside the school during Meyer's tenure.[24] Suschitzky's early training in photography occurred at a time when a more politicized pedagogy led a number of Bauhaus students to subordinate modernist techniques to realist methods focused on the task of political mobilization.[25]

By October 1930, Edith Suschitzky was back in London, coming to the attention of Special Branch for the first time when she was spotted with CPGB leaders at a demonstration in support of the Workers' Charter in Trafalgar Square. Despite attempts to enlist the influence of both the mayor of Vienna, Karl Seitz, and the Cambridge economist Maurice Dobb, Suschitzky was expelled from Britain the following January.[26] She returned to Vienna and quickly found an assignment working as a photographer for the Soviet news agency TASS, a common enough role for Comintern activists. She appears also to have gained experience briefly in a commercial studio. Her published photo essays began to appear more regularly—the two best on poverty in London's East End, another on Vienna's bathing area, the Lobau—the work of a photographer struggling to shape her ambitions to the commercial and political parameters of the Social Democratic press (figs. 8 and 9).[27] The 150 or so surviving negatives from the Vienna years reveal a frugal and technically adroit photographer, exploring subjects of working-class deprivation and the reform-minded culture of Austrian Social Democracy, as well as the threat of militarist and fascist forces. Much of this section of Suschitzky's archive appears to have been confiscated or abandoned, but its remnants betray a nascent realist method, an attempt to construct a narrative of reality grounded in the antagonisms of class. Her imagery suggests a photographer already skilled at turning reportage into pictures, using a Rolleiflex camera held at waist height, allowing the motif to fill the frame to create an exchange with her subjects. (It is significant that Suschitzky never felt comfortable with a 35mm camera: the medium-format Rolleiflex, never quite the modernist camera-eye, allowed speed of execution in a way that encouraged dialogue with the person photographed. Instinctively, photography was a medium through which subject, photographer, and imagined audience might communicate.) Thus Suschitzky's photography was beginning to reveal a capacity for nuance increasingly absent from her politics. As she revealed in letters to Alexander Tudor-Hart in London, her Russian was coming along well: "the way to Moscow won't be very long for me—ha."[28]

1 This essay draws on my earlier publication, "Politics, Photography and Exile in the Life of Edith Tudor-Hart (1908–1973)," in *Arts in Exile in Britain 1933–1945: Politics and Cultural Identity,* vol. 6: *The Yearbook of the Research Centre for German and Austrian Exile Studies,* ed. Shulamith Behr and Marian Malet (Amsterdam and New York, 2005), pp. 45–87. Edith Tudor-Hart was born Edith Suschitzky in 1908, and I use her maiden name until the date of her marriage in 1933. During her lifetime she spelled her name with and without a hyphen. I have stuck to the former for consistency except where it appears otherwise in titles or original documents.

2 This and subsequent information about Suschitzky's arrest are taken from police reports, a microfilm copy of which is held by the Institut für Zeitgeschichte, University of Vienna, MF A/270, ff. 1355–1508.

3 The KPÖ was banned by the Austrian Cabinet on May 26, 1933. For the history of the Communist Party of Austria I have relied on Herbert Steiner, *Die kommunistische Partei Österreichs von 1918 bis 1933: Bibliographische Bemerkungen* (Meisenheim am Glan, 1968) and Barry McLoughlin et al., *Kommunismus in Österreich 1918–1938* (Innsbruck, 2009).

4 Eric Hobsbawm, *Interesting Times: A Twentieth-Century Life* (London, 2002), p. 13.

5 For a history of the Montessori movement in Austria, see Franz Hammerer, *Maria Montessoris pädagogisches Konzept: Anfänge der Realisierung in Österreich* (Vienna, 1997). For a contemporary description, see Rudolf Hauser, "Die Montessori-Bewegung in Österreich," *Vierteljahrsschrift für wissenschaftliche Pädagogik* 6 (1930), pp. 588–94.

6 See Wilfried Konnert, *Favoriten im Wandel der Zeit* (Vienna, 1974) and J. Robert Wegs, *Growing Up Working Class: Continuity and Change Among Viennese Youth, 1890–1938* (London, 1989).

7 For the history of the Suschitzky family, see Annette Lechner, "Die Wiener Verlagsbuchhandlung 'Anzengruber-Verlag, Brüder Suschitzky' (1901–1938) im Spiegel der Zeit," *Archiv für Geschichte des Buchwesens* 44 (1995), pp. 187–273.

8 As the social historian Geoff Eley has argued, these few years witnessed "the single most concentrated pan-European societal transformation since the French Revolution." See Geoff Eley, *Forging Democracy: The History of the Left in Europe, 1850–2000* (Oxford, 2002), p. 124. See also Helmut Gruber, *Red Vienna: Experiment in Working-Class Culture 1919–1934* (Oxford, 1991).

9 See Ernst Papanek, *The Austrian School Reform* (New York, 1962) and Georg Tidl, *Sozialistische Mittelschüler Österreichs 1918 bis 1938* (Vienna, 1977).

10 Robert Streibel, ed., *Eugenie Schwarzwald und ihr Kreis* (Vienna, 1996) and Deborah Holmes, *Langweile ist Gift: Das Leben der Eugenie Schwarzwald* (St. Pölten, 2012).

11 Friedrich Scheu, *Ein Band der Freundschaft: Schwarzwald-Kreis und Entstehung der Vereinigung Sozialistischer Mittelschüler* (Vienna, 1985), p. 165.

12 Genia Quittner, *Weiter Weg nach Krasnogorsk: Schicksalsbericht einer Frau* (Vienna, 1971), esp. pp. 19–23.

13 "Die Bilder selbst sind Kriegs- und Revolutionsillustrationen." Bruno Frei, *Das Elend Wiens* (Vienna, 1921), p. viii.

14 See Nigel West and Oleg Tsarev, *The Crown Jewels: The British Secrets at the Heart of the KGB Archives* (London, 1998), pp. 106 and 108, and John Costello and Oleg Tsarev, *Deadly Illusions* (London, 1993), pp. 133–34 and 137. For an account of Arnold Deutsch's work for the Soviets, see West and Tsarev 1998, pp. 103ff. and Christopher Andrew and Vasili Mitrokhin, *The Mitrokhin Archive: The KGB in Europe and the West* (London, 2000), pp. 73ff. Genrikh Borovik claims it was Deutsch who recruited Suschitzky in Vienna in 1929 in his book with Philip Knightley, *The Philby Files: The Secret Life of the Master Spy—KGB Archives Revealed* (London, 1994), p. 301.

15 Nigel West and Oleg Tsarev, *The Crown Jewels: The British Secrets at the Heart of the KGB Archives* (London, 1998), p. 273.

16 John Costello and Oleg Tsarev, *Deadly Illusions* (London, 1993), p. 448, footnote 48.

17 Victor Serge, *Memoirs of a Revolutionary* (Iowa City, 2002), p. 177.

18 See Monika Faber, ed., *Zeit ohne Zukunft: Photographie in Wien 1918–1938* (Vienna, 1998) and Iris Meder and Andrea Winklbauer, eds., *Vienna's Shooting Girls: Jüdische Fotografinnen aus Wien,* exh. cat. Jewish Museum (Vienna, 2012).

19 See in particular the special issue of the SDAP journal *Der jugendliche Arbeiter* 4 (April 1931) devoted to the photo in service of socialism. The edition included an article by *Der Kuckuck*'s editor, Siegfried Weyr, "Das Photo als Kampfmittel," pp. 8–10. For a detailed history of Vorwärts Verlag and *Der Kuckuck,* see Stefan Riesenfellner and Josef Seiter, *Der Kuckuck: Die moderne Bild-Illustrierte des Roten Wien* (Vienna, 1995).

20 Georg Lukács, *History and Class Consciousness* (Cambridge, MA, 1971), first published in 1923.

21 Edith Suschitzky, "Was will der neue Kindergarten?," *Der Kuckuck,* September 27, 1931, p. 10.

22 Correspondence with Lutz Schöbe, Bauhaus, Dessau, November 19, 2003. Suschitzky appears to have interrupted her studies in 1929 and was registered as a "guest student" at some point that year, possibly with Peterhans. Wolfgang Suschitzky states that she studied with Peterhans in *Edith Tudor Hart: The Eye of Conscience* (London, 1987), p. 10.

23 Edith Suschitzky, "A University of Commercial Art," *Commercial Art* (March 1931). The title, which misrepresents the tone of the article, is presumably not Suschitzky's. For an account of Meyer's directorship between 1928 and 1930, see Rainer K. Wick, *Teaching at the Bauhaus* (Ostfildern-Ruit, 2000), pp. 77–82.

24 Michael Siebenbrot, "Zur Rolle der Kommunisten und anderer fortschrittlicher Kräfte am Bauhaus," *Wissenschaftliche Zeitschrift der Hochschule für Architektur und Bauwesen* 23, no. 516 (1976), pp. 481–85. Meyer was dismissed from his directorship by Dessau's Social Democratic mayor, Fritz Hesse, because of the increased politicization of the school.

25 Herbert Molderings, "From the Bauhaus to Photojournalism," in *Photography at the Bauhaus,* ed. Jeannine Fiedler (London, 1990), pp. 265–85.

26 Intercepted letters from Wilhelm Suschitzky to Edith Suschitzky, November 28, 1930, and from Maurice Dobb to Alexander Tudor-Hart, December 2, 1930, The National Archives, United Kingdom, TNA KV 2/1012.

27 Edith Suschitzky, "Whitechapel: Londons Elendsviertel," *Der Kuckuck,* March 29, 1931, p. 14; "Der Markt des nackten Elends," *Der Kuckuck,* October 4, 1931, p. 15; and "Wildbaden in der Lobau," *Der Kuckuck,* August 21, 1932, p. 4.

28 Intercepted letter, Edith Suschitzky to Alexander Tudor-Hart, undated (probably March 1931), TNA KV 2/1012.

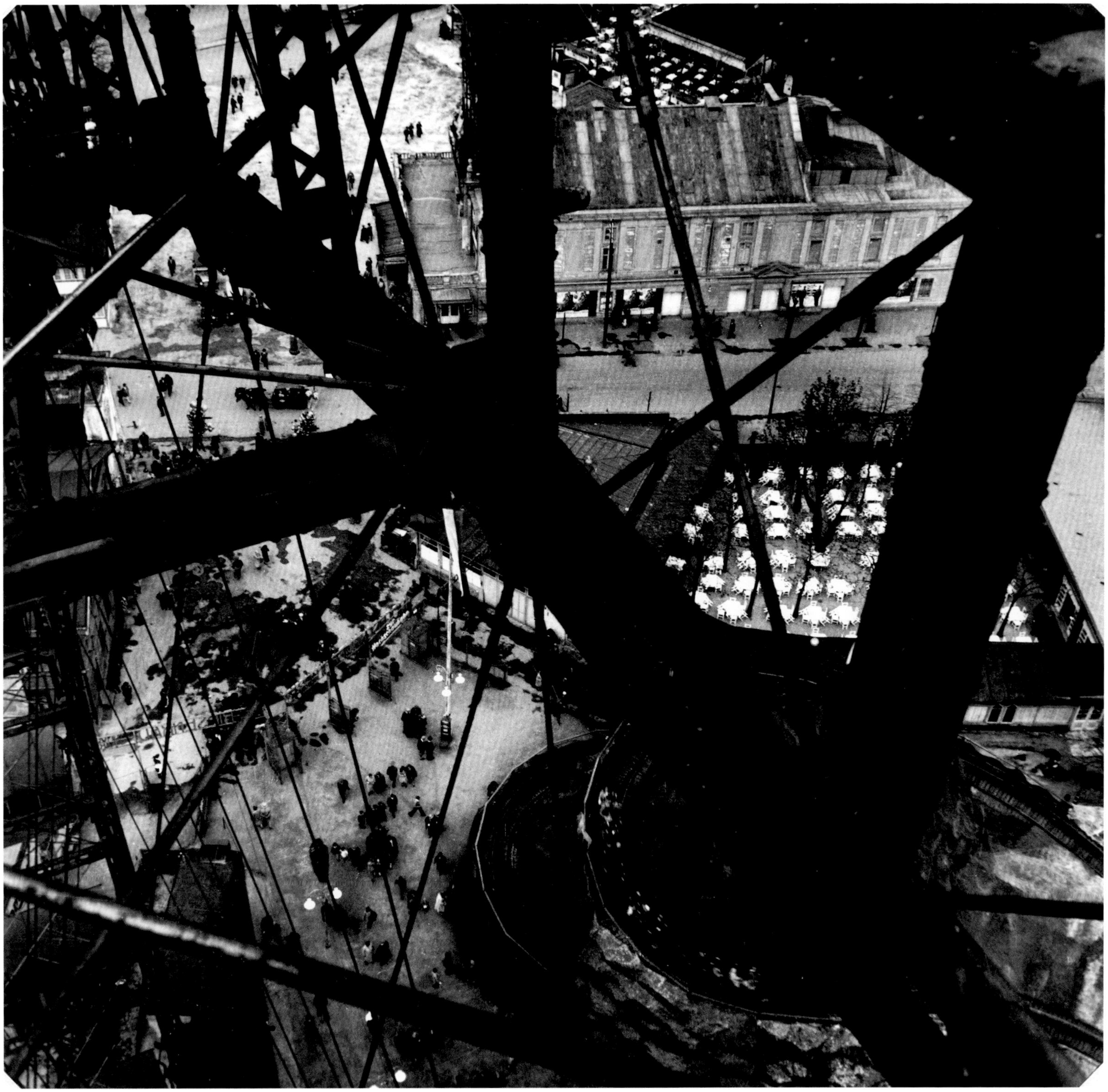

Edith Suschitzky
Prater Ferris Wheel, Vienna, 1931
Modern silver-gelatin print, 29.3 × 29.2 cm
National Galleries of Scotland, PGP 279.1

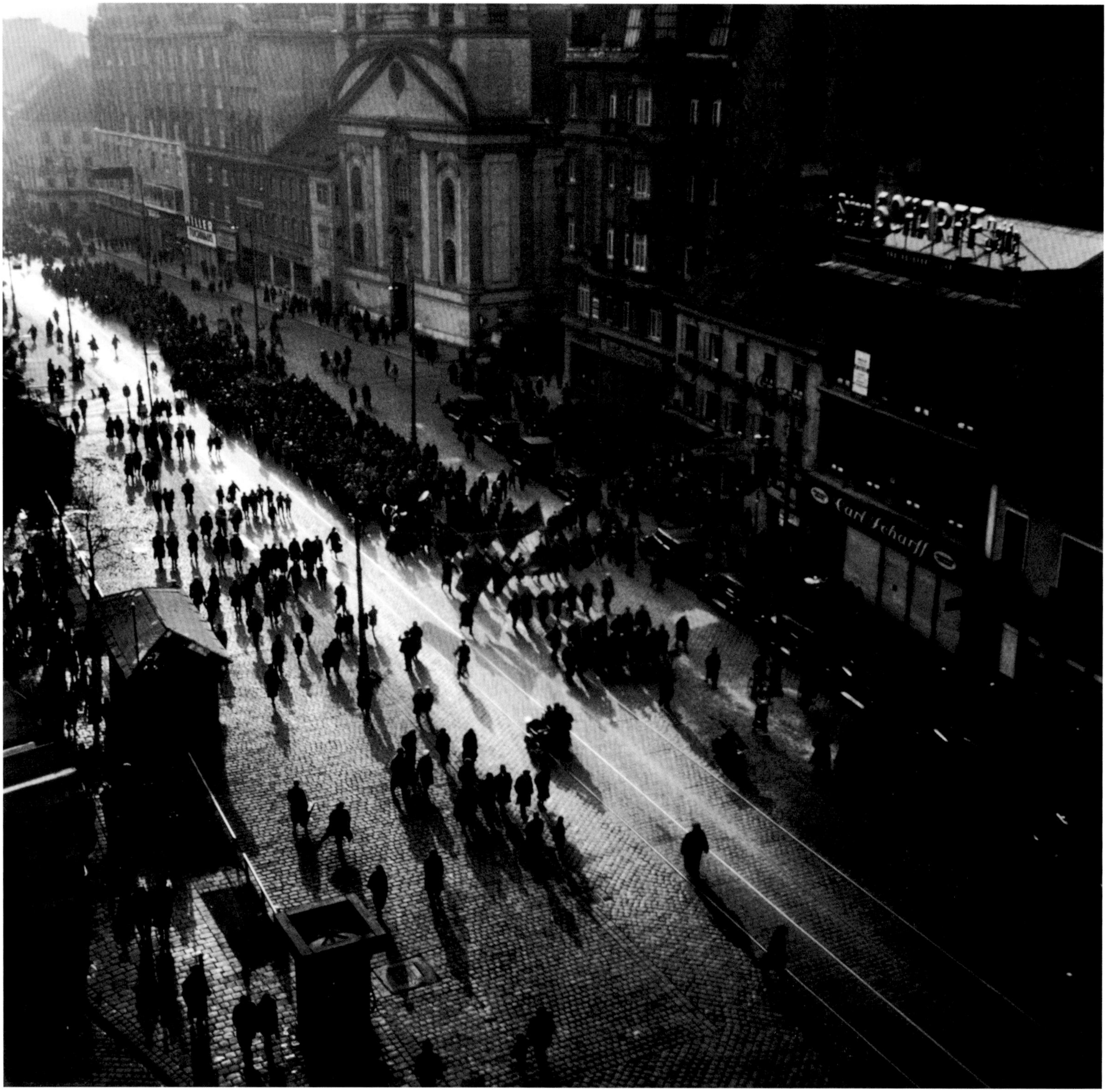

Edith Suschitzky
May Day March, Landstrasse, Vienna, 1931
Modern silver-gelatin print, 27.7 × 27.7 cm
National Galleries of Scotland, PGP 279.10

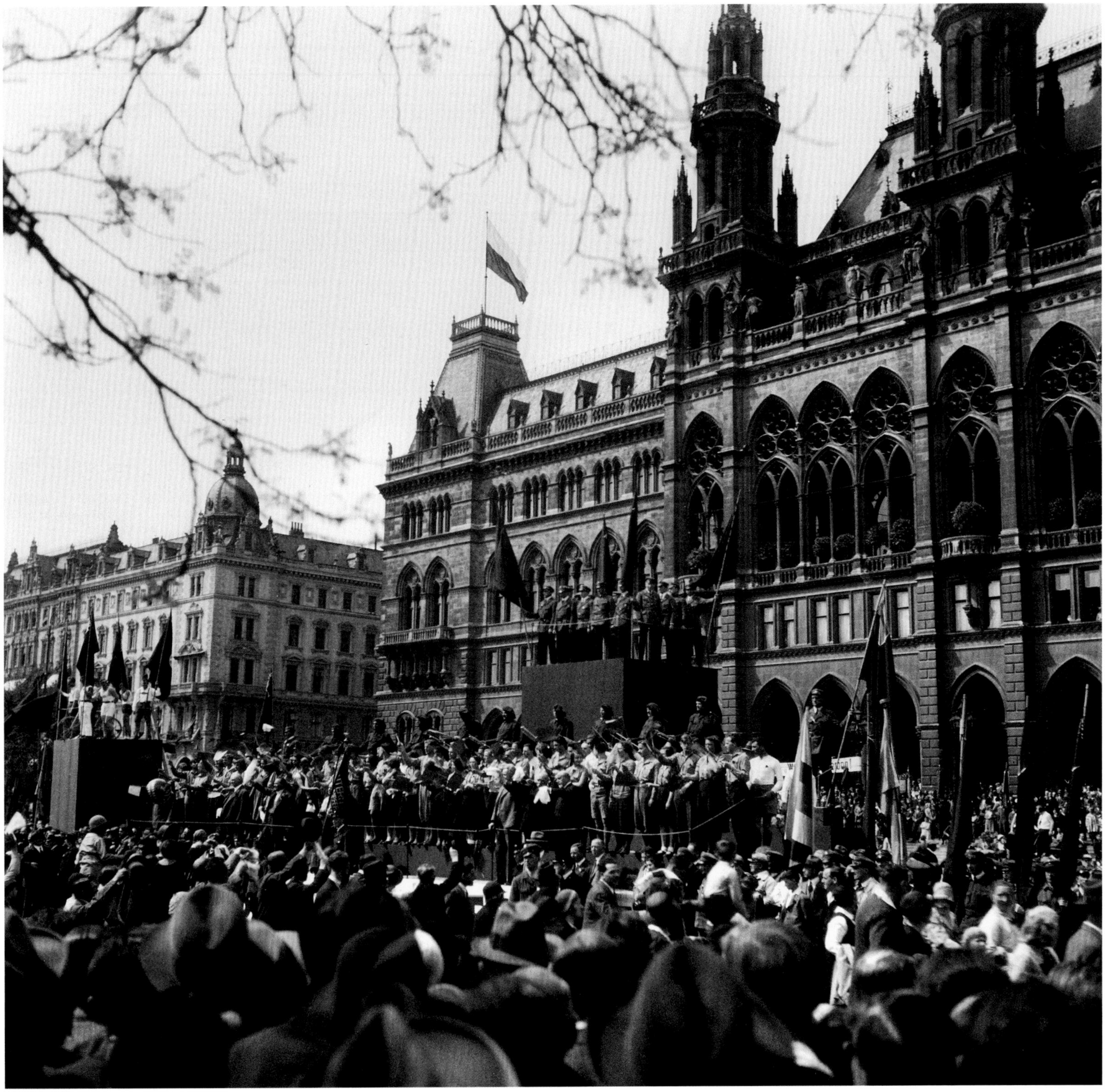

Edith Suschitzky
May Day Gathering Outside the City Hall, Vienna, 1931
Modern silver-gelatin print, 30.1 × 30.1 cm
National Galleries of Scotland, PGP 279.24

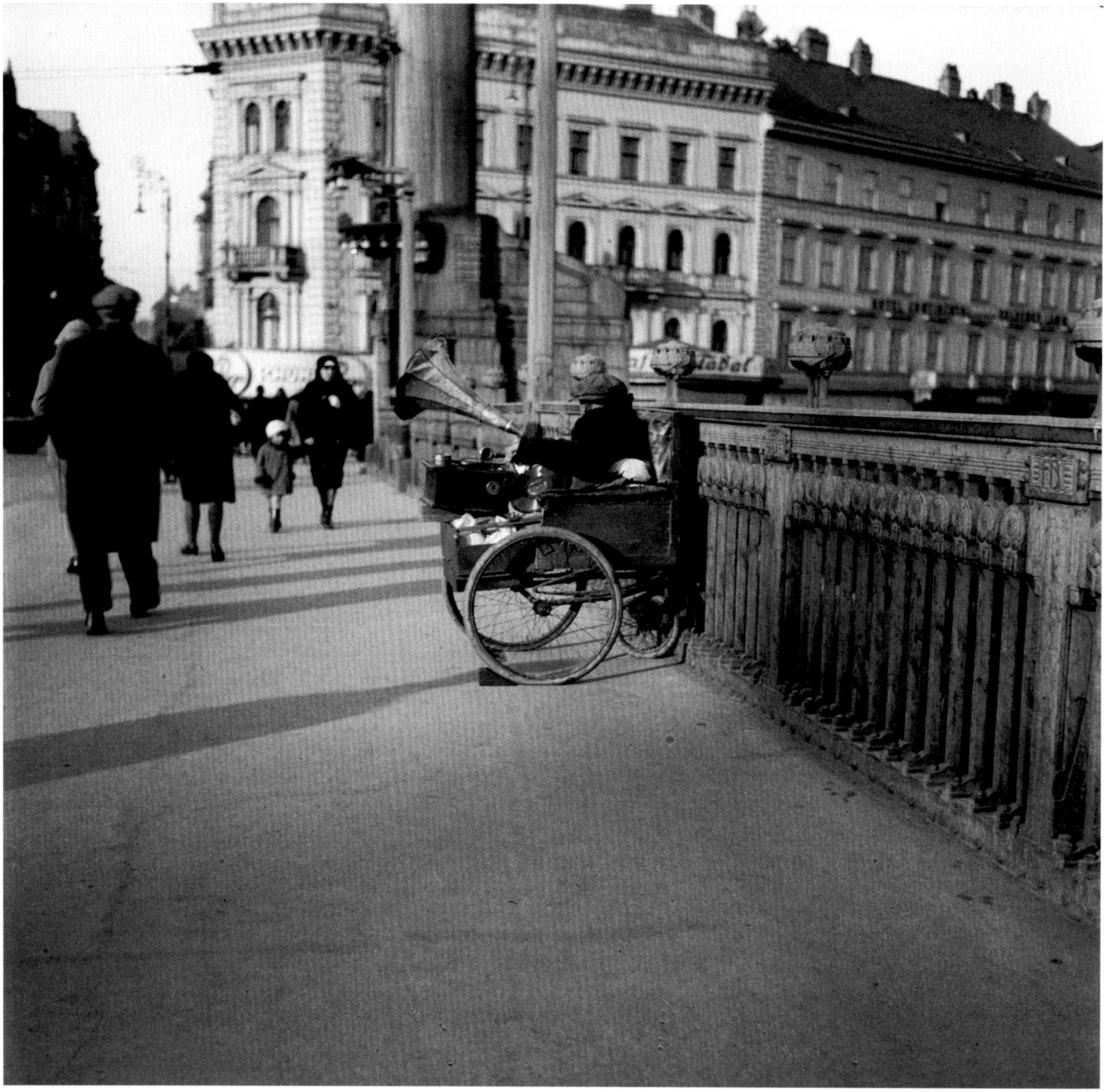

Edith Suschitzky
First World War Veteran, Vienna, ca. 1930
Digital inkjet print, 30.1 × 29.9 cm
National Galleries of Scotland, PGP 279.83

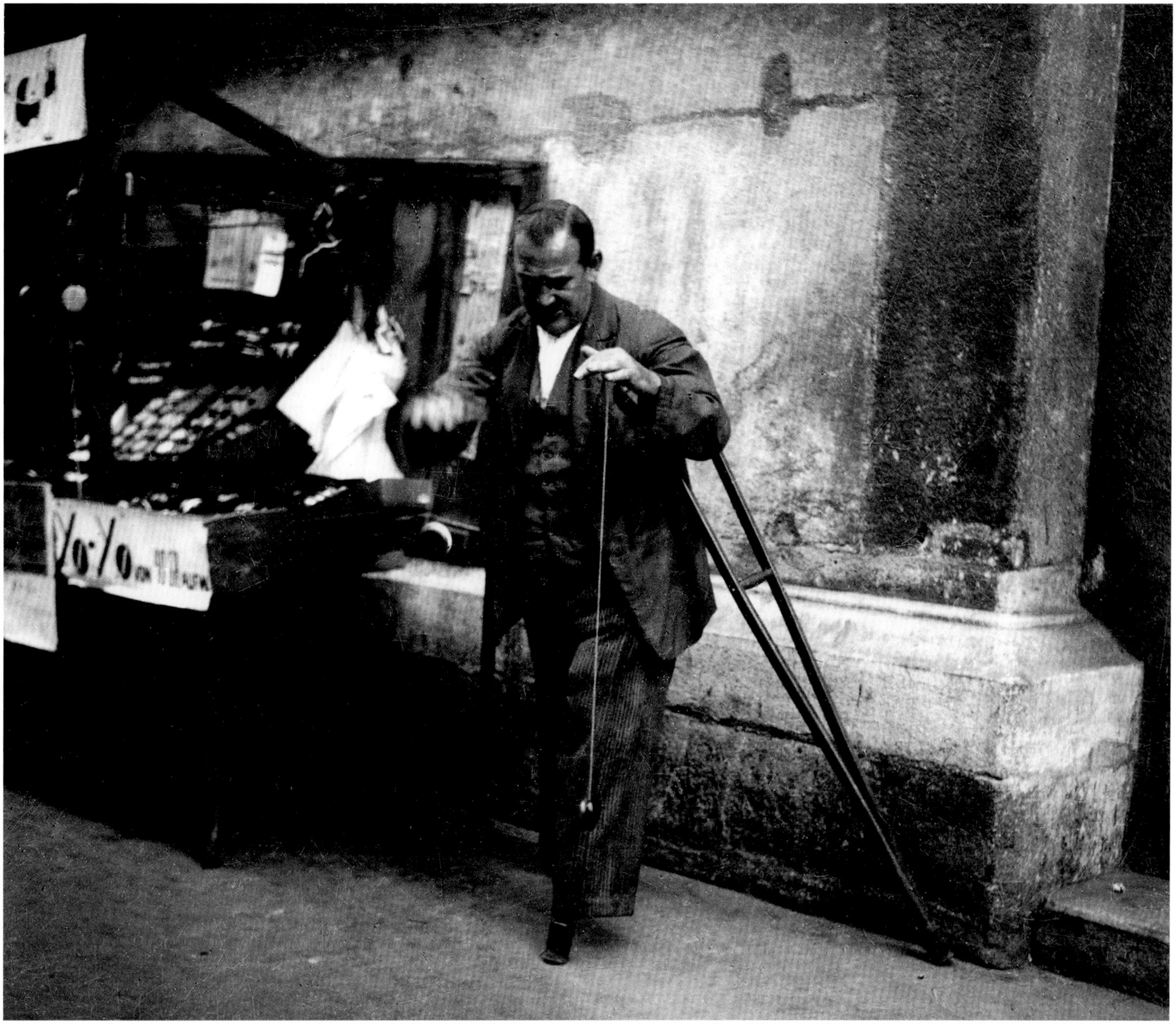

Edith Suschitzky
First World War Veteran Selling Yo-yos, ca. 1930
Silver-gelatin print, 19.6 × 21.9 cm
Galerie Johannes Faber

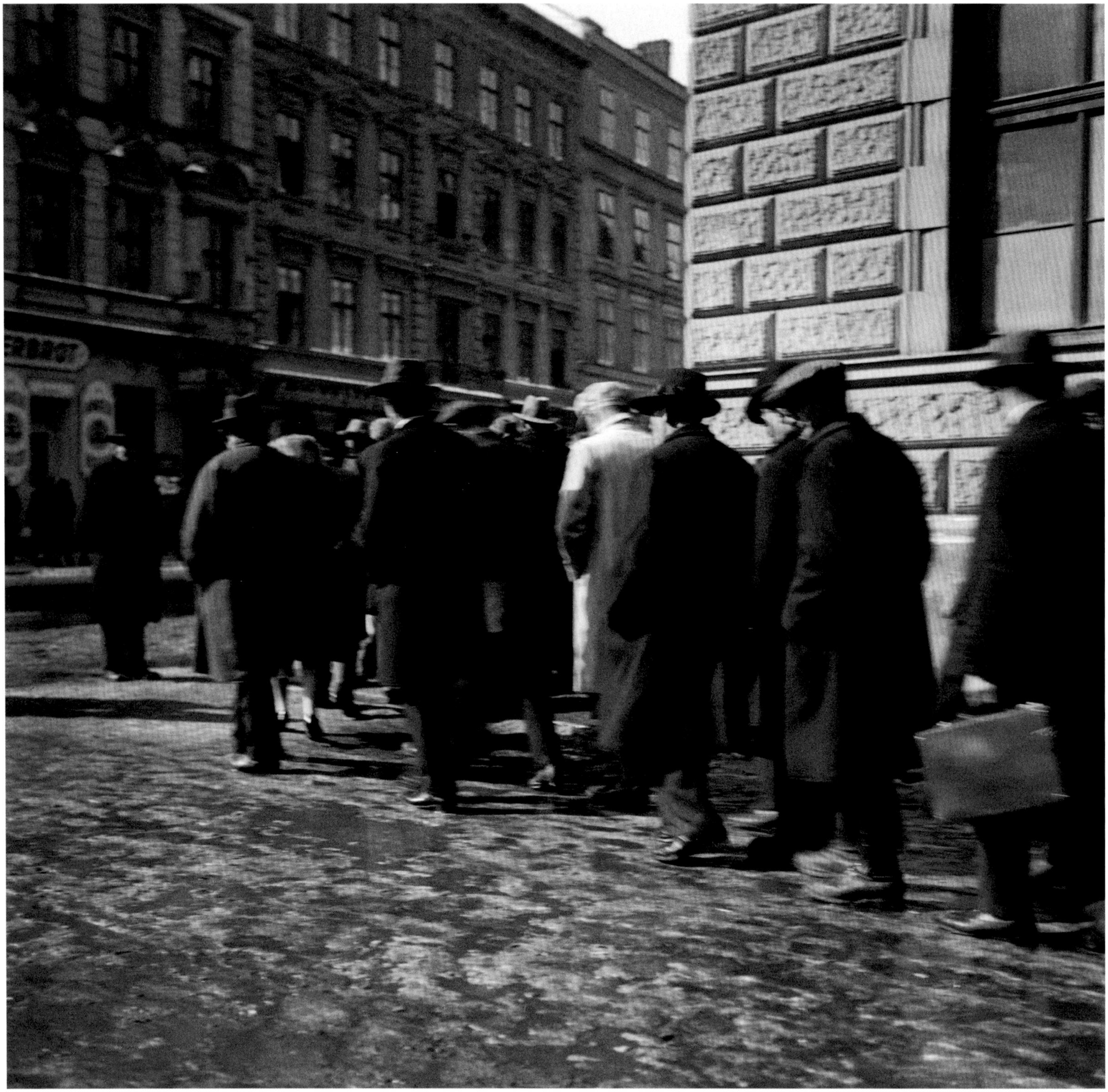

Edith Suschitzky
Queue of Unemployed, Vienna, ca. 1930
Digital inkjet print, 30.2 × 29.9 cm
National Galleries of Scotland, PGP 279.84

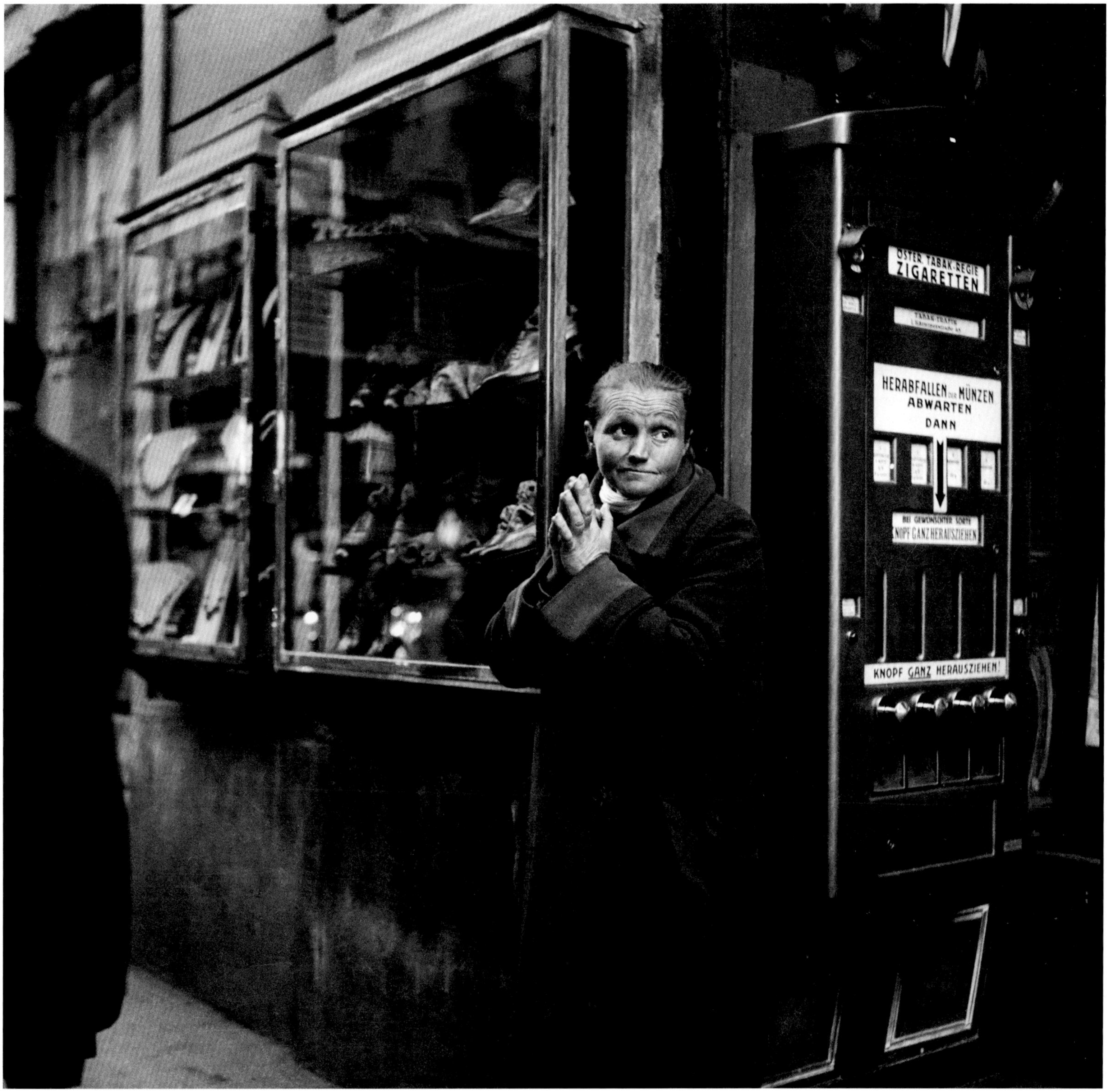

Edith Suschitzky
Woman, Vienna, ca. 1930
Digital inkjet print, 30.2 × 29.9 cm
National Galleries of Scotland, PGP 279.85

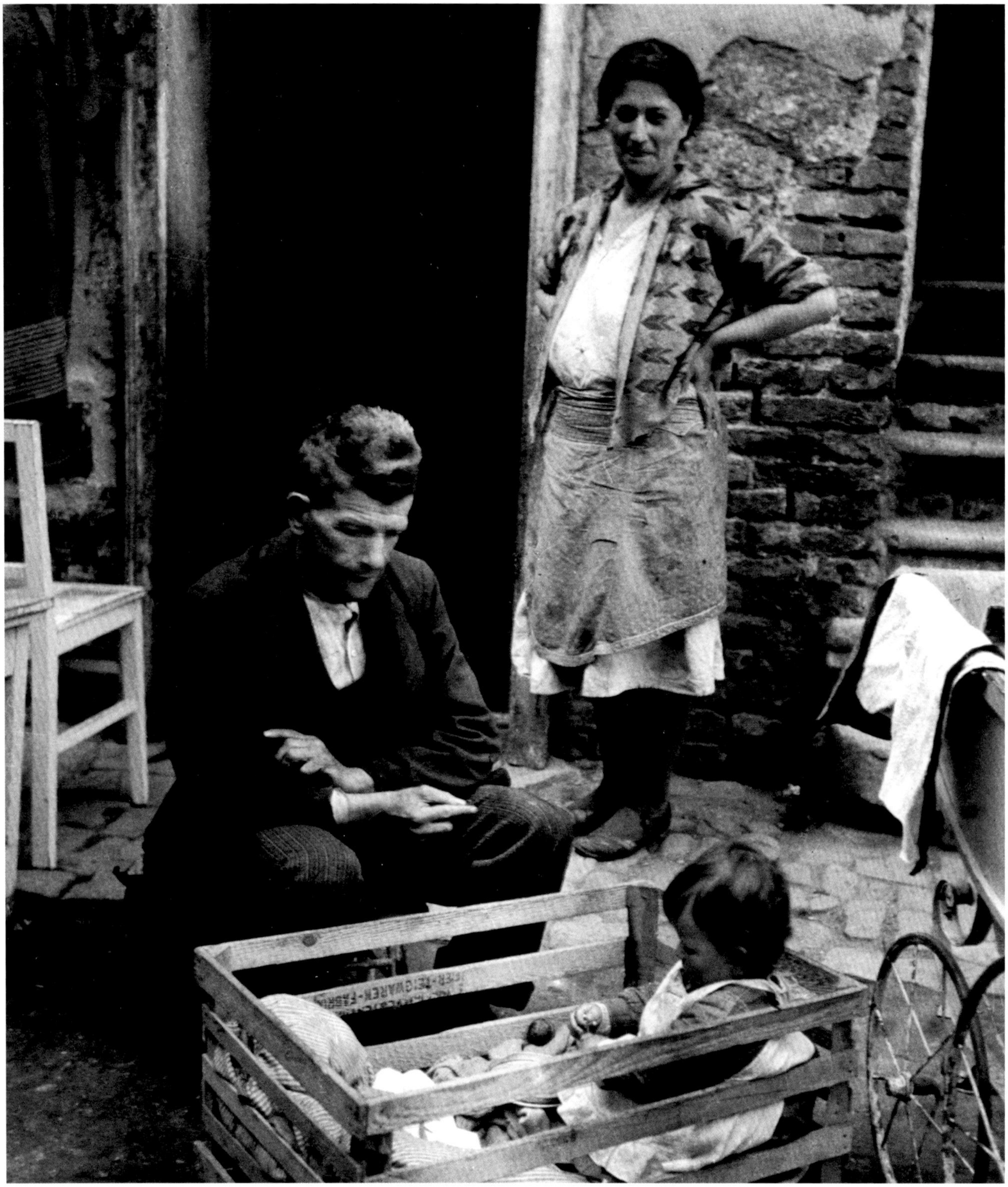

Edith Suschitzky
Unemployed Family, Vienna, 1930
Silver-gelatin print, 23.7 × 19.5 cm
Wien Museum, 204463

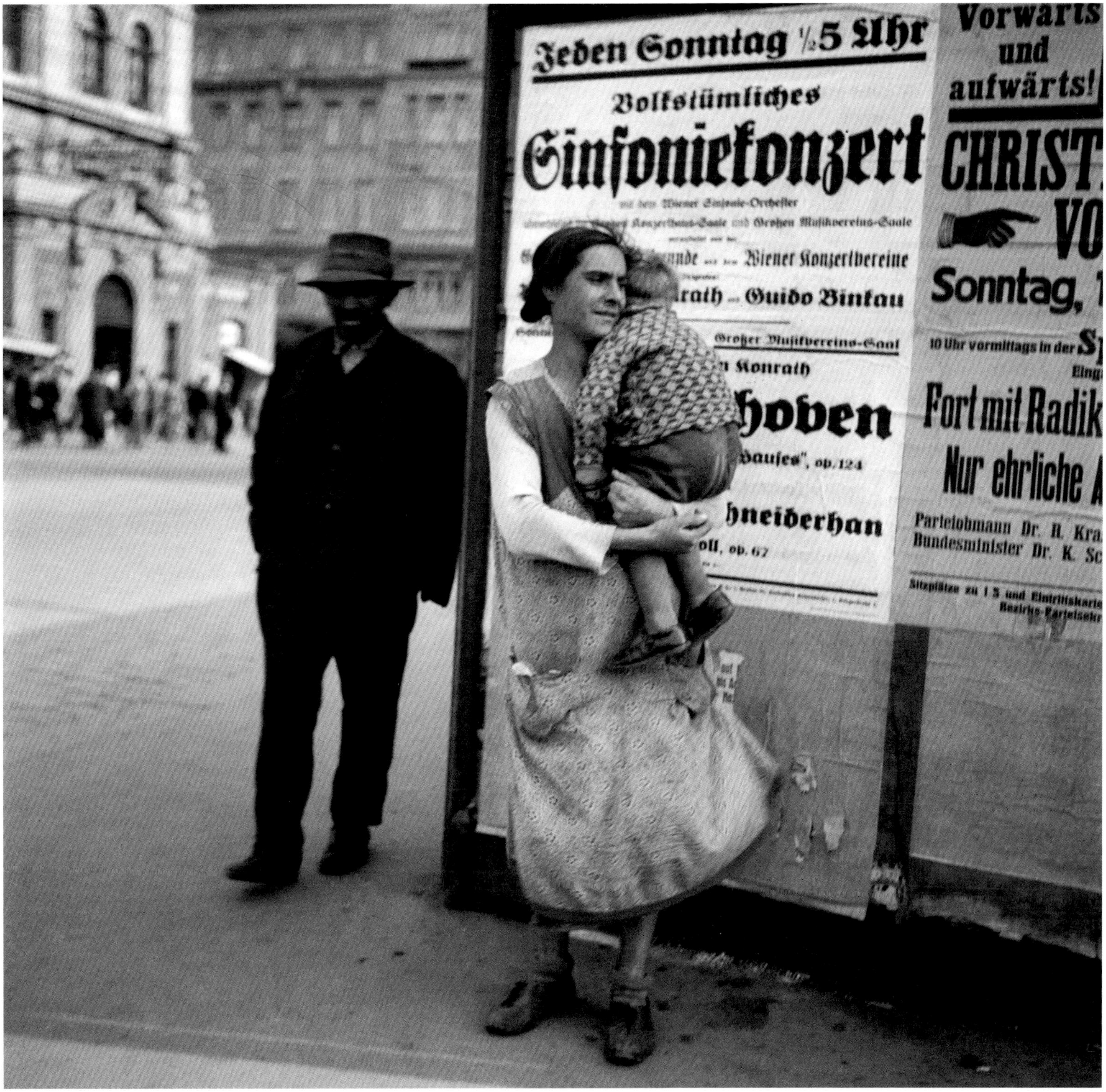

Edith Suschitzky
Woman and Child, Vienna, ca. 1930
Digital inkjet print, 30.5 × 30 cm
National Galleries of Scotland, PGP 279.86

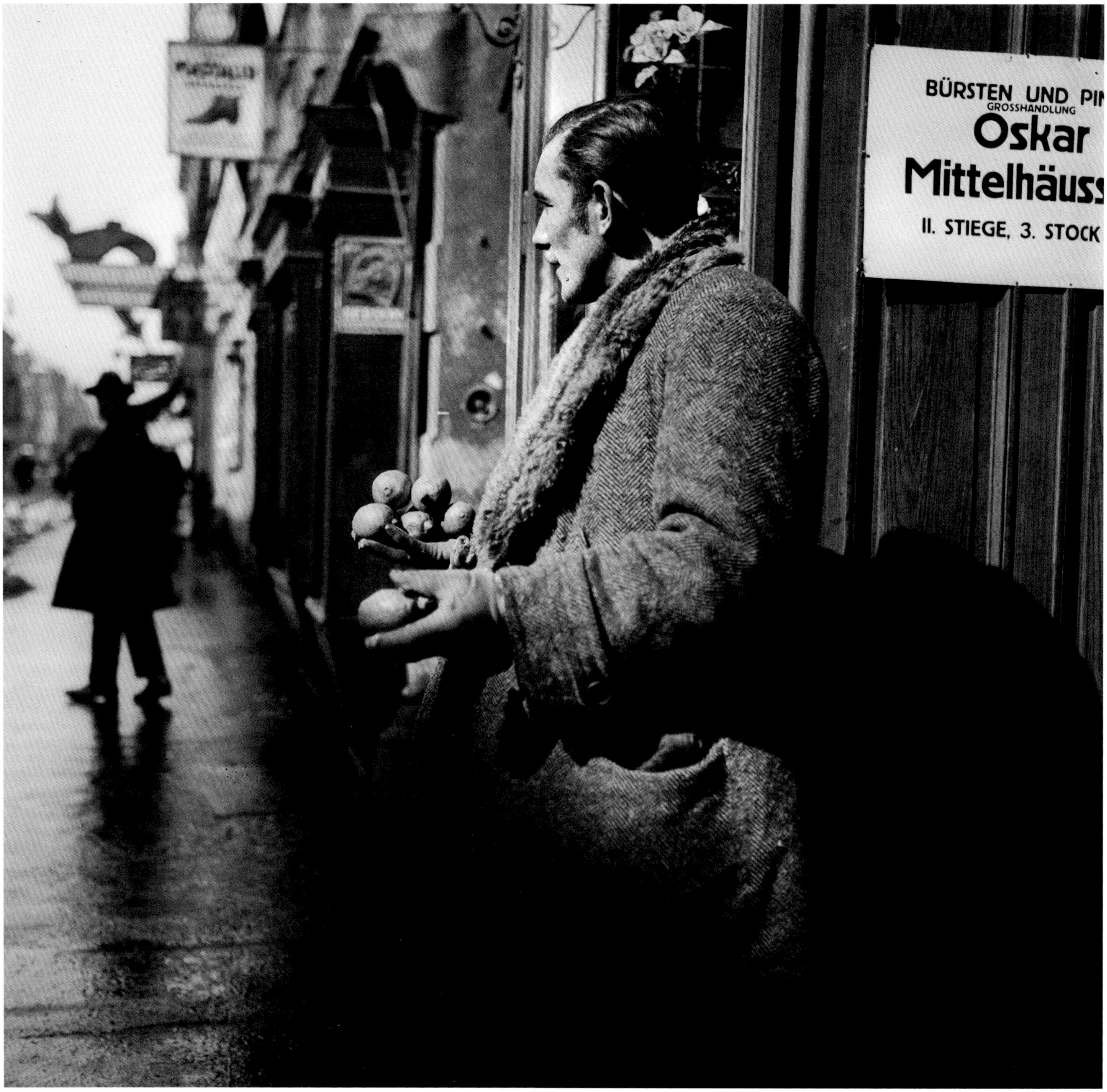

Edith Suschitzky
Man Selling Fruit, Vienna, ca. 1930
Modern silver-gelatin print, 30.3 × 30 cm
National Galleries of Scotland, PGP 279.17

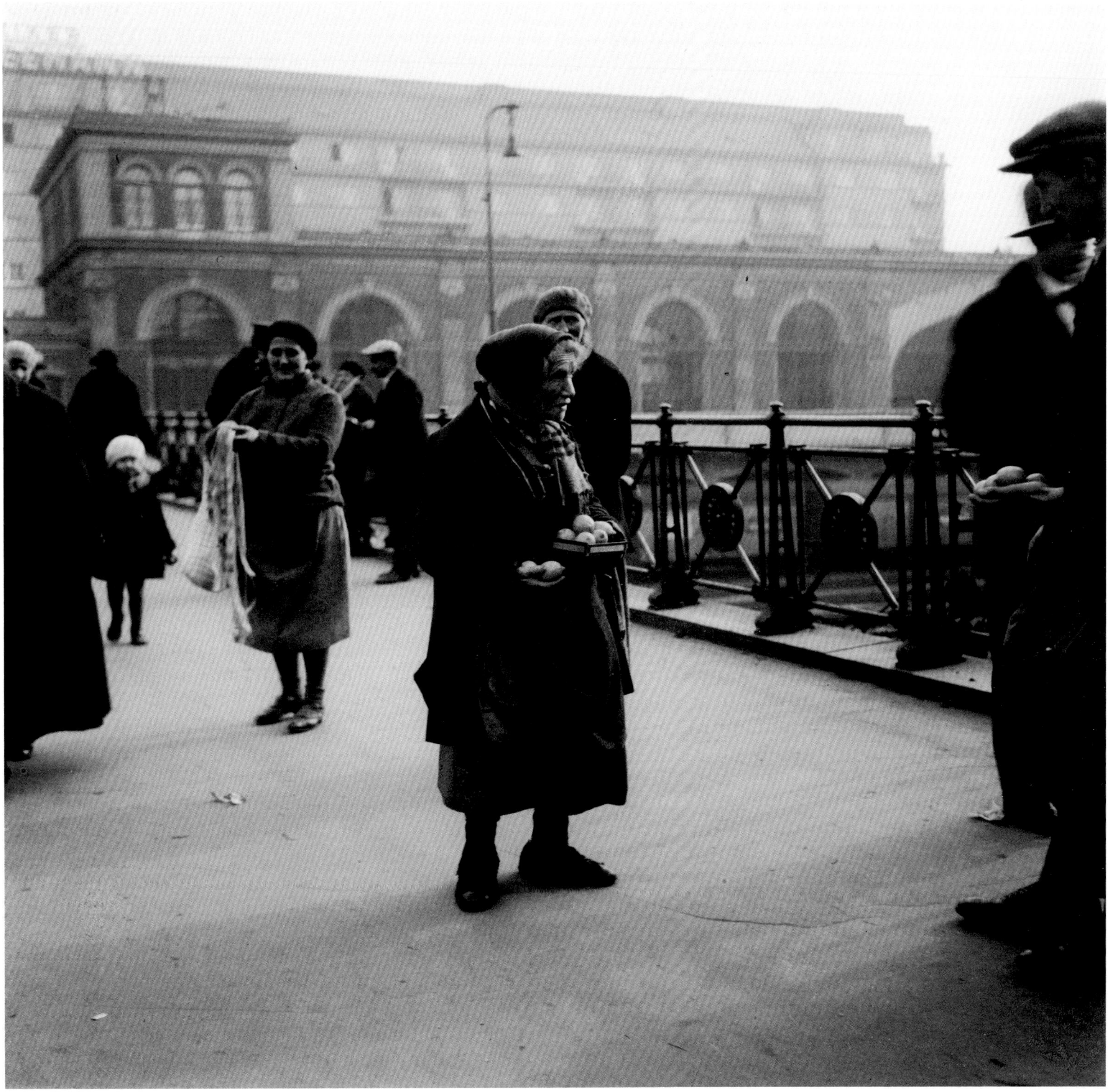

Edith Suschitzky
Woman Selling Fruit, Vienna, ca. 1930
Modern silver-gelatin print, 25.1 × 25 cm
National Galleries of Scotland, PGP 279.6

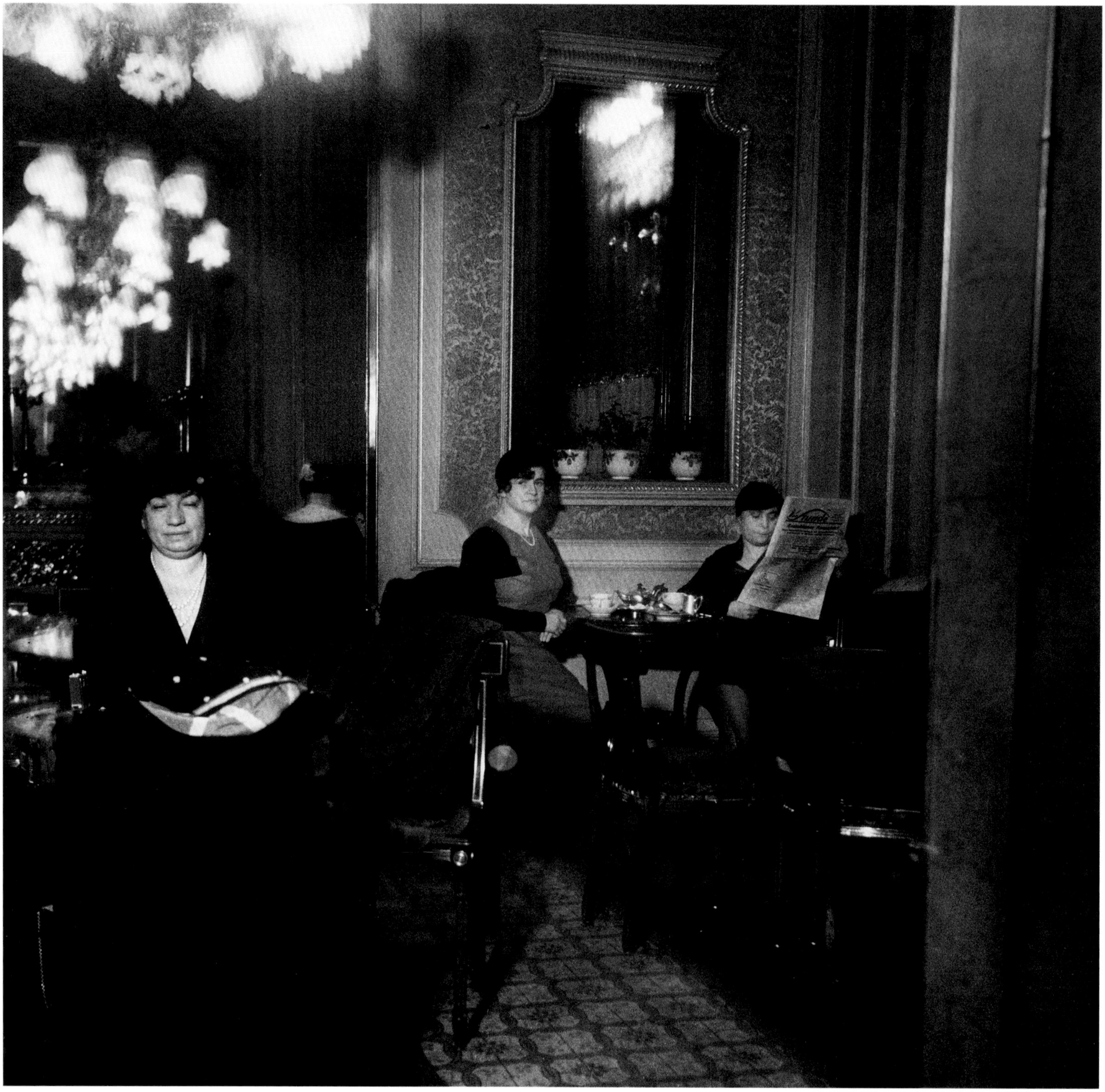

Edith Suschitzky
Café Interior, Vienna, 1932
Modern silver-gelatin print, 30.2 × 30.1 cm
National Galleries of Scotland, PGP 279.5

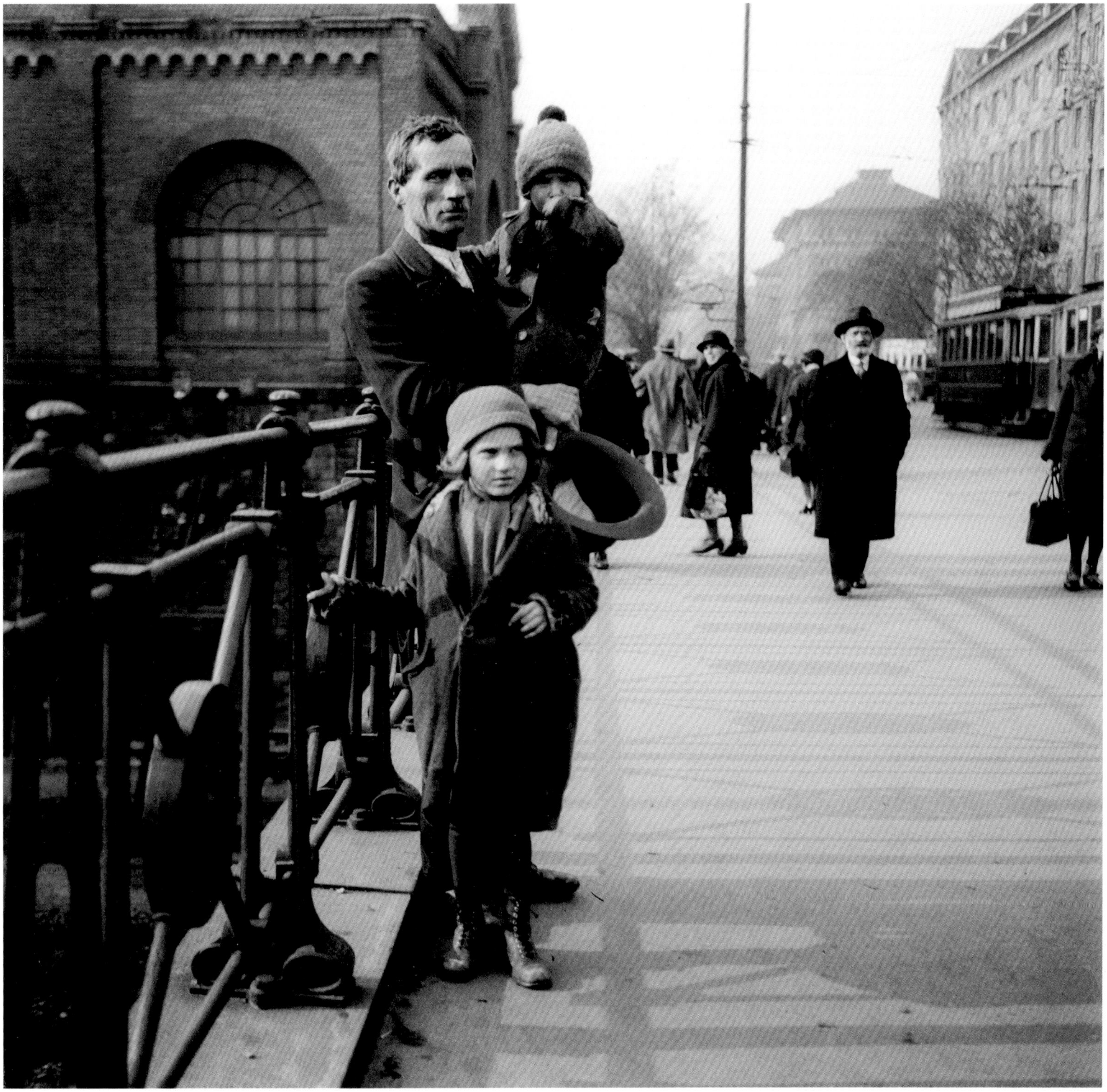

Edith Suschitzky
Man with Children Begging, Vienna, ca. 1930
Modern silver-gelatin print, 27.7 × 27.5 cm
National Galleries of Scotland, PGP 279.19

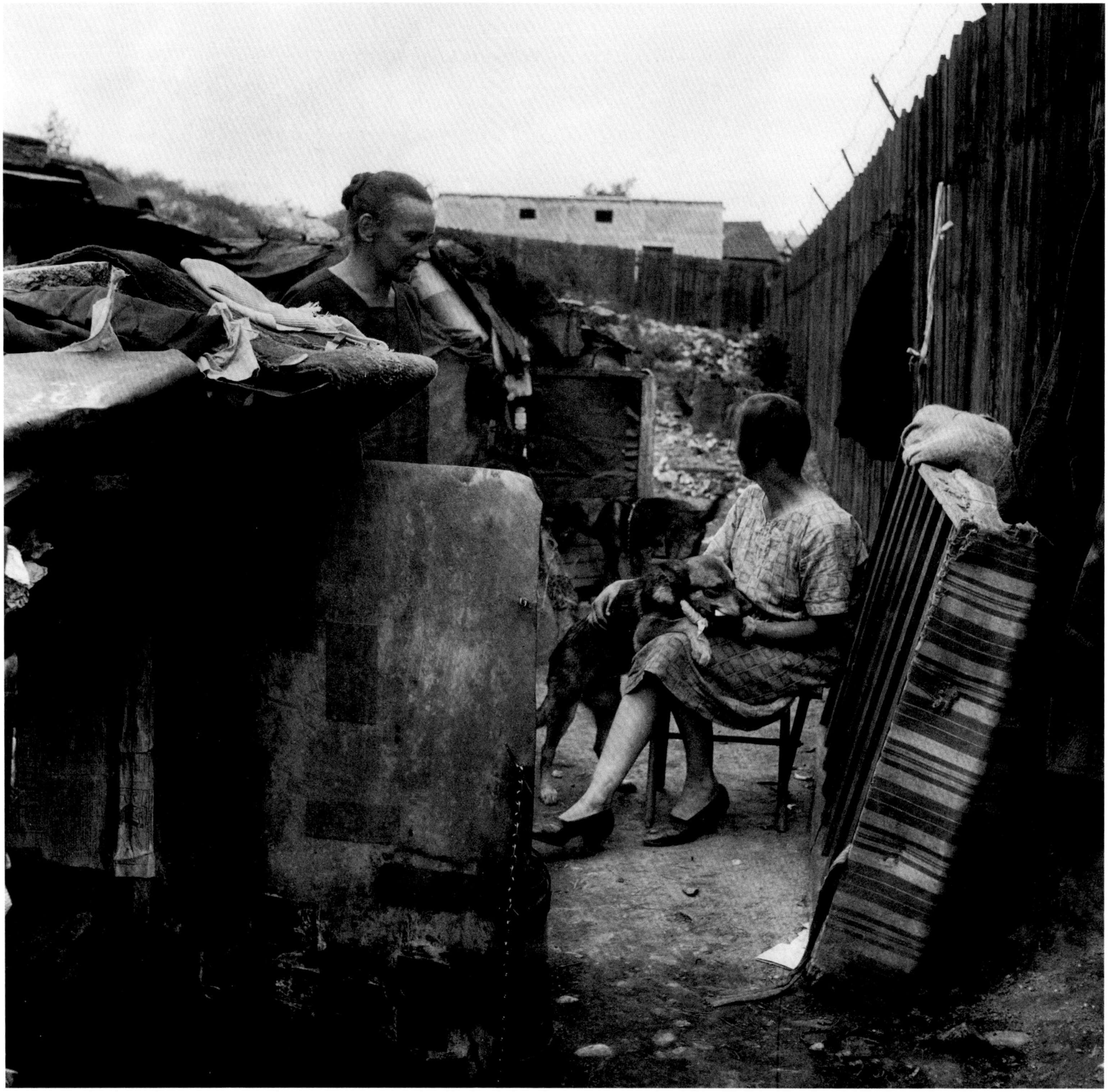

Edith Suschitzky
Slum Housing, Vienna, ca. 1930
Modern silver-gelatin print, 30.3 × 30.1 cm
National Galleries of Scotland, PGP 279.27

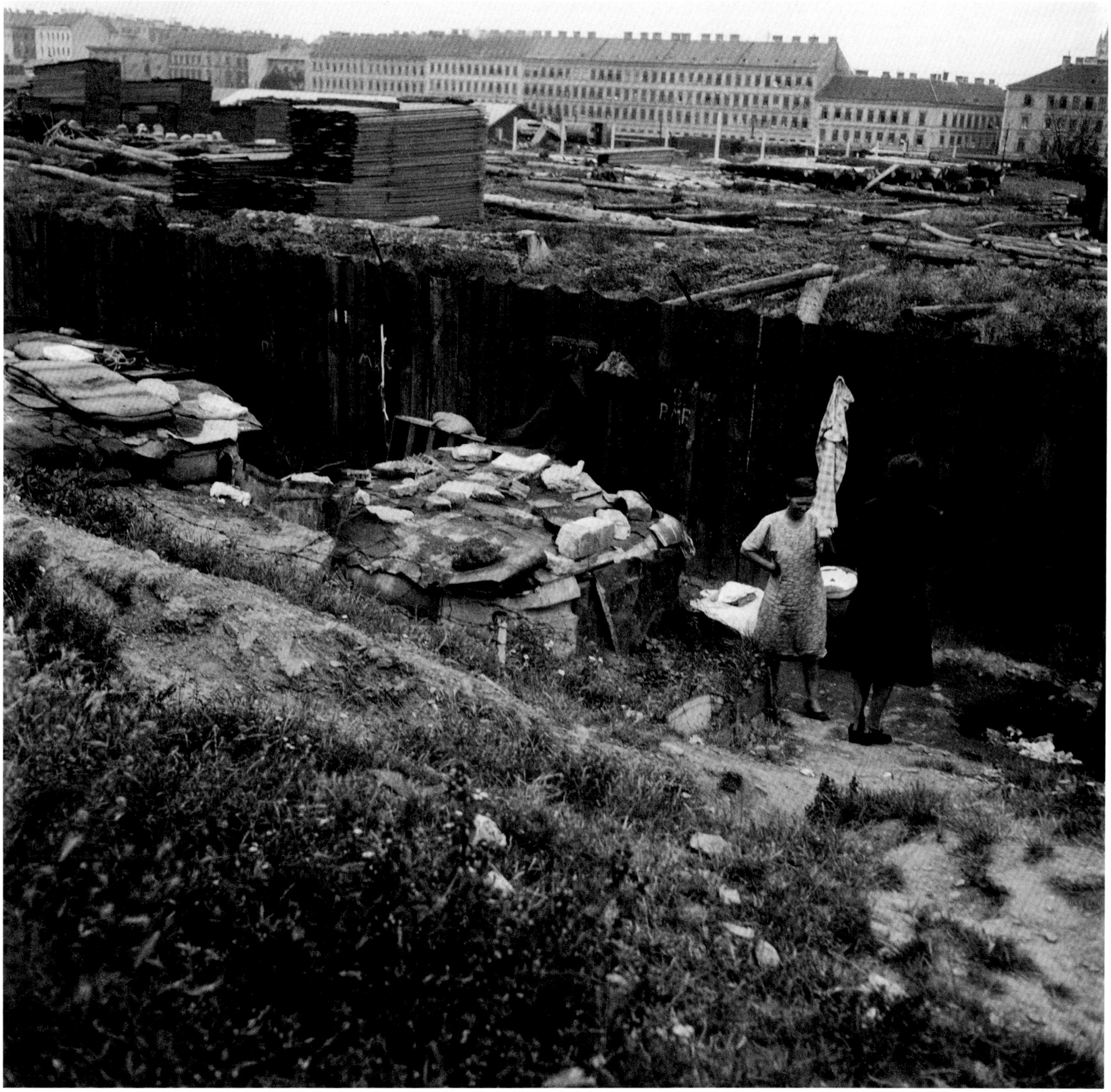

Edith Suschitzky
Slum Housing, Vienna, ca. 1930
Digital inkjet print, 30.5 × 30 cm
National Galleries of Scotland, PGP 279.87

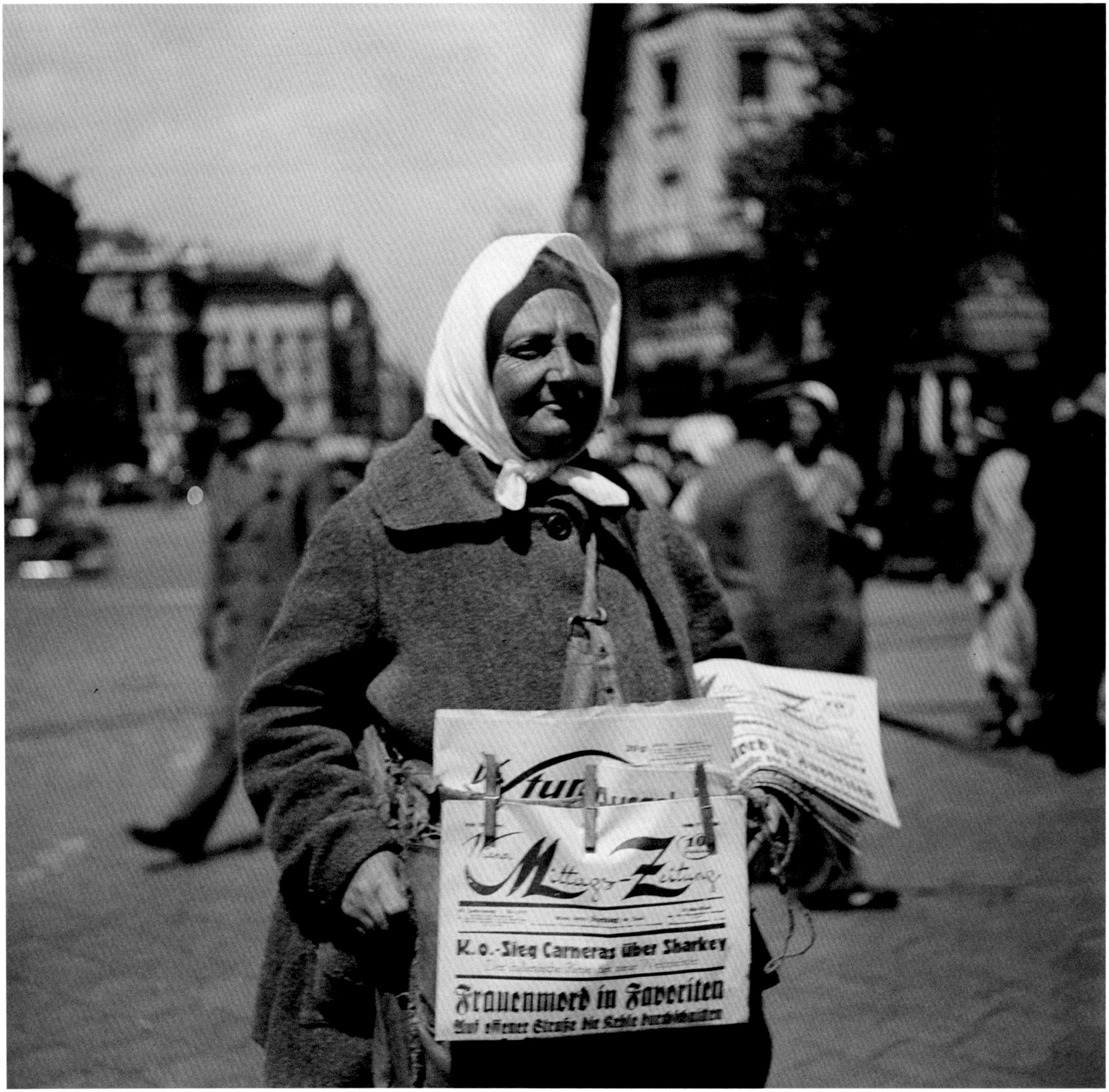

Edith Suschitzky
Newspaper Seller, Vienna, 1933
Digital inkjet print, 30.4 × 30 cm
National Galleries of Scotland, PGP 279.88

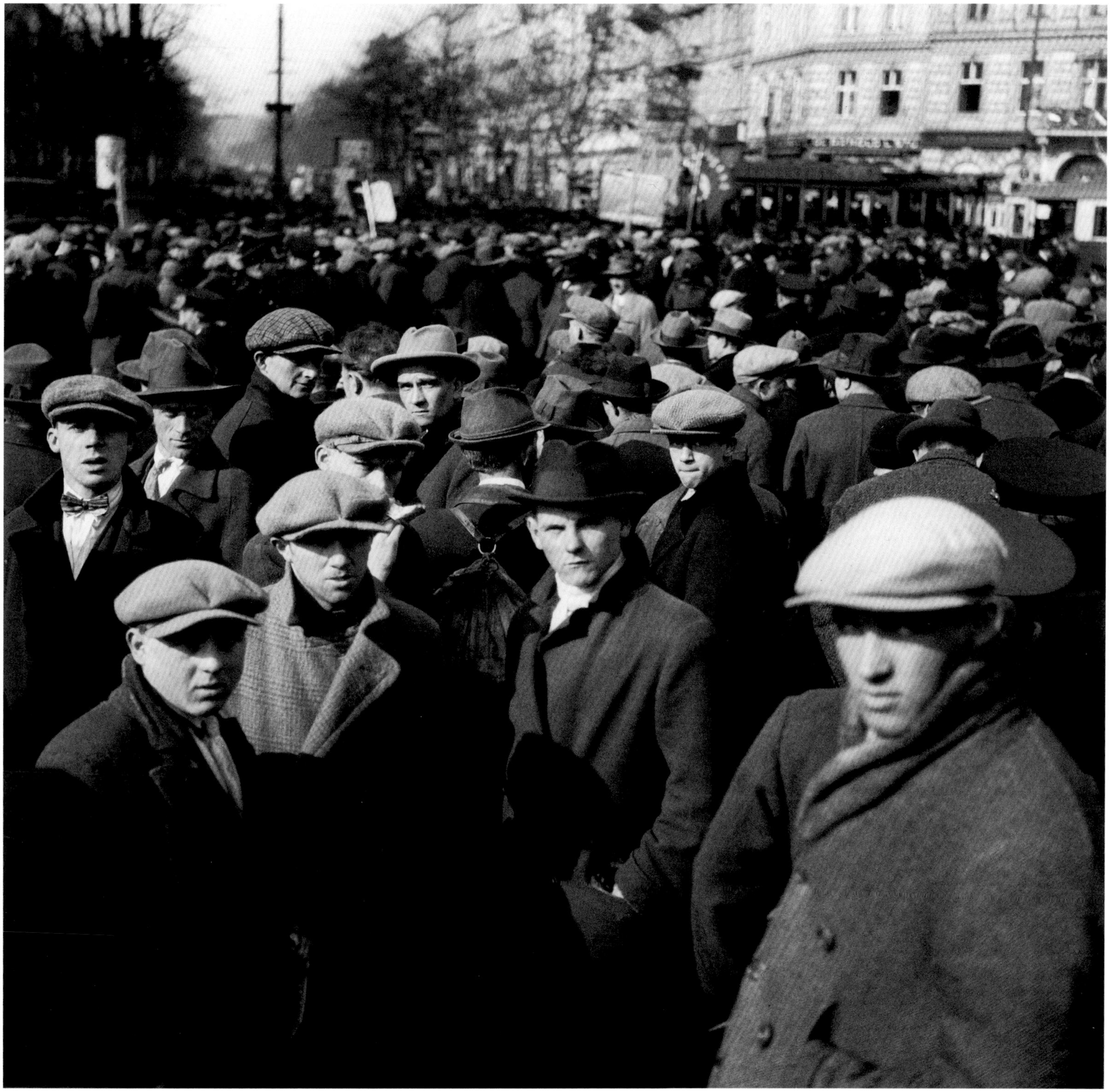

Edith Suschitzky
Unemployed Workers' Demonstration, Vienna, 1932
Modern silver-gelatin print, 30.3 × 30 cm
National Galleries of Scotland, PGP 279.20

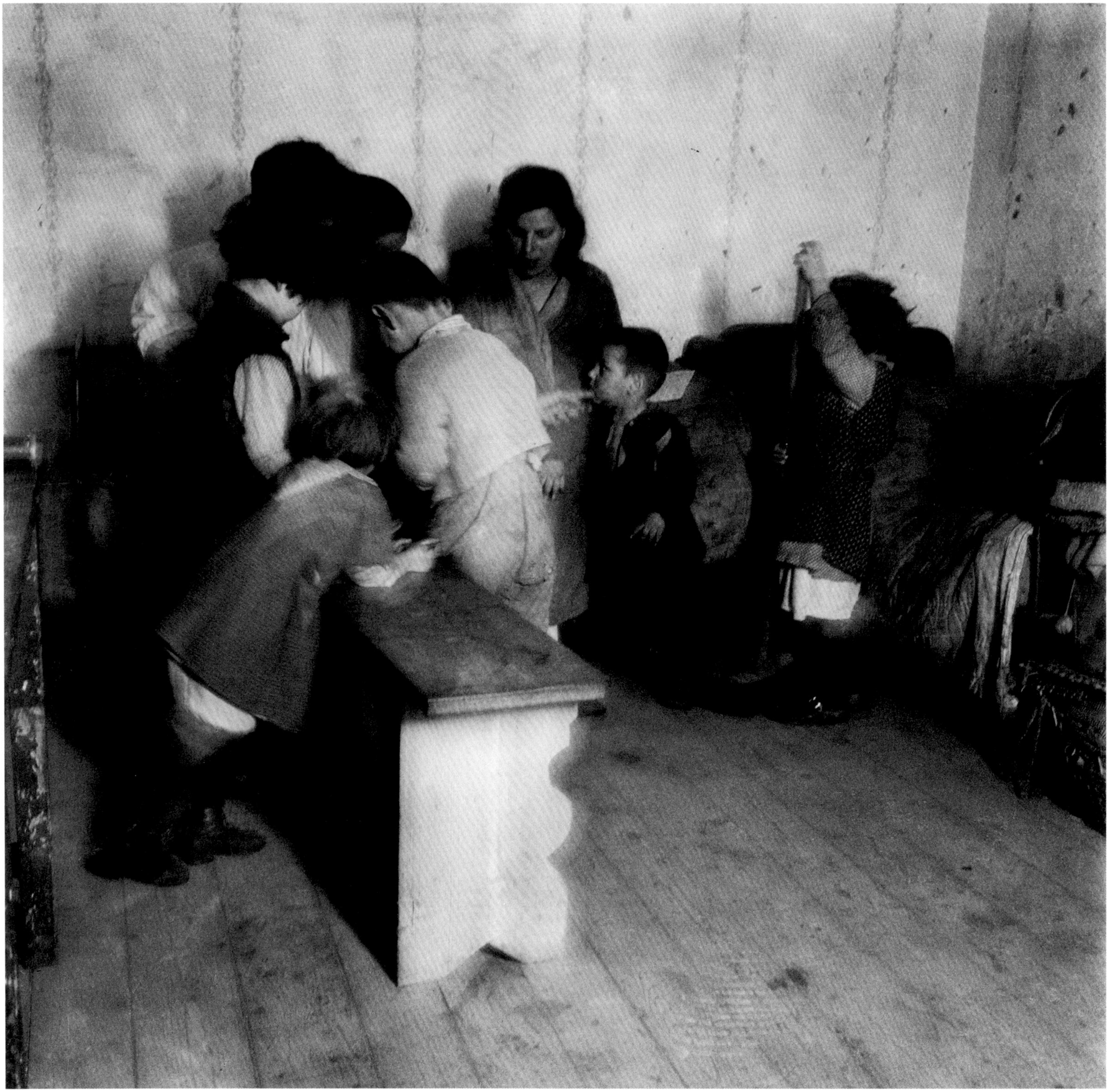

Edith Suschitzky
Working-Class Home, Vienna, ca. 1930
Modern silver-gelatin print, 27.7 × 27.5 cm
National Galleries of Scotland, PGP 279.16

Activist with a Camera
Edith Suschitzky in the Context of the Viennese Photo Scene around 1930

Anton Holzer

Edith Suschitzky, who called herself Edith Tudor-Hart following her marriage in 1933, published her first photographs in the illustrated press around 1930, when she was in her early twenties. A series of her reportages appeared in *Der Kuckuck,* a Social Democratic illustrated magazine, while other photographs of hers were published in *Die Bühne,* a liberal monthly. These publications provided the young woman, who had been active in the Communist movement since the late nineteen-twenties,[1] with a welcome source of extra income. It is not certain, however, whether Suschitzky was aiming for a career as a photojournalist. She and her photographs appeared only occasionally, rather than continually, in the newspapers and illustrated magazines, and most of the pictures she took in Vienna remained unpublished. What is more, her journalistic activity in Vienna lasted only a few years. Shortly after the publication of her first photographs, the political situation in Austria radically changed. The country's liberal democracy, in which the Social Democrats—at least in Vienna—had held a strong position, was gradually dismantled by Engelbert Dollfuss's Christian Social government in 1933 and 1934. Thus, in July 1933, both the Communist and the National Socialist party newspapers were banned, while in February 1934 the Social Democratic opposition and its press were forcibly shut down, and the state reorganized into a dictatorial regime. Against this background, Suschitzky's room for maneuver increasingly narrowed. In May 1933 she was briefly arrested; in the same year she married the English doctor Alexander Tudor-Hart, moving with him to London in April 1934, that is, immediately after Austria's transition to dictatorship.

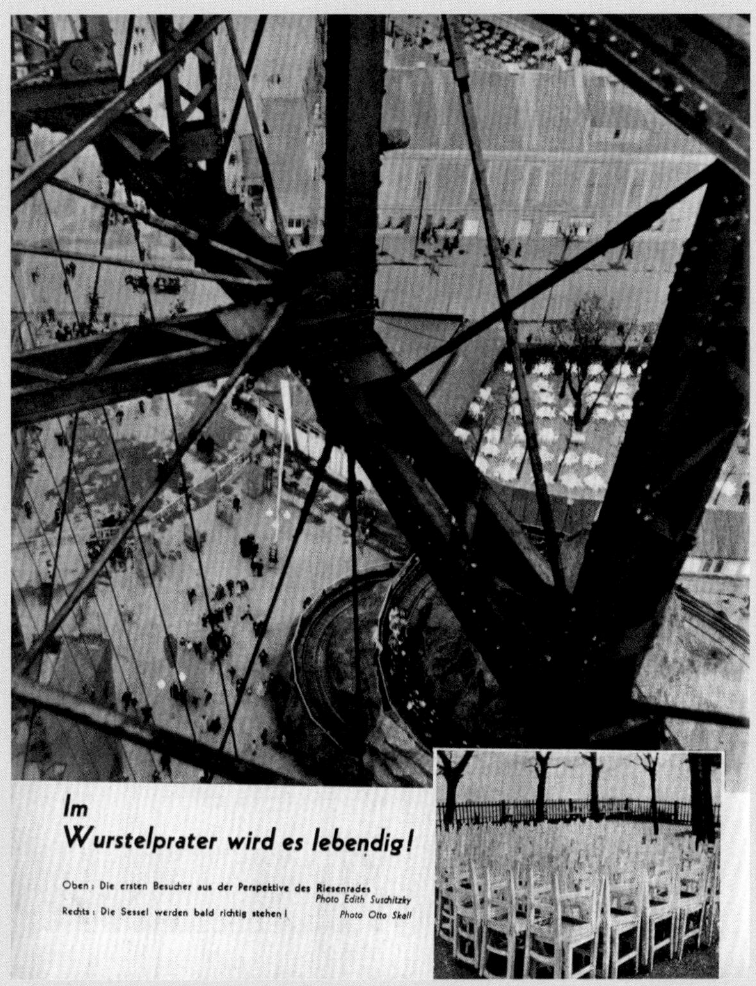
Im
Wurstelprater wird es lebendig!

Oben: Die ersten Besucher aus der Perspektive des Riesenrades
Photo Edith Suschitzky
Rechts: Die Sessel werden bald richtig stehen!
Photo Otto Skall

Fig. 10
Edith Suschitzky, "The Vienna Prater with the Giant Ferris Wheel, Taken from Above," *Die Bühne,* second April issue of 1933, p. 14. Photo (bottom): Otto Skall

Reception of the Avant-Garde in Vienna around 1930

What was the milieu in which Edith Suschitzky moved while working as a photographer in Vienna? And what were her photographic influences? To answer these questions, it is necessary to outline more precisely two photographic movements that left a visible impact on her work around 1930: on the one hand, the photography of the avant-garde, especially of the *Neues Sehen* (New Vision), and, on the other, the socially critical photography of the worker photography movement. As we shall see, the latter exerted a more powerful influence on her work than the avant-garde, which appears as a clear point of reference in only a few of her photographs. Personal connections linked Suschitzky with both: her political involvement in the Communist movement had brought her into contact with the worker photography movement, while she had encountered the photographic avant-garde during her studies at the Bauhaus in Dessau from 1928 to 1930. After returning to Vienna in 1930, Suschitzky produced a number of photographs in which she experimented with the formal principles of *Neues Sehen,* such as unusual camera angles. One of these pictures, published in the magazine *Die Bühne* in April 1933, is taken from a gondola at the top of Vienna's giant Ferris wheel (fig. 10).[2] The wheel's iron struts, which cut diagonally across the foreground of the picture, appear as an abstract pattern. The camera is pointed almost vertically downward from a great height. Far below on the ground people can be seen, small as ants, hurrying across the grounds of the Prater, Vienna's central park. This might be compared with a similar image that was also taken from a gondola of the Ferris wheel about a year and a half before by the amateur Viennese photographer Sepp Nowak (fig. 11), who was also influenced by the *Neues Sehen.*[3] Vienna in the late twenties could hardly have been described as a citadel of the avant-garde—rather the opposite. Nevertheless, under the Social Democratic government a climate of cultural openness and curiosity had been established, which attracted all manner of progressive cultural projects.[4] Among these were the artistic, theatrical, and photographic scenes of the young and revolutionary Soviet Union. In March 1928—ten years after the Russian Revolution—an exhibition of Soviet Russian art was shown by Vienna's Hagenbund, an association of progressive artists. Innovative theater productions could also be seen in Vienna, as well as modernist poster design and graphic works. At the same time, between 1927 and 1929, the film distribution company NEWA showed a large number of so-called "Russian films" in Vienna.[5] On the other hand, there was also an intensive exchange between Vienna and the progressive Czech cultural scene. In 1928 a large exhibition of contemporary culture was held in the Czech city of Brno, which excited a great deal of interest in Austria. In the thirties a number of modern Czech photographers, as well as some filmmakers, were in contact with Vienna, among them Jan Lukas, Václav Jiru, and Alexandr Hackenschmied (later Hammid). Others, like Willy Riethof or Otto Skall, were of Czech origin but mostly lived and worked in Vienna.

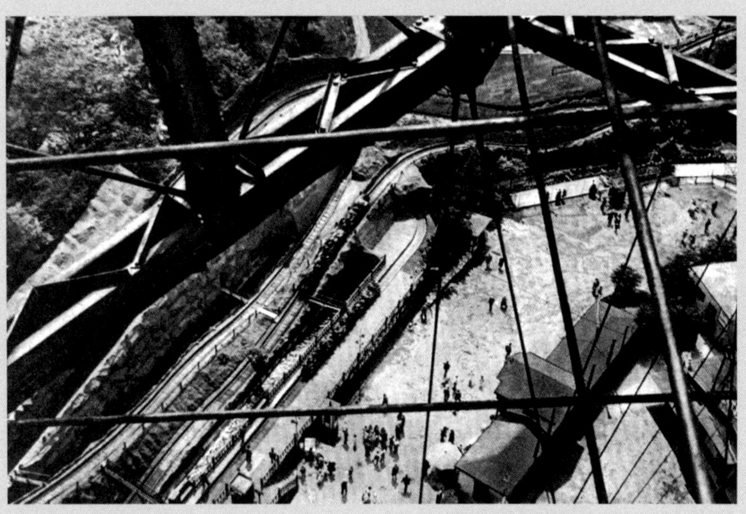

Fig. 11
Sepp Nowak, "Vienna's Giant Ferris Wheel," *Die Bühne,* second November issue of 1931, p. 26

The avant-garde German films of the nineteen-twenties were also known in Vienna. In 1927, for example, Walter Ruttmann's film *Berlin: Die Sinfonie der Grossstadt* (Berlin: Symphony of the Metropolis) premiered in Vienna, at almost the same time that it came out in Berlin. The German Bauhaus also exerted an influence. As we have seen, Suschitzky had studied in Germany in the late twenties. A few other Austrian artists also studied at the Bauhaus, such as Friedl Dicker, Herbert Bayer, and Erich Komeriner, who had been born in Vienna but grew up in Berlin.

On the other hand, some German Bauhaus photographers occasionally worked in Vienna. For example, Fritz Heinze, who had been studying at the Bauhaus since 1927, spent the summer of 1930 in the city.[6] One of his photographs shows the opera house on the corner of Vienna's Ringstrasse at night (fig. 12).[7] This almost abstract street scene is a long way from traditional images of Vienna, and it bathes the city in an experimental light that had not been seen before. It is entirely possible that Heinze, who like Suschitzky was active in the Communist movement, knew the Viennese photographer from their student days in Dessau. A small group of Bauhaus students, Heinze among them, actively participated in the Dessau group of the German Association of Worker Photographers.[8] Whether Suschitzky was also a member of the Dessau group is not known.

A Manifesto of Modern Photography: The *Film und Foto* Exhibition in Vienna

In 1930, enthusiasm for the "new" photography reached a high point.[9] This was the year in which the legendary Werkbund (Work Federation) exhibition *Film und Foto,* known as *FiFo* for short, came to Vienna. The Vienna show was held between February 20 and March 31, 1930 in the Austrian Museum of Art and Industry on the Ringstrasse (today the Austrian Museum of Applied Arts / Contemporary Art or MAK). Although Edith Suschitzky was not among the photographers whose work was exhibited at the show, it may safely be assumed that she saw it. Both *Der Kuckuck* and *Die Bühne,* which were publishing her pictures at this time, gave detailed and extremely positive reviews of the exhibition.[10]

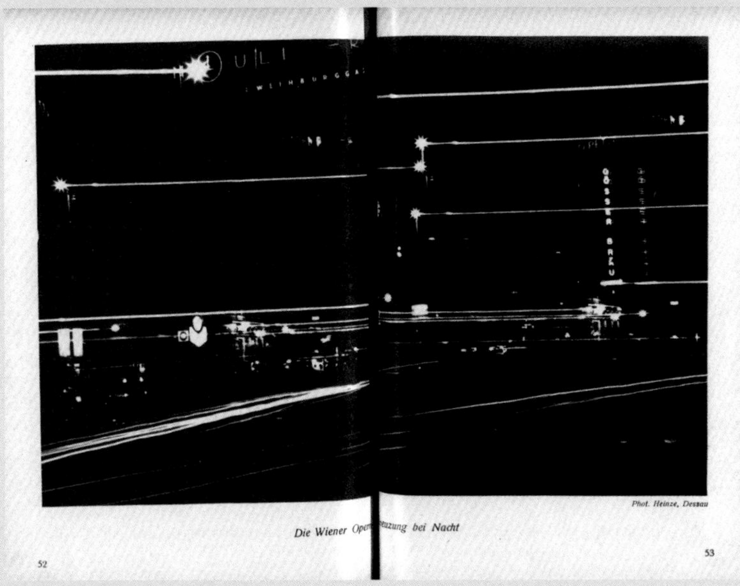

Fig. 12
Fritz Heinze, "Junction at the Vienna Opera by Night," *Wiener Magazin* 11, November 1930, pp. 52–53

Alongside the international stars of modern photography, whose work could already be seen in Germany (El Lissitzky, Alexander Rodchenko, John Heartfield, Hannah Höch, Helmar Lerski, Germaine Krull, László Moholy-Nagy, André Kertész, Man Ray, Aenne Biermann, Charles Sheeler, Edward Weston, Sasha Stone, Piet Zwart, and many others), the Vienna exhibition also included an additional section showing the work of thirteen Austrian photographers.[11] Alongside the various representatives of *Neues Sehen* or *Neue Sachlichkeit* (New Objectivity)—such as Richard Träger, Willy Riethof, Hans Cechal, and Franz Meyer—the Austrian section showed works that might at best be defined as "moderate modernism," for instance by Trude Fleischmann, Trude Geiringer and Dora Horowitz, Grete Kolliner, Hertha Müller, Ilona Kiss, Otto Skall, and others. Even traditional photographic art studies, such as those by Maximilian Karnitschnigg, were shown.

It is very clear from the Austrian works added to the *Film und Foto* exhibition of 1930 that its organizer, the Österreichischer Werkbund (Austrian Work Federation), held differing ideas about what modern photography was. The factional disputes and conflicts between the moderns and traditionalists came through in the selection of photographs. Among the Austrian photographers whose work could be described as modern, it was clear that the moderate modernists had prevailed over the more radical innovators. Many representatives of contemporary photography united both modern and traditional elements, depending on their approach to their subject, their aims, and their intentions. This was just as true of studio photographers as it was of press photographers, but it also applied to the amateurs, who still tended to be more ready to work experimentally. The Viennese amateur photographers who were active around 1930, and whose work showed a greater openness to modern photography, included, to name just a few, Franz Senkinc, Sepp Nowak, Albert Karplus, Ferdinand Hodek, Josef Schramek, Otto Exinger, Franz Spreng, Otto Weber, Willy Eggarter, Willy Riethof, Rudolf Spiegel, Kurt Husnik, Hans Grabkovicz, Otto Dobrowolny, Oskar Kuhn, Hans Madensky, Annie Schulz, Lotte Meitner-Graf, Otto Skall, Robert Haas, Niklaus Schwarz, Ludwig Szabo, Hans Casparius, Franz Mayer, Kurt Husnk, Walther Schneider, Felix Braun, and Ernst Kassowitz. It is true that most of them were not avant-gardists in the narrow sense of the word. But the influence of *Neue Sachlichkeit* or *Neues Sehen* repeatedly recurs in their photo reportages, their commercial photography, and their still lifes.

Suschitzky undoubtedly knew the works of this "moderately modernist" group of photographers, which were shown in exhibitions and published in magazines. No record has survived of whether she had any closer contact with its individual members. She must also have been very aware that in Vienna the new photography was in a precarious position. Radical photographic experiments of the kind that were carried out at the Bauhaus in the late twenties met with little response in Vienna.[12] What is more, around 1930 a fierce conflict was raging between the supporters of modern photography and the traditionalists. It was being fought out in the press, but also in the photography magazines and yearbooks, almost all of which were firmly in conservative hands.[13] It was broadly won by the traditionalists not long after the Work Federation's *Film und Foto* exhibition. By 1931–32, the avant-gardists' spirit had largely been broken, and traditionalist and conservative positions were setting the tone once more.

The Camera as a Means of Political Engagement

For Edith Suschitzky, the avant-garde's artistic experiments were evidently nothing more than a kind of formal gimmickry, in which she would from time to time indulge. The artistic principles of *Neues Sehen* scarcely play any further role in the overwhelming part of her Vienna work, nor in the later social documentary work she did in England. Although she shot a number of street scenes from an elevated window, she did this less in order to experiment with unusual camera angles than, for example, to be able to capture all the marchers in a demonstration. Only occasionally did she shoot her street photographs at a slight angle, above all in her English works from the nineteen-thirties. In this way she produced slightly estranged images with diagonal perspectives, which challenged the everyday perception of things, but which were a far cry from the avant-garde's radical visual innovations.

In her early social documentary images, which show such things as street demonstrations, social living conditions among ordinary people, or the misery of the underclass, but also in most of her scenes of everyday life, taken in Vienna's Prater or on the Danube, Suschitzky almost invariably chose a factual and documentary visual language. In her eyes, photography was first and foremost a documentary means for conveying social and political concerns. In a reportage that appeared in *Der Kuckuck* in early October 1931, she portrayed the "Caledonian market" in London, "an emporium for the poorest of the poor," as she put it (fig. 13).[14] The photographer had brought the pictures back from one of her trips to London. They offer sober, clear, and unadorned visual documentation, whose aim was to capture the depressing social reality of the subject. The text is also by Suschitzky and describes the poverty and deprivation of both shoppers and traders:

> In contrast to most of the world's other marketplaces, the Caledonian market is utterly colorless and devoid of romance; it might be said to embody, in concentrated form, the bleakness of London's working class districts, where the sun literally never shines. The traders are principally working class women and the unemployed, who, after wandering around for some time, are able to bargain for themselves a tattered pair of trousers. Eccentric figures with very large hats are also sometimes to be seen, but in general very few people from the other side of London actually stray into this malodorous world.[15]

This example shows that Suschitzky did not use photography as a means of poetically representing reality, but principally as a way of documenting social injustices. In her eyes, the camera was a "weapon" in the political struggle. This position had been developed in the twenties by the worker photography movement. Since Suschitzky was closely associated with the Communist movement, and was publishing her pictures in *Der Kuckuck,* the magazine of the Social Democratic party, she was very well acquainted with this photographic movement. Worker photography groups, organized along party political lines, emerged in Germany in the mid-twenties and spread to several other European countries.[16]

The Austrian Worker Photography Movement

In March 1926, the Communist *Arbeiter-Illustrierte-Zeitung* (AIZ), published in Germany, announced its first photo competition for worker photographers. Its editors' declared aim was "to put the photo correspondents of the bourgeois press completely out of business, and replace them with photographs by workers that depict working class life."[17] When the Social Democratic journalist Julius Braunthal founded the Austrian Social Democratic illustrated magazine *Der Kuckuck* in 1929 (fig. 14), it not only based its layout on the *AIZ* but also adopted its worker photography competitions. In July 1930, the editors of *Der Kuckuck* made a programmatic appeal to worker photographers:

> We consider it important that workers reflect on the world of their daily lives and learn to reproduce it in photographs. We consider it important that they look around themselves, see their daily routine for what it is, and give it visual form by means of a camera. We aim to bring out the beauty of life, wherever it may be. The subjects we would like to see dealt with can only

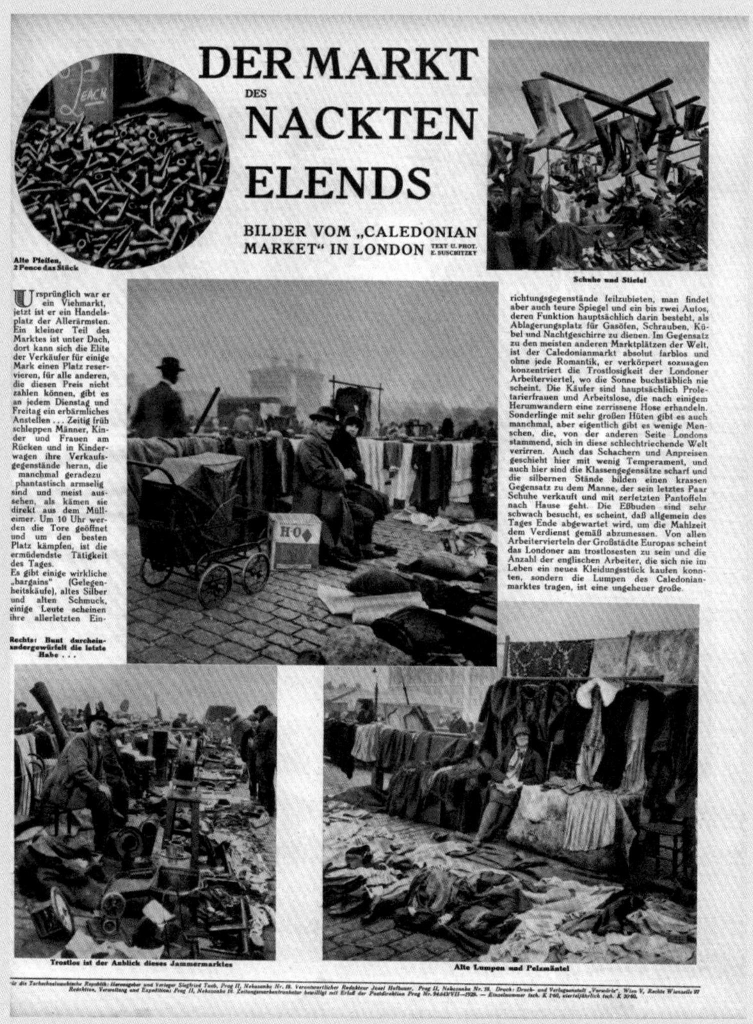

DER MARKT DES NACKTEN ELENDS

BILDER VOM „CALEDONIAN MARKET" IN LONDON

TEXT U. PHOT. E. SUSCHITZKY

Alte Pfeifen, 2 Pence das Stück

Ursprünglich war er ein Viehmarkt, jetzt ist er ein Handelsplatz der Allerärmsten. Ein kleiner Teil des Marktes ist unter Dach, dort kann sich die Elite der Verkäufer für einige Mark einen Platz reservieren, für alle anderen, die diesen Preis nicht zahlen können, gibt es an jedem Dienstag und Freitag ein erbärmliches Anstellen ... Zeitig früh schleppen Männer, Kinder und Frauen am Rücken und in Kinderwagen ihre Verkaufsgegenstände heran, die manchmal geradezu phantastisch armselig sind und meist aussehen, als kämen sie direkt aus dem Mülleimer. Um 10 Uhr werden die Tore geöffnet und um den besten Platz kämpfen, ist die ermüdendste Tätigkeit des Tages.
Es gibt einige wirkliche „bargains" (Gelegenheitskäufe), altes Silber und alten Schmuck, einige Leute scheinen ihre allerletzten Einrichtungsgegenstände feilzubieten, man findet aber auch teure Spiegel und ein bis zwei Autos, deren Funktion hauptsächlich darin besteht, als Ablagerungsplatz für Gasöfen, Schrauben, Kübel und Nachtgeschirre zu dienen. Im Gegensatz zu den meisten anderen Marktplätzen der Welt, ist der Caledonianmarkt absolut farblos und ohne jede Romantik, er verkörpert sozusagen konzentriert die Trostlosigkeit der Londoner Arbeiterviertel, wo die Sonne buchstäblich nie scheint. Die Käufer sind hauptsächlich Proletarierfrauen und Arbeitslose, die nach einigem Herumwandern eine zerrissene Hose erhandeln. Sonderlinge mit sehr großen Hüten gibt es auch manchmal, aber eigentlich gibt es wenige Menschen, die, von der anderen Seite Londons stammend, sich in diese schlechtriechende Welt verirren. Auch das Schachern und Anpreisen geschieht hier mit wenig Temperament, und auch hier sind die Klassengegensätze scharf und die silbernen Stände bilden einen krassen Gegensatz zu dem Manne, der sein letztes Paar Schuhe verkauft und mit zerfetzten Pantoffeln nach Hause geht. Die Eßbuden sind sehr schwach besucht, es scheint, daß allgemein des Tages Ende abgewartet wird, um die Mahlzeit dem Verdienst gemäß abzumessen. Von allen Arbeitervierteln der Großstädte Europas scheint das Londoner am trostlosesten zu sein und die Anzahl der englischen Arbeiter, die sich nie im Leben ein neues Kleidungsstück kaufen konnten, sondern die Lumpen des Caledonianmarktes tragen, ist eine ungeheuer große.

Schuhe und Stiefel

Rechts: Bunt durcheinandergewürfelt die letzte Habe ...

Trostlos ist der Anblick dieses Jammermarktes

Alte Lumpen und Pelzmäntel

Fig. 13
Edith Suschitzky (photos and text), "The Market of Naked Misery: Images of the 'Caledonian Market' in London," *Der Kuckuck,* October 4, 1931, p. 15

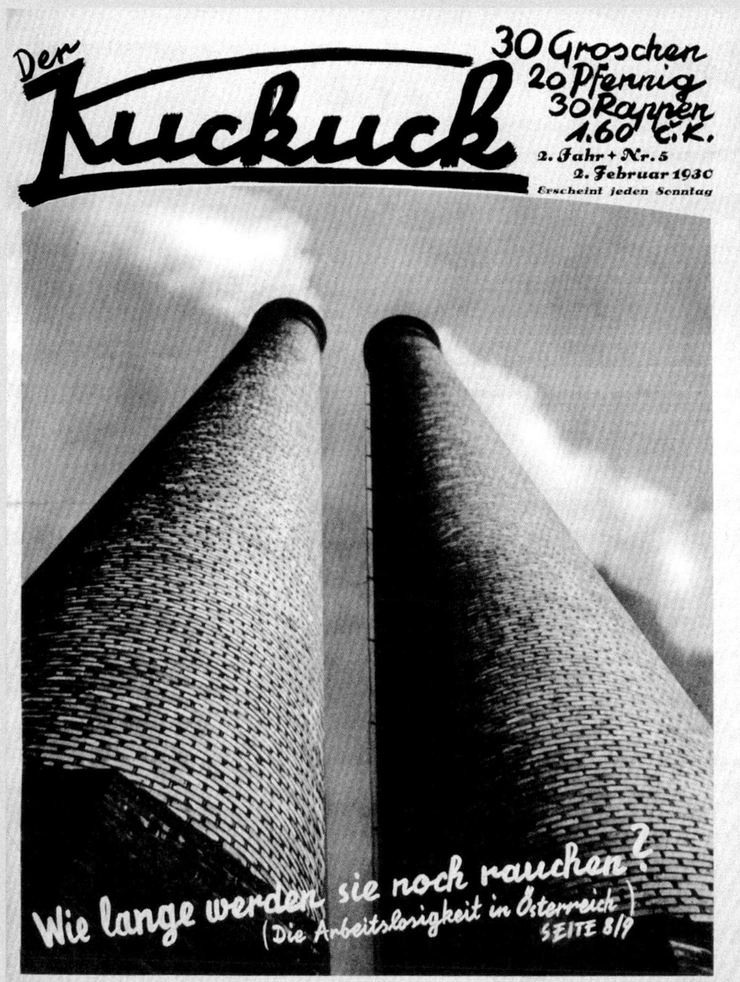

Fig. 14
"How Long Will They Continue to Emit Smoke? (Unemployment in Austria)," front cover of the Social Democratic magazine *Der Kuckuck,* February 2, 1930. Photo: Hans Cechal

> be sketched out in general terms: workplaces, work itself, the journey to work, the home, the street, the child, the body, the world of the child, esoterica, the objects of everyday life, social life, etc. We are only interested in showing landscapes if they are distinguished by outstanding visual qualities.[18]

Although Suschitzky was a Communist rather than a Social Democrat, she also shared the attitude expressed by Siegfried Weyr, the editor-in-chief of *Der Kuckuck*. In the summer of 1932 she took part in one of *Der Kuckuck*'s regularly announced photo competitions. The competition's winning works were published in the paper, and the photographers were promised remuneration of five schillings a picture. Suschitzky's entry, a reportage on the daily life of the Prater, was published in August 1932.[19] One of her pictures shows a *Watschenmann,* or popular fairground dummy, which emitted a sound when given a *Watschn,* or clip round the ears (fig. 15).

Why did Suschitzky publish her work in *Der Kuckuck,* a Social Democratic paper, and not in a Communist one? Compared to the Social Democrats, the Austrian Communist Party was tiny. In elections to the National Council during the nineteen-twenties, it consistently gained less than one percent of the vote, while over the same period the Social Democratic Workers' Party (Sozialdemokratische Arbeiterpartei or SDAP) gained between 35.9 percent (1920) and 42.3 percent (1927), thus establishing itself as the second largest party after the Christian Social Party. These inequalities of political power also had ramifications for the world of the party political newspapers, especially the field of the illustrated press. In 1929, the first year of its publication, *Der Kuckuck* had a weekly edition of just over 50,000 copies, which was a respectable circulation even by the standards of the bourgeois press.[20] The Communists had little to set against this journalistic power. The *Illustrierte Rote Woche,* which was associated with the Communist Party, was founded in early 1932 and ran for only a year and a half. It was banned in late July 1933. Printed on cheap newspaper and produced by the simplest of means, it could not hope to compete with *Der Kuckuck* in terms of either content or design. The Communist Party therefore had no suitable platform for high-quality photo reportage. So it is not surprising that Suschitzky turned to the Social Democratic *Kuckuck,* especially as the magazine's photographic policy closely coincided with her own ideas.

Around 1930 some Austrian Communists made hesitant attempts toward developing a party-affiliated worker photography movement based on the German model. In 1931 the Association of Austrian Worker Photographers was founded, but it never amounted to anything significant.[21] The *Illustrierte Rote Woche* announced "photography prizes" for worker photographers, but hardly any pictures by such photographers were published. The editors even openly admitted that the Communist worker photography movement had met with little success up to that point. As they wrote in June 1932:

> Our worker photographers have failed as photojournalists to the extent that they were incapable of capturing momentary situations. Photographing a slum dwelling is not difficult. All you need is the owner's permission. It is in clandestinely photographing places like the factory workshop, the labor exchange, or the welfare office that real skill is needed. This is also the reason why there are so few pictures showing workers' struggles. Photographers effectively limit themselves to reporting revolutionary demonstrations. But the kind of pictures they should be taking would be of families fighting an eviction, of workers

> resisting a saber attack by mounted police, or thwarted attempts to seize a peasant's small holding. While there were no important pictures of this kind, we did receive a number of group photographs, which of course cannot tell the viewer anything. Even from a technical point of view, most of the pictures sent in to us were of very poor quality. For example, one comrade sent us a picture of a worker's flat. The flat is a dingy basement, but the comrade took the picture from an entirely unsuitable point of view, which does not convey the fact that this basement is actually someone's home. The worker photographer also needs to develop an eye for correctly capturing a photographic image.[22]

The Social Democrats, by contrast, had access to a wide-reaching organizational and cultural network, both through *Der Kuckuck* and through their capillary party structure. In the nineteen-twenties and early thirties, the worker photography movement was firmly in the hands of Social Democrats. Photographers more or less closely associated with the party, for instance organizing themselves in the "photo clubs" of the Naturfreunde, a Social Democratic "tourist association" that had been founded in 1895. From the mid-twenties onward, such associations were revived and developed an active organizational life. Especially active among them, and open to modern photography, was the photo club of the Naturfreunde Meidling, the branch of the association based in the Meidling district of Vienna.[23] At the same time, worker photography groups were also set up in Vienna's adult education colleges (*Volkshochschulen*) during the twenties. Finally, there were a number of professional and amateur photographers who mostly published their work in the press, and who also felt themselves to be members of the worker photography movement.[24] The Social Democratic illustrated magazine *Der Kuckuck* formed the most important journalistic platform for all of these different groups.

Against the Idyll: Suschitzky as a Politically and Socially Critical Photographer of City Life

As far as we know, Edith Suschitzky was not an active member of any worker photography group in Vienna. Nevertheless, she was active in the cultural life associated with the movement. Her social documentary works were often much closer to the programmatic guidelines of *Der Kuckuck*'s editorial board than many of the contributions from the Social Democratic worker photography groups. In a review of an exhibition by the Ottakring worker photographers in February 1931, *Der Kuckuck* criticized the fact that:

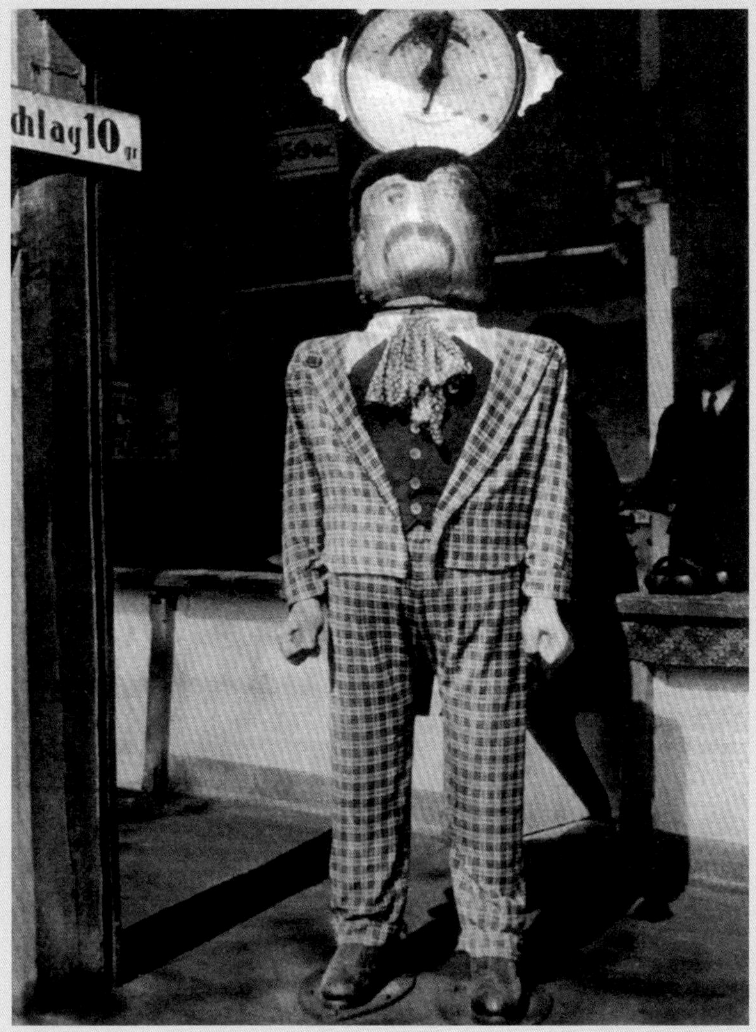

Fig. 15
Edith Suschitzky, "The 'Watschenmann,' a Fairground Dummy at Vienna's Prater," *Der Kuckuck,* August 14, 1932, p. 9

> Vienna's worker photographers [lack] an appreciation of what constitutes a political photograph. By this we don't mean a visual report of a public ceremony, demonstration or personality, but rather an idea captured in a visual detail. It is precisely photography that is capable of expressing militarism, exploitation, starvation wages, "rationalization," unemployment, class conflict, etc., in an unprecedented way. . . . And this is quite apart from the fact that, in the hands of a politically conscious worker photographer, the camera can contribute to bringing the image of the world offered by the illustrated magazine ever closer to the truth. For it is easy to imagine that the business interests of the various photo agencies supplying visual material for the illustrated magazines force on them a reactionary position, whereby they noticeably and quite deliberately avoid dealing with anything that is detested by the bourgeoisie.[25]

Writing in *Der Kuckuck,* Weyr repeatedly criticized the basically conservative tenor of many of the contributions from worker photography groups. They did not show the "truth" of the social and political situation, but rather idealized images typified by idyllic genre pictures and captivating landscapes. Images such as these also belonged to the standard repertoire of bourgeois amateur photographers. Nothing of this kind is to be found in Suschitzky's work. Neither in Vienna nor later in England did she make any excursions to places of natural beauty; rather, she remained committed to documenting the lives of the city's ordinary inhabitants.[26] She was, at least in her early years in Vienna, a photographer of the metropolis.

When we consider Suschitzky's photographs from her Vienna years, it becomes clear that, even in this early phase of her career, she created a substantial and distinct body of work. No other Austrian photographer of this period, male or female, photographed the everyday social and political life of Vienna so determinedly and with such a committed, socially critical vision. Edith Suschitzky documented the political struggles of Vienna's worker movement, showing the way of life of its working class population, but also the misery of the poor and the socially excluded. Alongside these she produced marvelous snapshots of daily city life as it played out on Vienna's streets or in the Prater, the ordinary people's entertainment district. She would tenaciously persevere with this photography of social criticism following her emigration to England.

1 See also Duncan Forbes's remarks in this catalogue.

2 *Die Bühne,* April 2, 1933, p. 14. The report on the Prater continues a few pages later in the magazine (p. 16), with more photographs by Suschitzky, among others.

3 *Die Bühne,* November 2, 1921, p. 26.

4 A recent large-scale exhibition project at the Wien Museum cast light on various aspects of Vienna's political and cultural atmosphere around 1930, which moved between tradition and rupture. See Wolfgang Kos, ed., *Kampf um die Stadt: Politik, Kunst und Alltag um 1930,* exh. cat. Wien Museum (Vienna, 2010).

5 Armin Loacker, "Die 'Newa' und der 'Russenfilm' in Wien," in *Arbeiterkino: Linke Filmkultur der Ersten Republik,* ed. Christian Dewald (Vienna, 2007), pp. 215–20.

6 See Anton Holzer, "Avantgarde und gemässigte Moderne: Fotografische Aufbrüche in Österreich um 1930," *Fotogeschichte* 123 (2012), pp. 51–60, esp. p. 59.

7 *Wiener Magazin,* November 11, 1930, pp. 52–53.

8 See also Korinna Lorz, "'foto-bauhäusler, werdet arbeiter-fotografen!': Fotografie am Bauhaus zwischen Avantgarde und Agitation; Ein Werkstattbericht," in "Fotografie im Klassenkampf: Arbeiterfotografie in Deutschland, Österreich und der Schweiz," ed. Wolfgang Hesse, special issue, *Fotogeschichte* 127 (2013), pp. 31–44.

9 For more on Austrian avant-garde photography around 1930, see Anton Holzer, "Avantgarde und gemässigte Moderne: Fotografische Aufbrüche in Österreich um 1930," *Fotogeschichte* 123 (2012), pp. 51–60.

10 See, for example, Wolfgang Born (W.B.), "Film und Foto: Vorschau auf die Werkbundausstellung," *Die Bühne,* February 15, 1930, pp. 42–43. *Der Kuckuck* devoted a great deal of space to the *Film und Foto* exhibition and described the show as pointing the way for the modern conception of photography. See *Der Kuckuck,* February 23, 1930, p. 15. Pictures in the style of *Neue Sachlichkeit* or *Neues Sehen* appeared regularly in *Der Kuckuck* from 1930 onward. See, for example, "Das neue Bild," *Der Kuckuck,* March 23, 1930, p. 15.

11 See *Internationale Ausstellung Film und Foto,* published by the Österreichischer Werkbund (Austrian Work Federation), a traveling exhibition by the Deutscher Werkbund (German Work Federation), exh. cat. Österreichisches Museum, February 20 to March 31, 1930 (Vienna, n.d. [1930]).

12 For the photography of the Bauhaus, see Jeannine Fiedler, *Fotografie am Bauhaus* (Berlin, 1990); Lutz Schöbe, ed., *Bauhaus: Fotografie aus der Sammlung der Stiftung Bauhaus Dessau* (Florence, 2004).

13 For more on this, see Anton Holzer, "Avantgarde und gemässigte Moderne: Fotografische Aufbrüche in Österreich um 1930," *Fotogeschichte* 123 (2012), pp. 51–60, esp. pp. 58–59.

14 *Der Kuckuck,* October 4, 1931, p. 15. Text and photos by Edith Suschitzky.

15 Ibid.

16 For the European worker photography movement of the interwar years, see Jorge Ribalta, ed., *The Worker Photography Movement 1926–1939: Essays and Documents* (Madrid, 2011). For the worker photography movement in the German-speaking countries, see "Fotografie im Klassenkampf: Arbeiterfotografie in Deutschland, Österreich und der Schweiz," ed. Wolfgang Hesse, special issue, *Fotogeschichte* 127 (2013), pp. 31–44.

17 *Arbeiter-Illustrierte-Zeitung* 8, 1926, p. 6.

18 *Der Kuckuck,* July 20, 1930, p. 9. For more on *Der Kuckuck*'s photo competitions, see Marion Krammer, *Bissige Bilder: Die Fotomontage als visuelles Propagandainstrument der Sozialdemokratie in den Jahren 1929–1934,* diploma thesis (University of Vienna, 2008).

19 *Der Kuckuck,* August 14, 1932, p. 9. The image-and-text reportage, which appeared in several parts, was published under the title "Wurstelprater vormittags." The pictures were taken by Edith Suschitzky and Nikolaus Schwarz, among others.

20 In 1929 the print run of *Der Kuckuck* ran to 56,000 copies a week; in 1930 it was at 44,500, in 1931 at 33,600, and in 1932 at 29,000 copies. See Stefan Riesenfellner and Josef Seiter, *Der Kuckuck: Die moderne Bild-Illustrierte des Roten Wien* (Vienna, 1995), p. 42.

21 In 1931 *Der Arbeiter-Fotograf,* the journal of the Association of German Worker Photographers, reported the founding of the Communist Association of Austrian Worker Photographers, which took place on April 1, 1931. Photographs are said to have been taken together on May 1. See *Der Arbeiter Fotograf* 5, 1931, p. 110. I would like to thank Wolfgang Hesse for this reference.

22 *Illustrierte Rote Woche,* June 5, 1932, n.p., esp. last page.

23 Compared with other worker photography groups around 1930, the Meidling photo club pursued the modernist tendency of *Neue Sachlichkeit* most consistently. The modernist representatives of the Meidling group included, among others, Hans Cechal, Franz Tesarik, Otto Weber, Josef Hufnagel, J. Halpern, Ferdinand Hodek, Otto Sadler, Karl Bauer, Ferdinand Bareder, and the Swiss photographer Martin Imboden, who lived in Vienna in the early nineteen-thirties.

24 For details on the Austrian worker photography movement, see Anton Holzer, "Vorwärts! Die österreichische Arbeiterfotografiebewegung der Zwischenkriegszeit," in "Fotografie im Klassenkampf: Arbeiterfotografie in Deutschland, Österreich und der Schweiz," ed. Wolfgang Hesse, special issue, *Fotogeschichte* 127 (2013), pp. 17–30.

25 *Der Kuckuck,* February 1, 1931, p. 16.

26 In the early years of her career, Suschitzky occasionally photographed in the country, such as at the beginning of the thirties in Monfalcone, Italy, when she made a reportage about a gypsy family on the outskirts of the town. Yet here, too, she was concerned with documenting social hardship and not with taking snapshots of the idyllic countryside. See Wolf Suschitzky, *Edith Tudor-Hart: The Eye of Conscience,* vol. 1: *Photo Pocket Book* (London, 1987), p. 9.

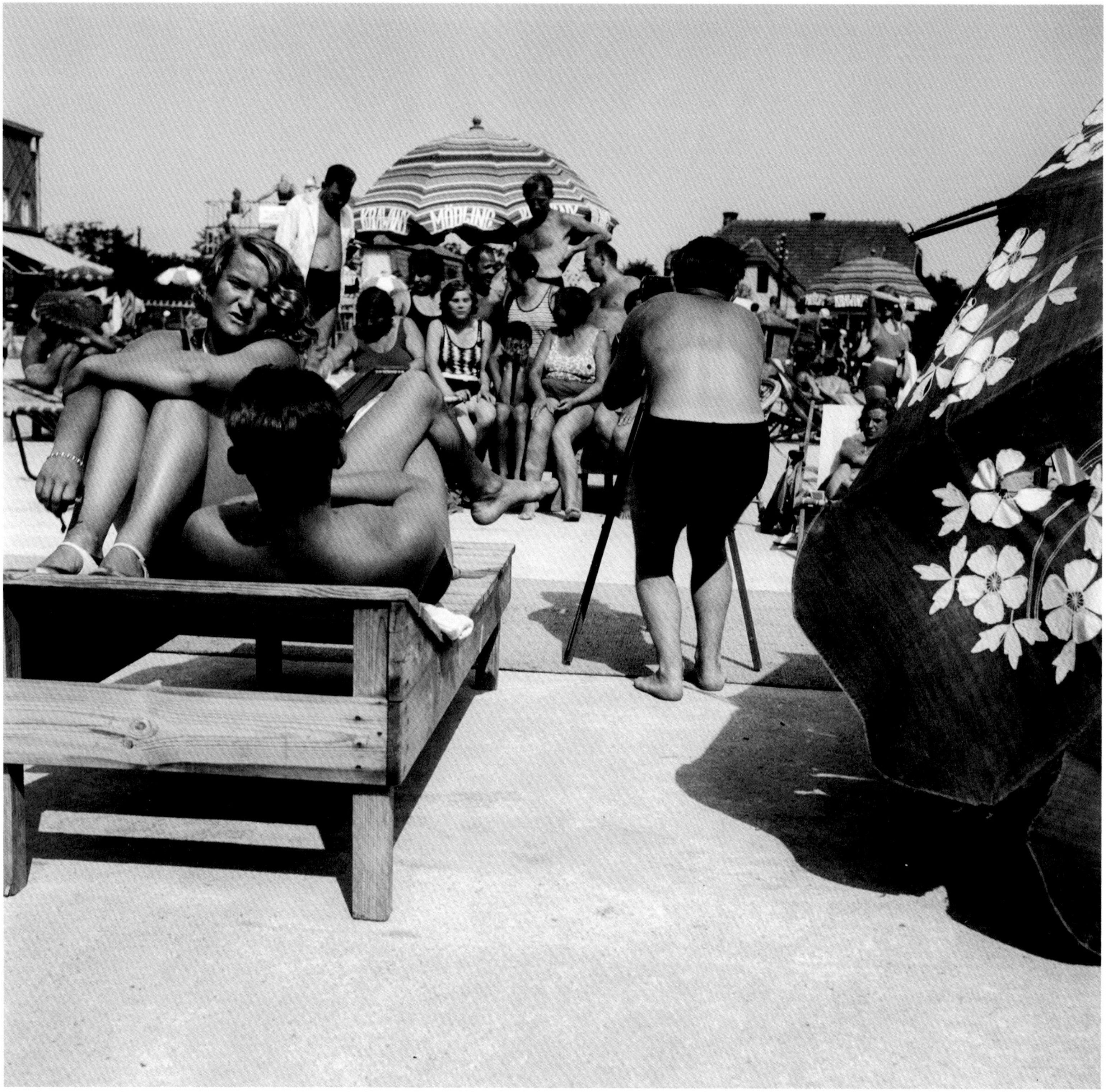

Edith Suschitzky
Lido, Mödling, near Vienna, ca. 1932
Silver-gelatin print, 30.2 × 30.1 cm
National Galleries of Scotland, PGP 279.21

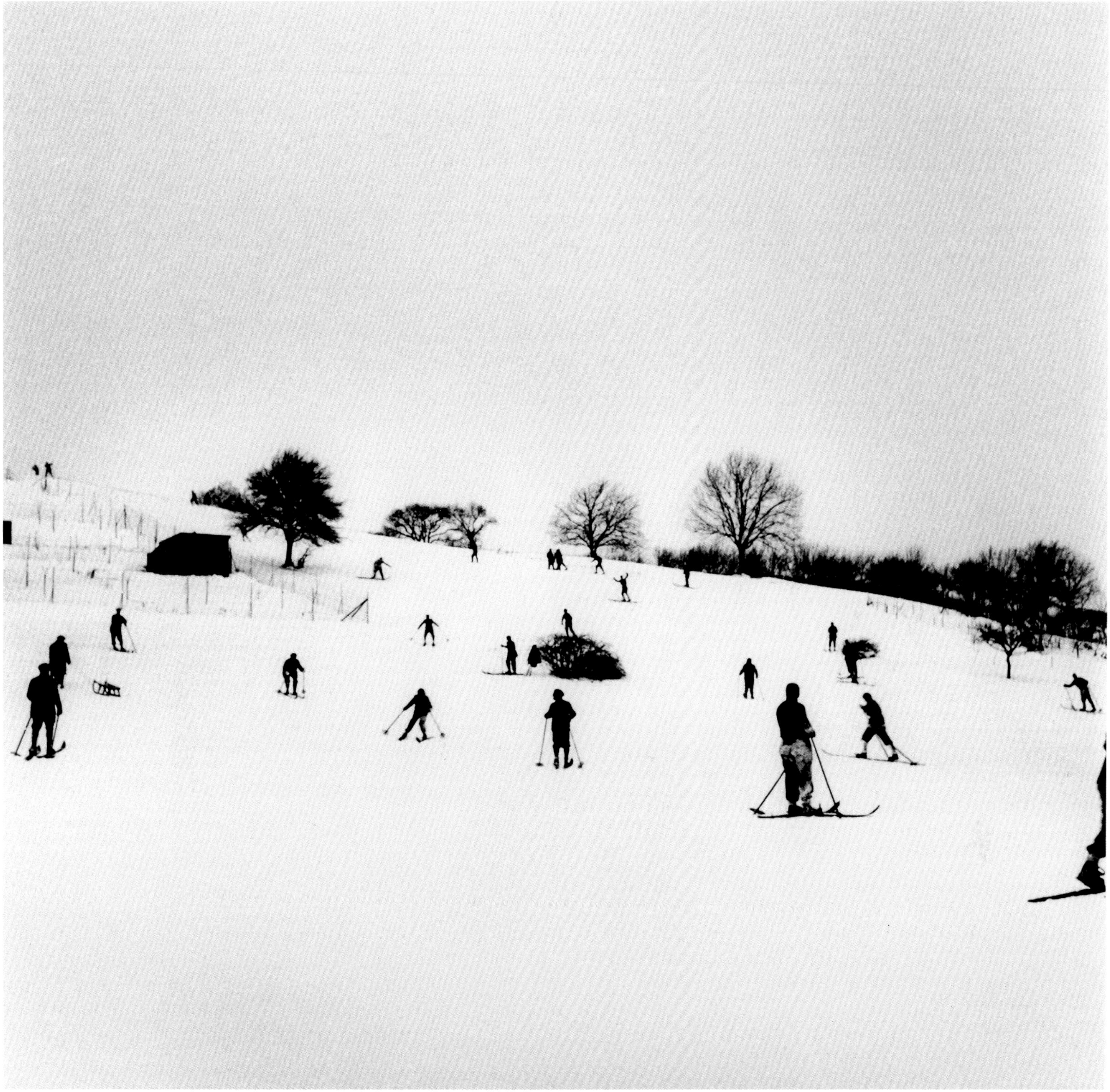

Edith Suschitzky
Skiing, Location Unknown, ca. 1932
Modern silver-gelatin print, 30.2 × 30.1 cm
National Galleries of Scotland, PGP 279.8

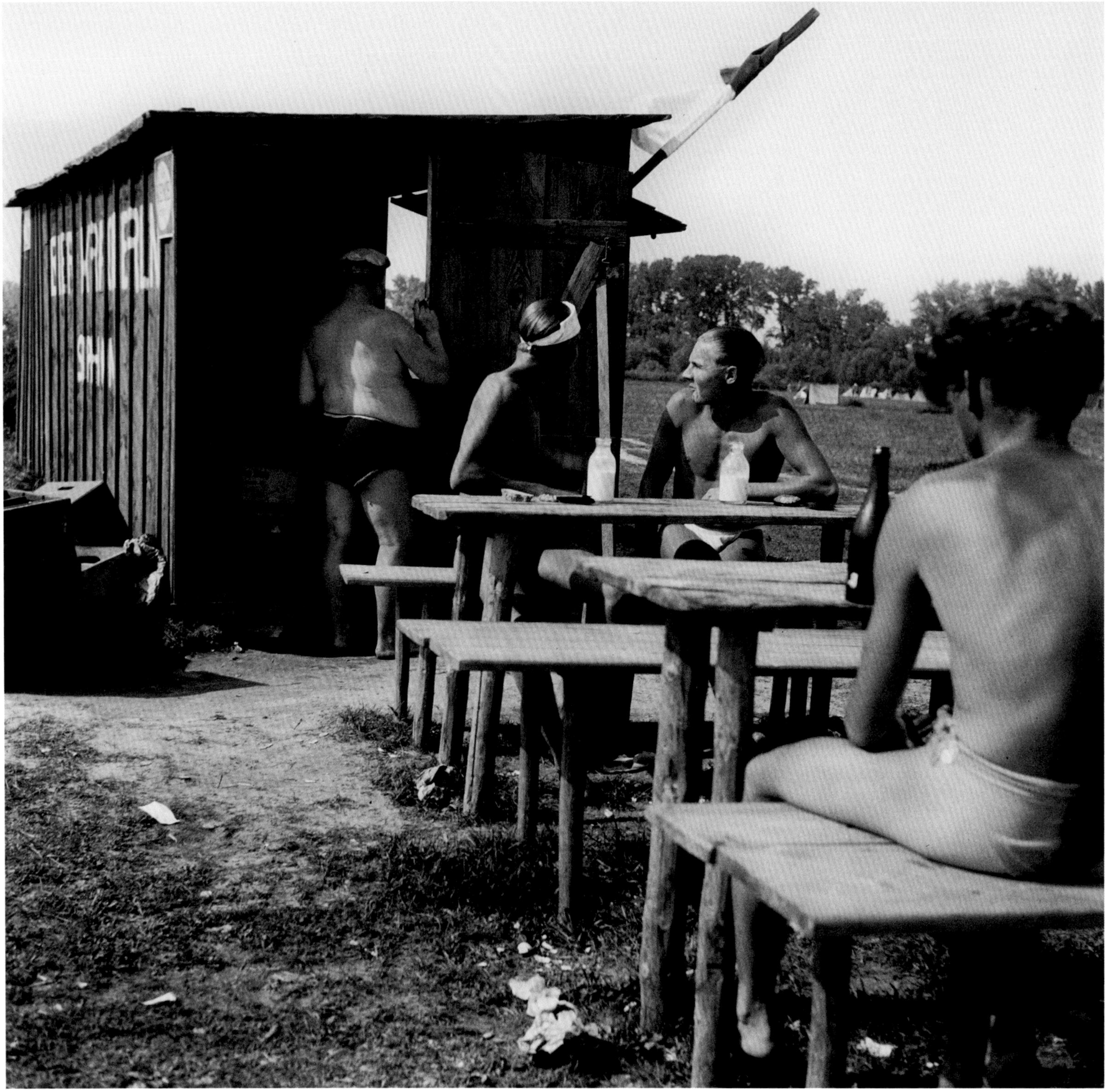

Edith Suschitzky
Refreshment Kiosk, the Lobau, Vienna, 1932
Modern silver-gelatin print, 30.2 × 30 cm
National Galleries of Scotland, PGP 279.23

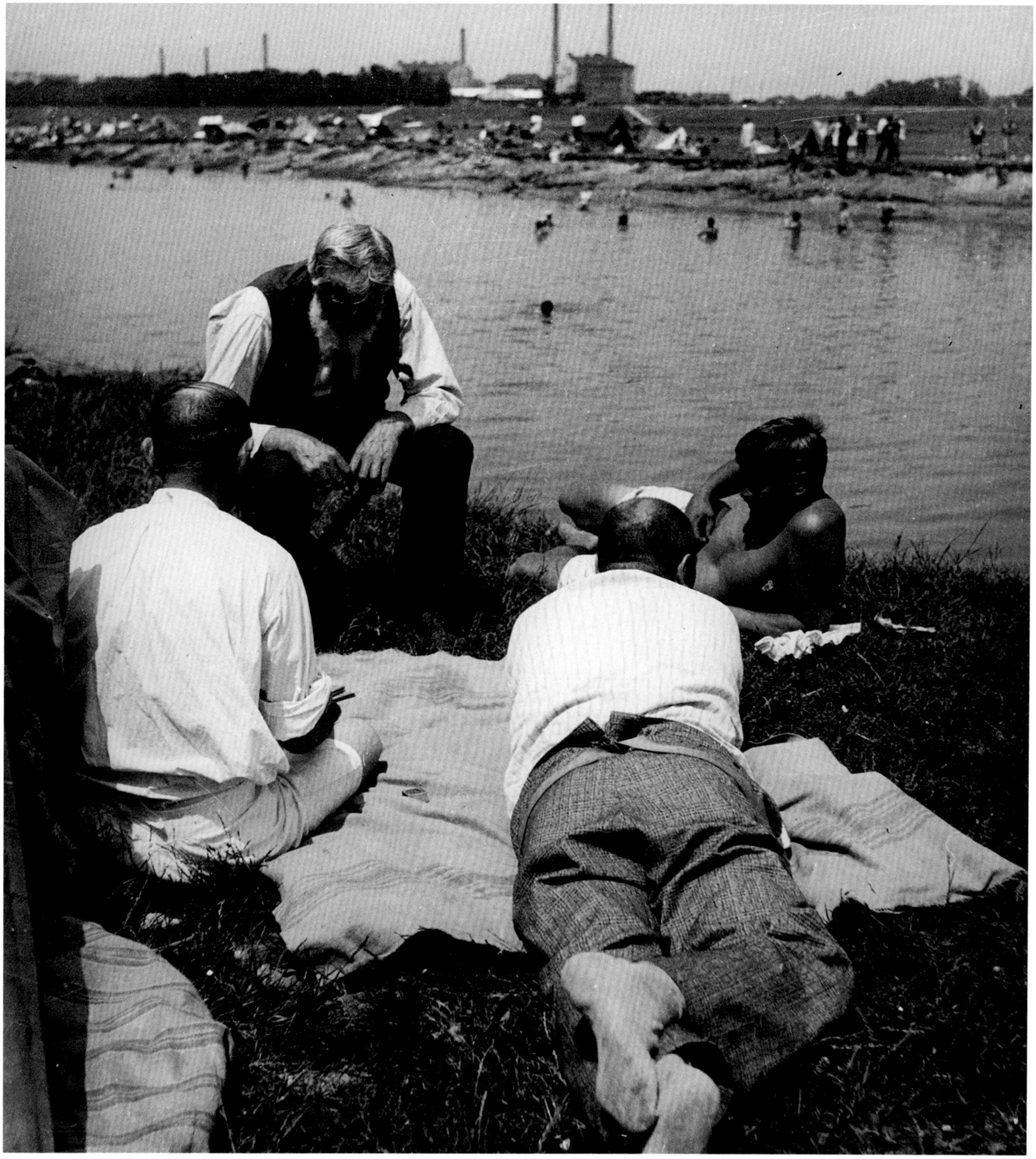

Edith Suschitzky
Sunbathing, the Lobau, Vienna, 1932
Silver-gelatin print, 21.9 × 19.1 cm
Galerie Johannes Faber

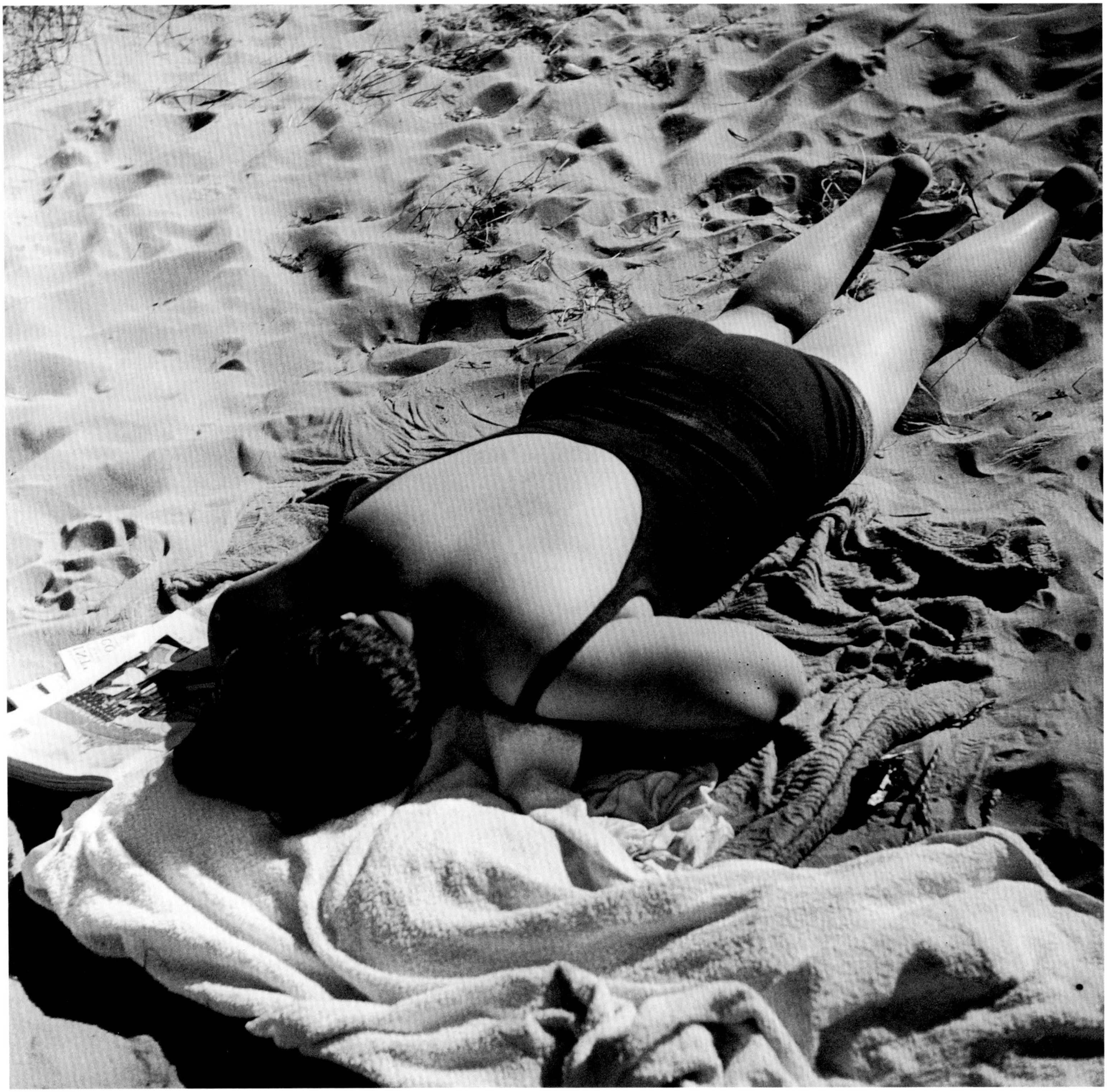

Edith Suschitzky
Woman Asleep on the Sand, possibly the Lobau, Vienna, 1932
Modern silver-gelatin print, 30.2 × 30.1 cm
National Galleries of Scotland, PGP 279.22

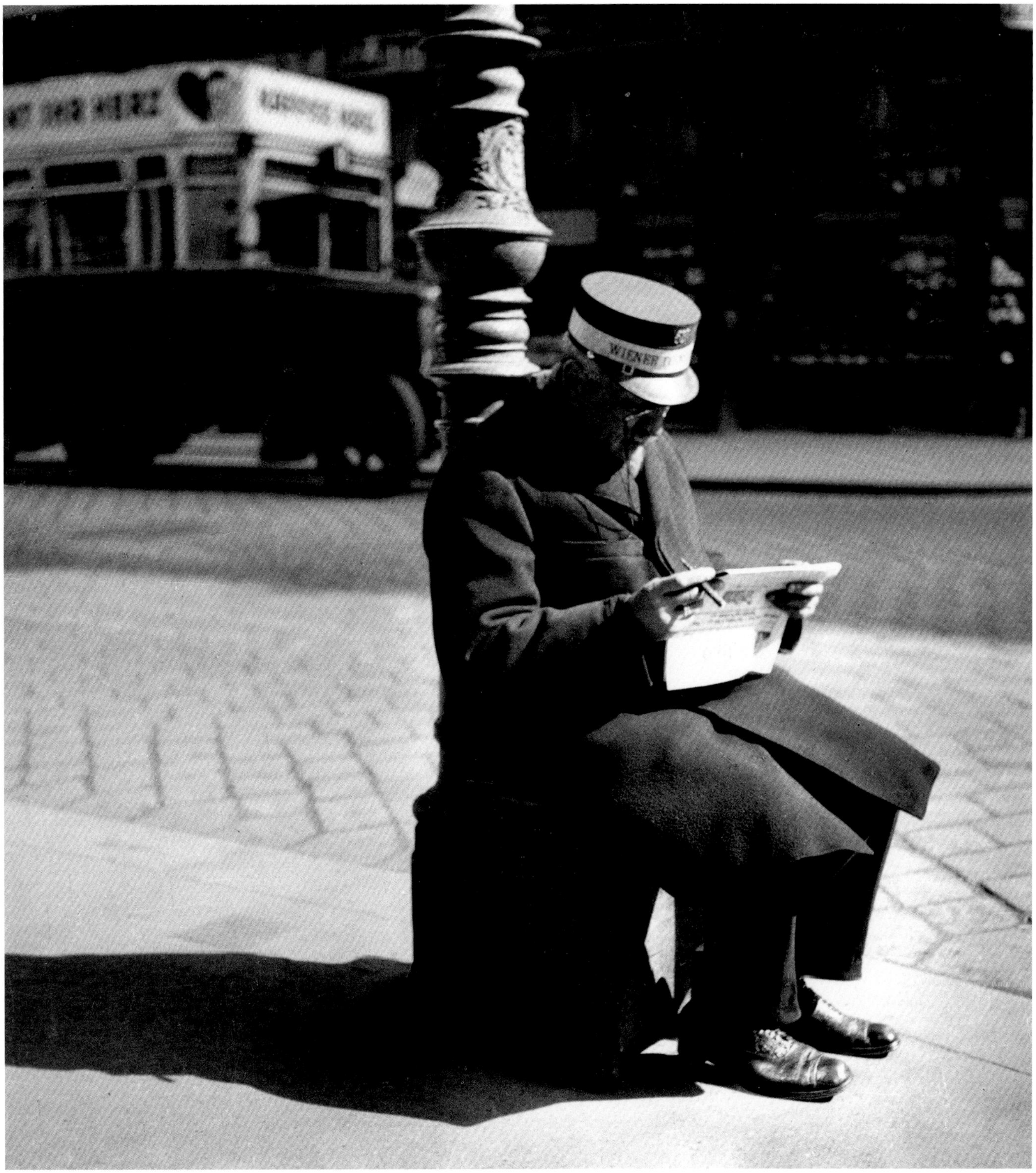

Edith Suschitzky
Porter, Vienna, 1929
Silver-gelatin print, 22.5 × 19.7 cm
Wien Museum, 204462

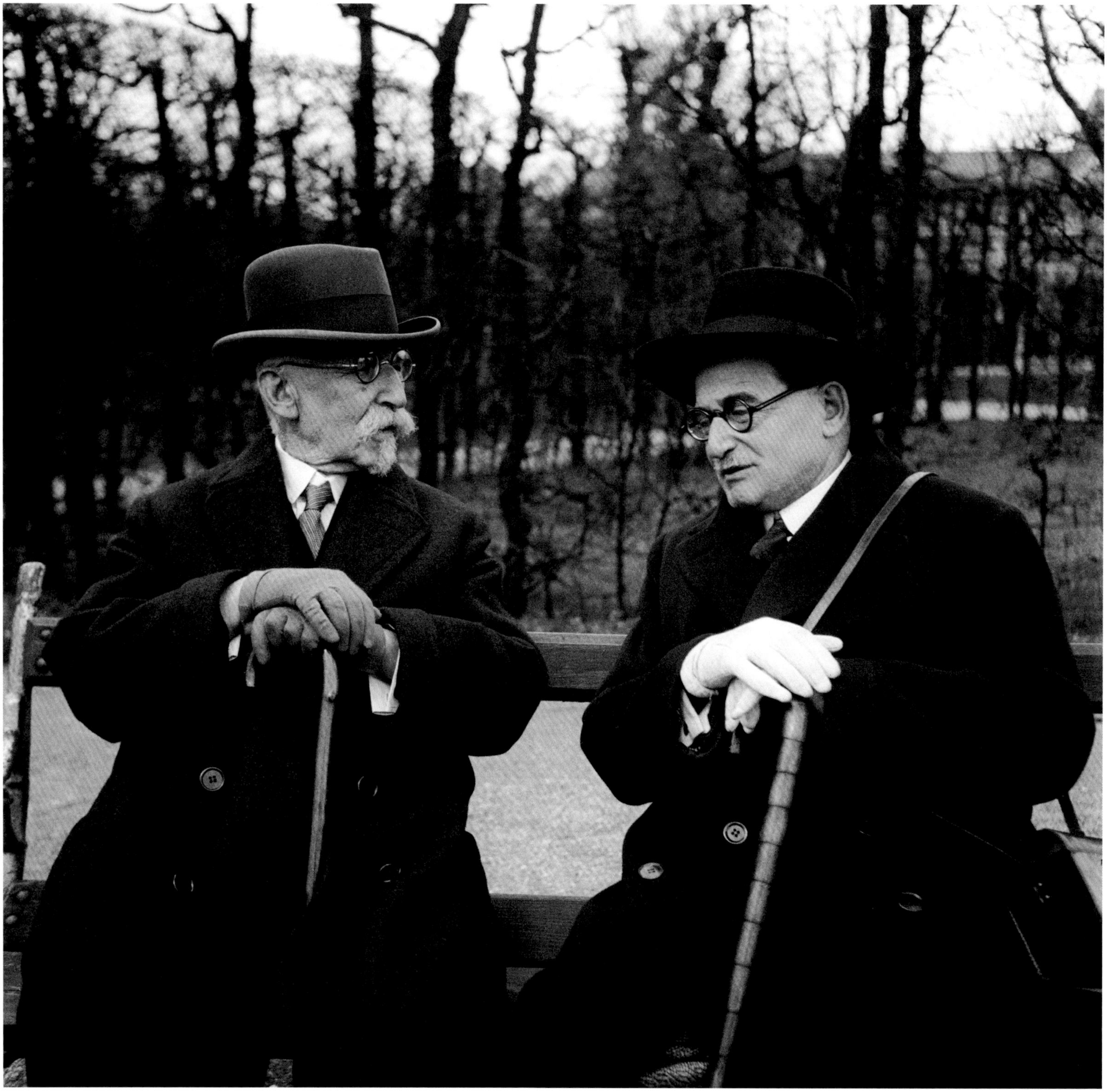

Edith Suschitzky
Unknown Man and Wilhelm Suschitzky, ca. 1930
Digital inkjet print, 30 × 29.9 cm
National Galleries of Scotland, PGP 279.71

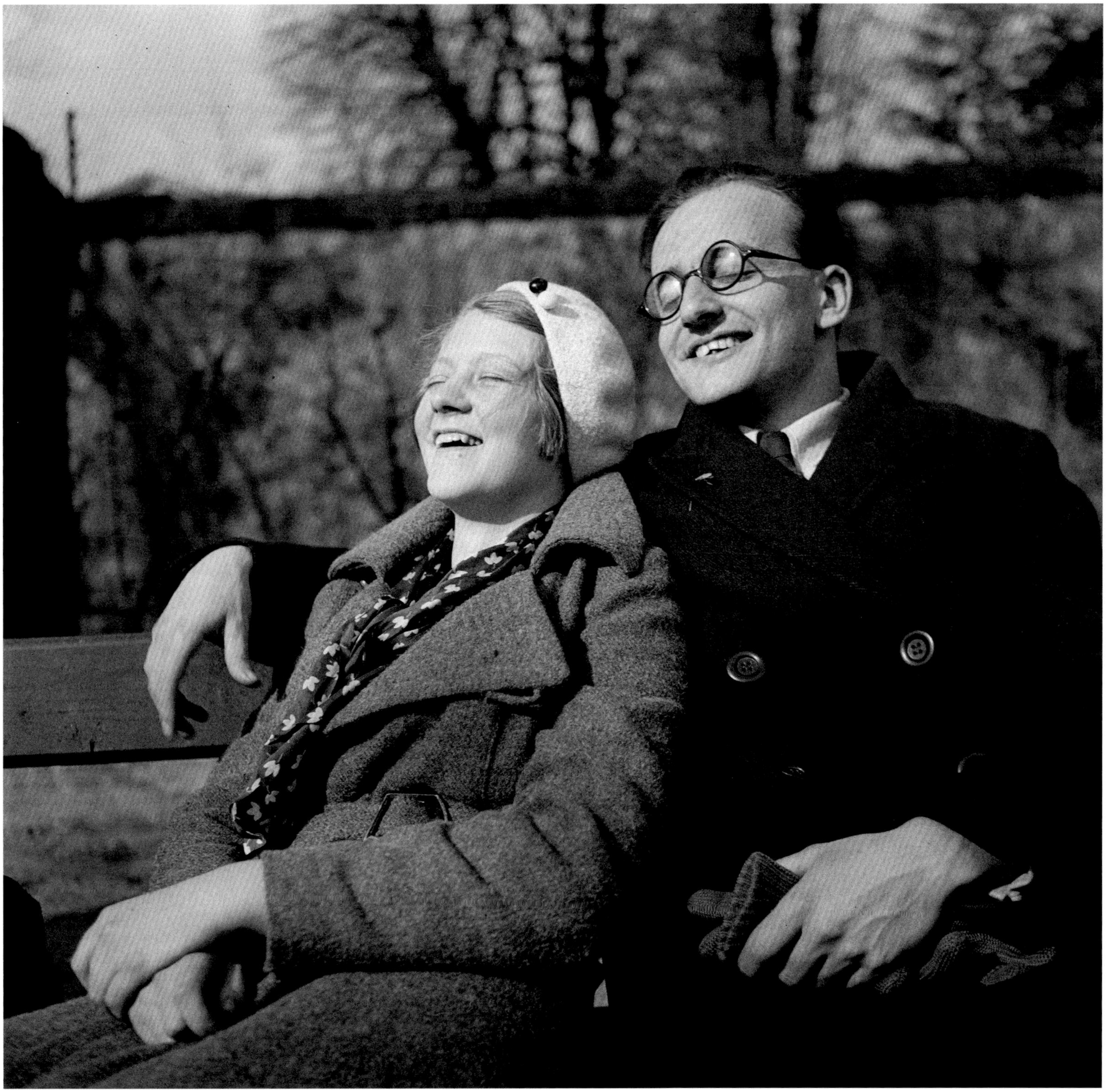

Edith Tudor-Hart
Puckée Voûte and Wolfgang Suschitzky,
Location Unknown, ca. 1934
Digital inkjet print, 30.1 × 30 cm
National Galleries of Scotland, PGP 279.72

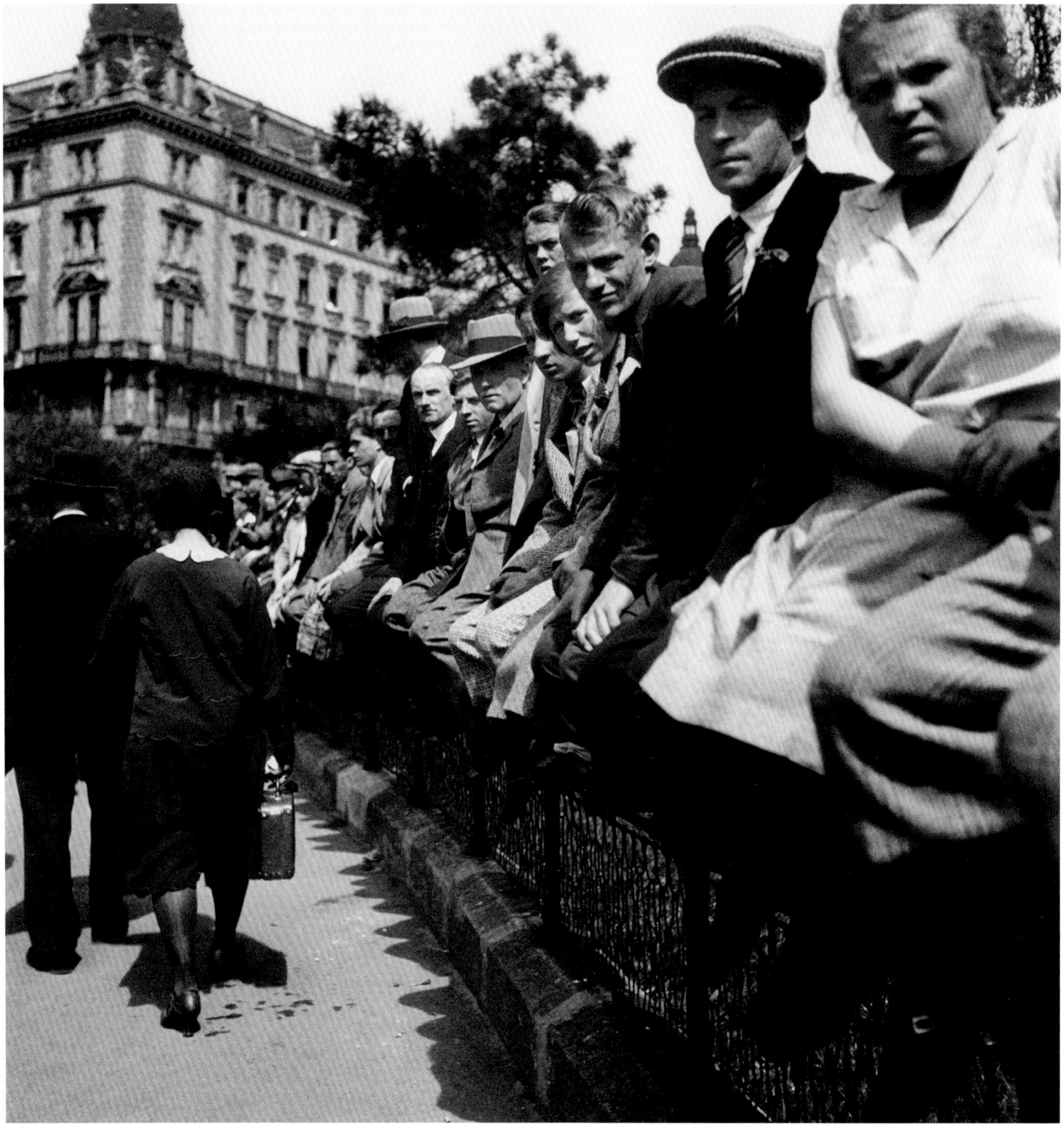

Edith Suschitzky
Crowd Sitting on a Fence, Vienna, ca. 1930
Modern silver-gelatin print, 26.2 × 24.1 cm
National Galleries of Scotland, PGP 279.14

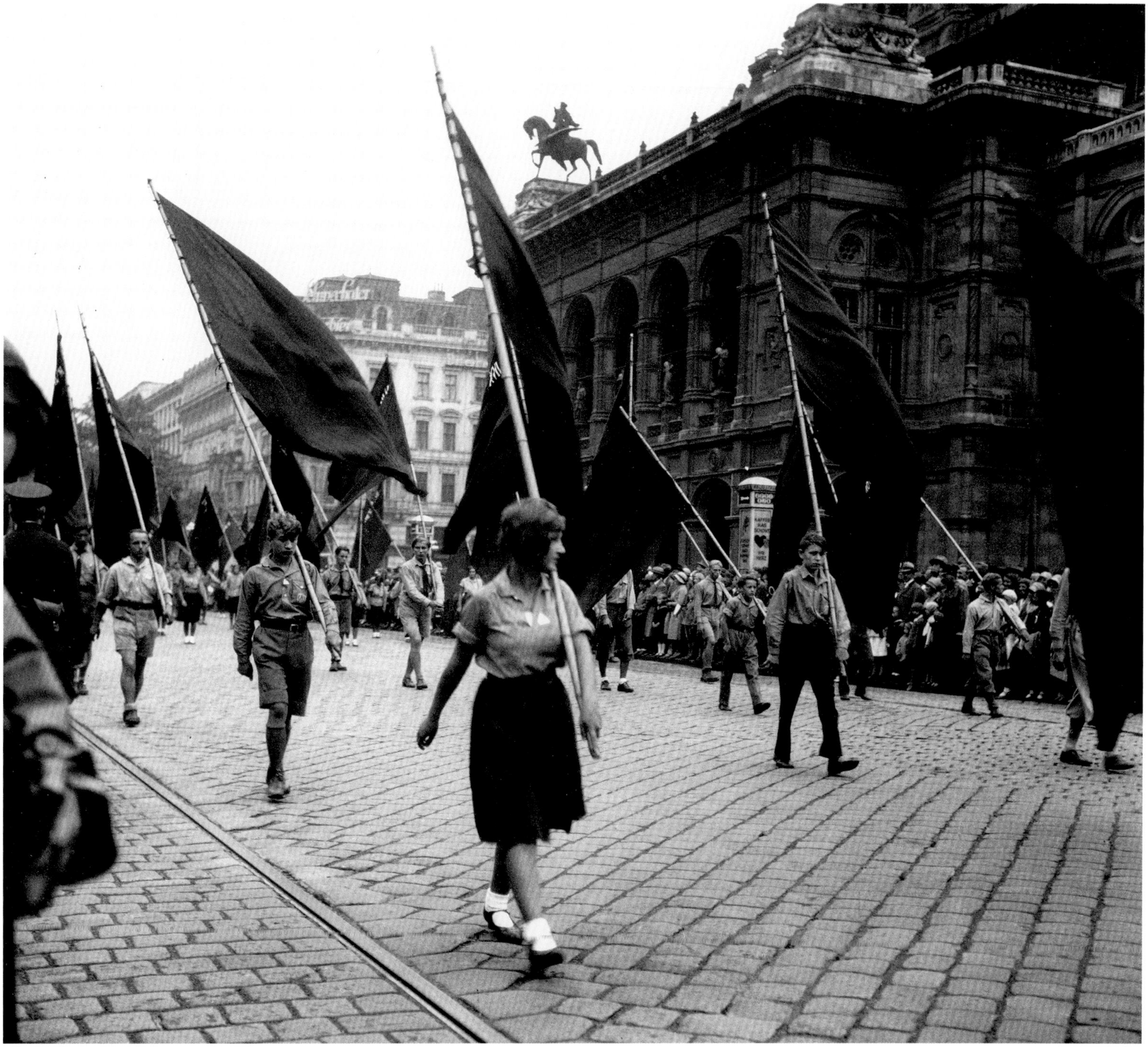

Edith Suschitzky
Members of the Social-Democratic Youth Movement Marching
Past the Opera House, Opernring, Vienna, ca. 1928
Modern silver-gelatin print, 28 × 30 cm
National Galleries of Scotland, PGP 279.9

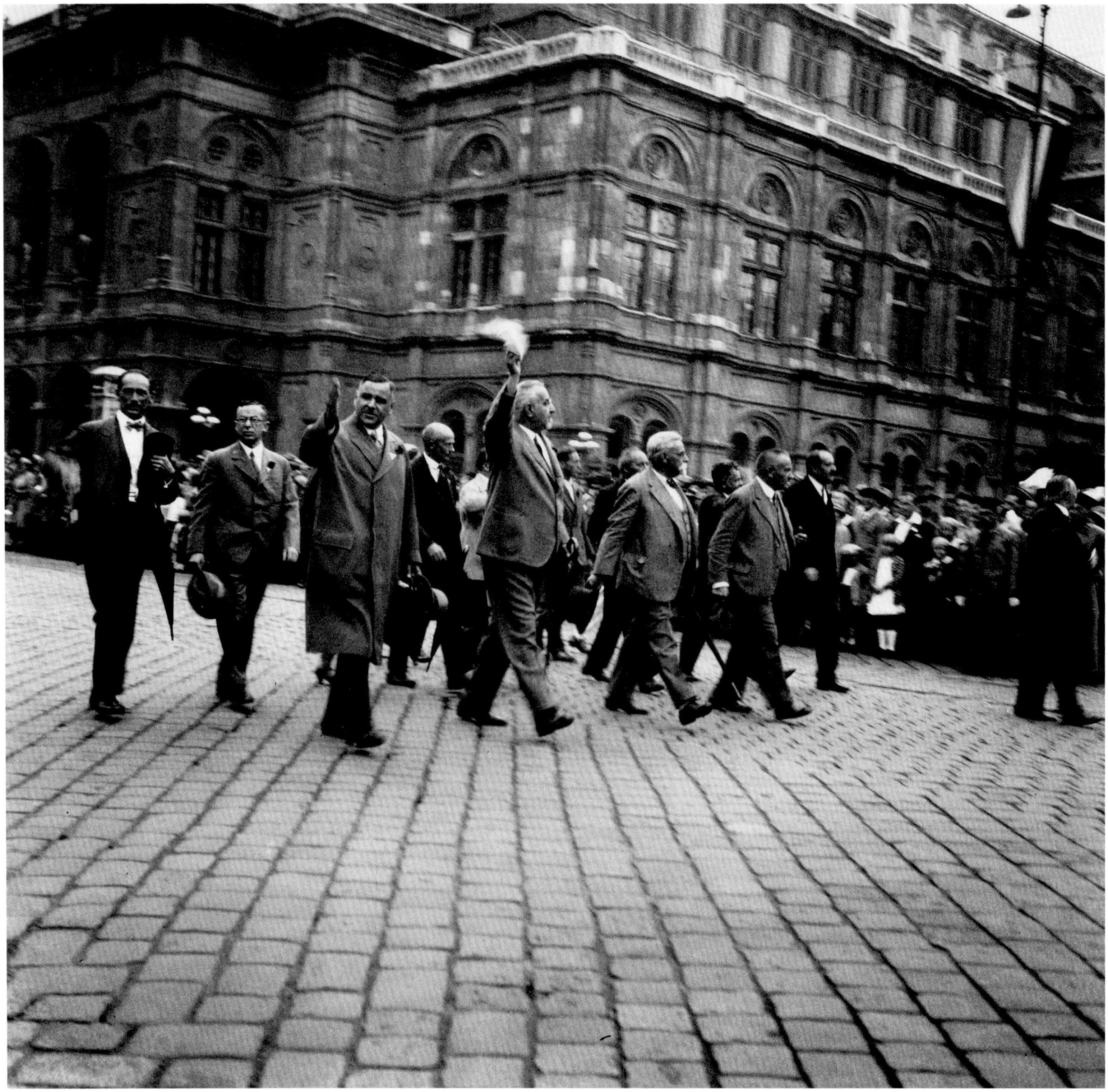

Edith Suschitzky
Unknown Political Delegation, Ringstrasse, Vienna, ca. 1928
Modern silver-gelatin print, 30.1 × 30.1 cm
National Galleries of Scotland, PGP 279.15

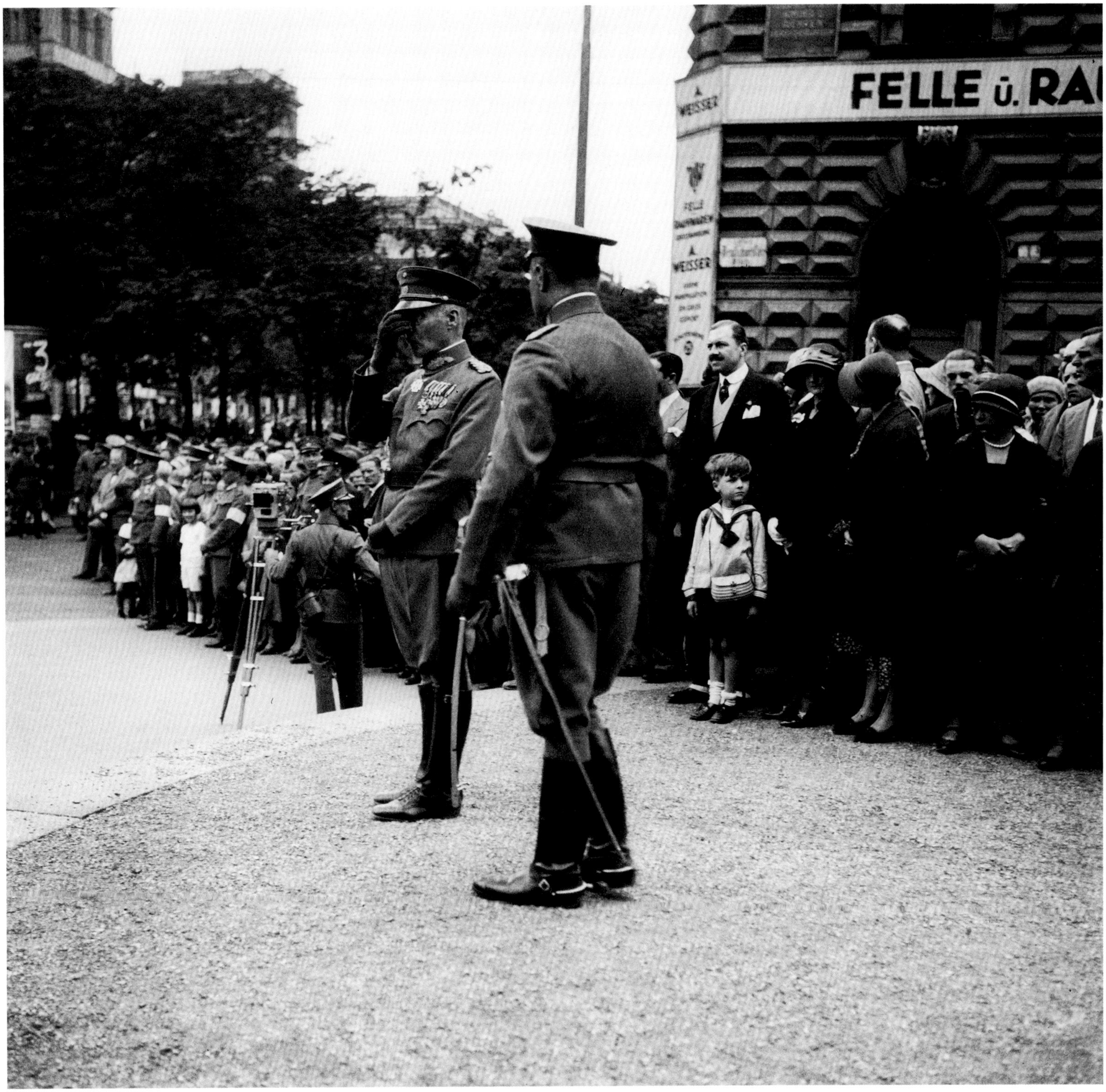

Edith Suschitzky
Officers of the Austrian Army, Vienna, ca. 1930
Modern silver-gelatin print, 30.2 × 30 cm
National Galleries of Scotland, PGP 279.25

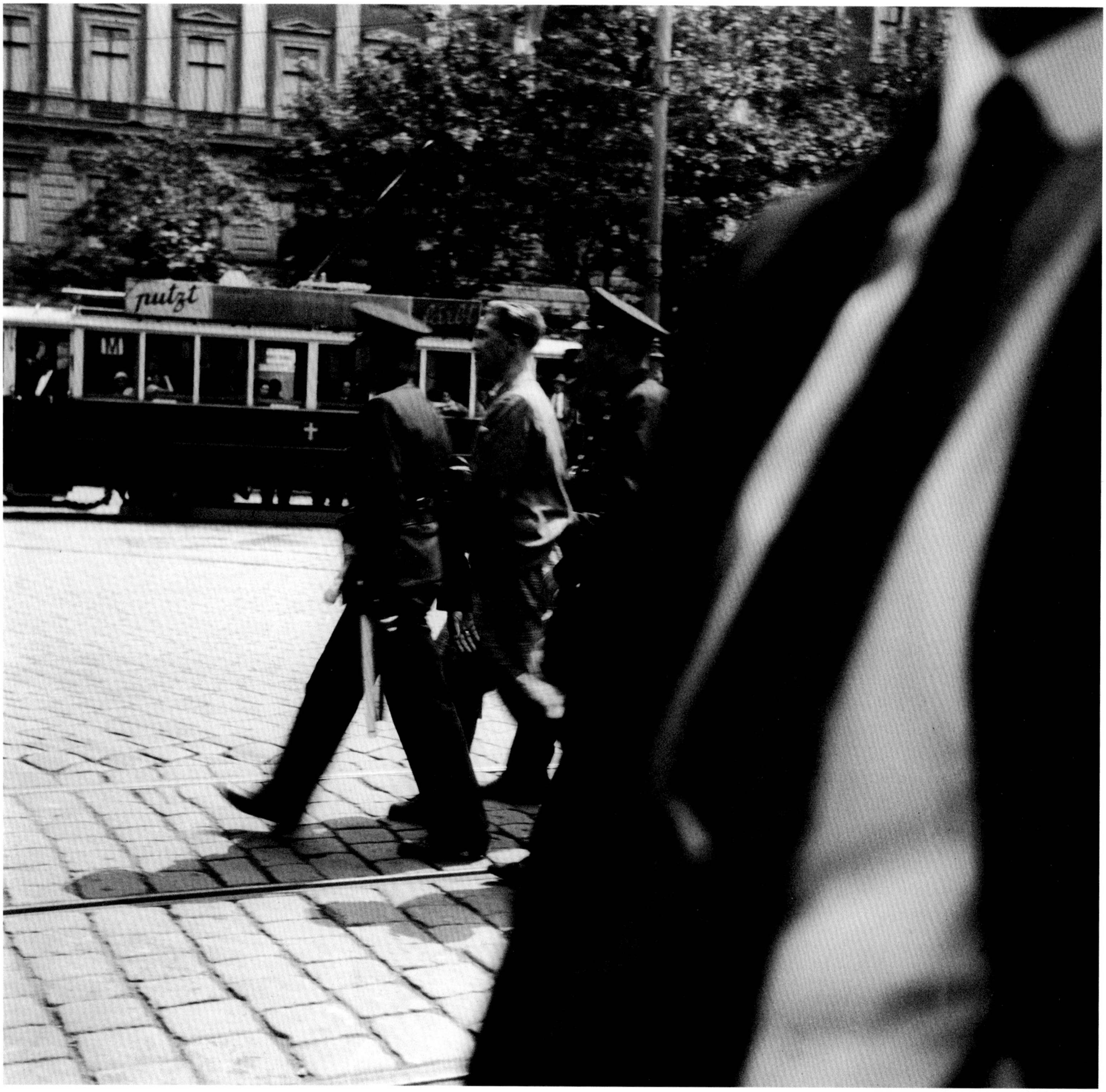

Edith Suschitzky
An Arrest, Vienna, 1933
Modern silver-gelatin print, 30.2 × 30.1 cm
National Galleries of Scotland, PGP 279.11

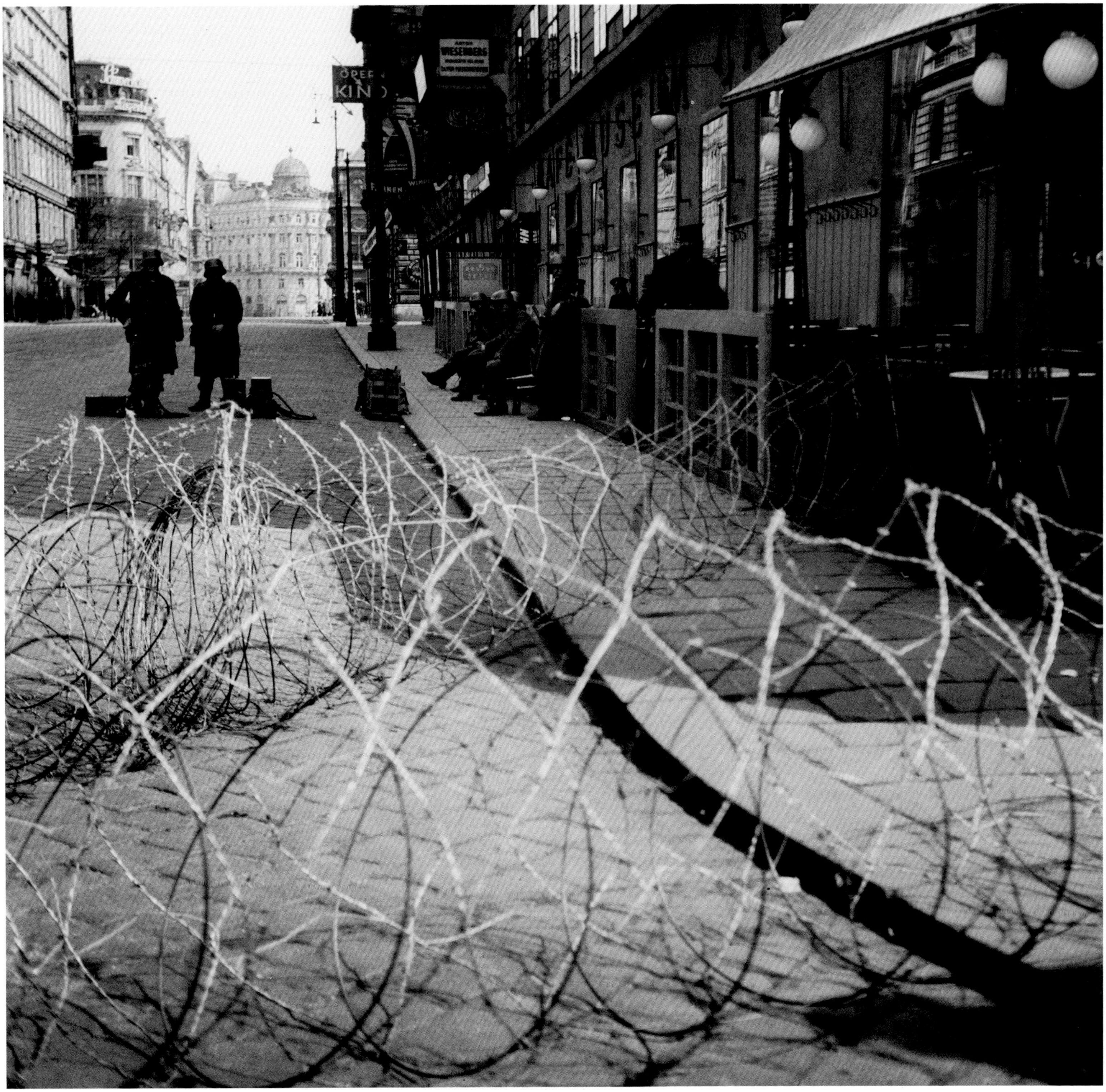

Edith Suschitzky
Barricade on the Operngasse, Vienna, 1933
Modern silver-gelatin print, 30.3 × 30 cm
National Galleries of Scotland, PGP 279.12

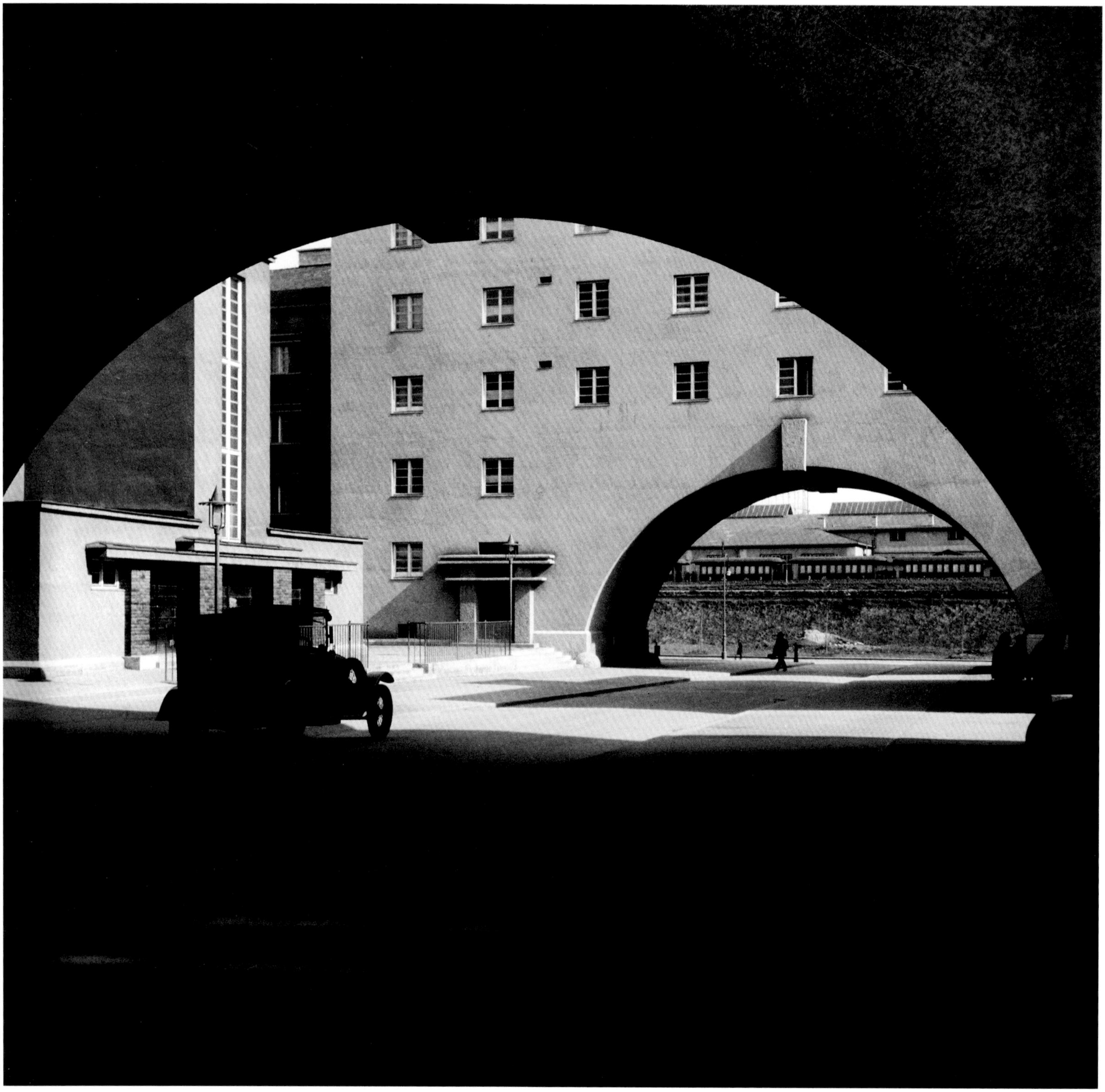

Edith Suschitzky
Karl-Marx-Hof, Vienna, 1933
Modern silver-gelatin print, 30.1 × 30 cm
National Galleries of Scotland, PGP 279.13

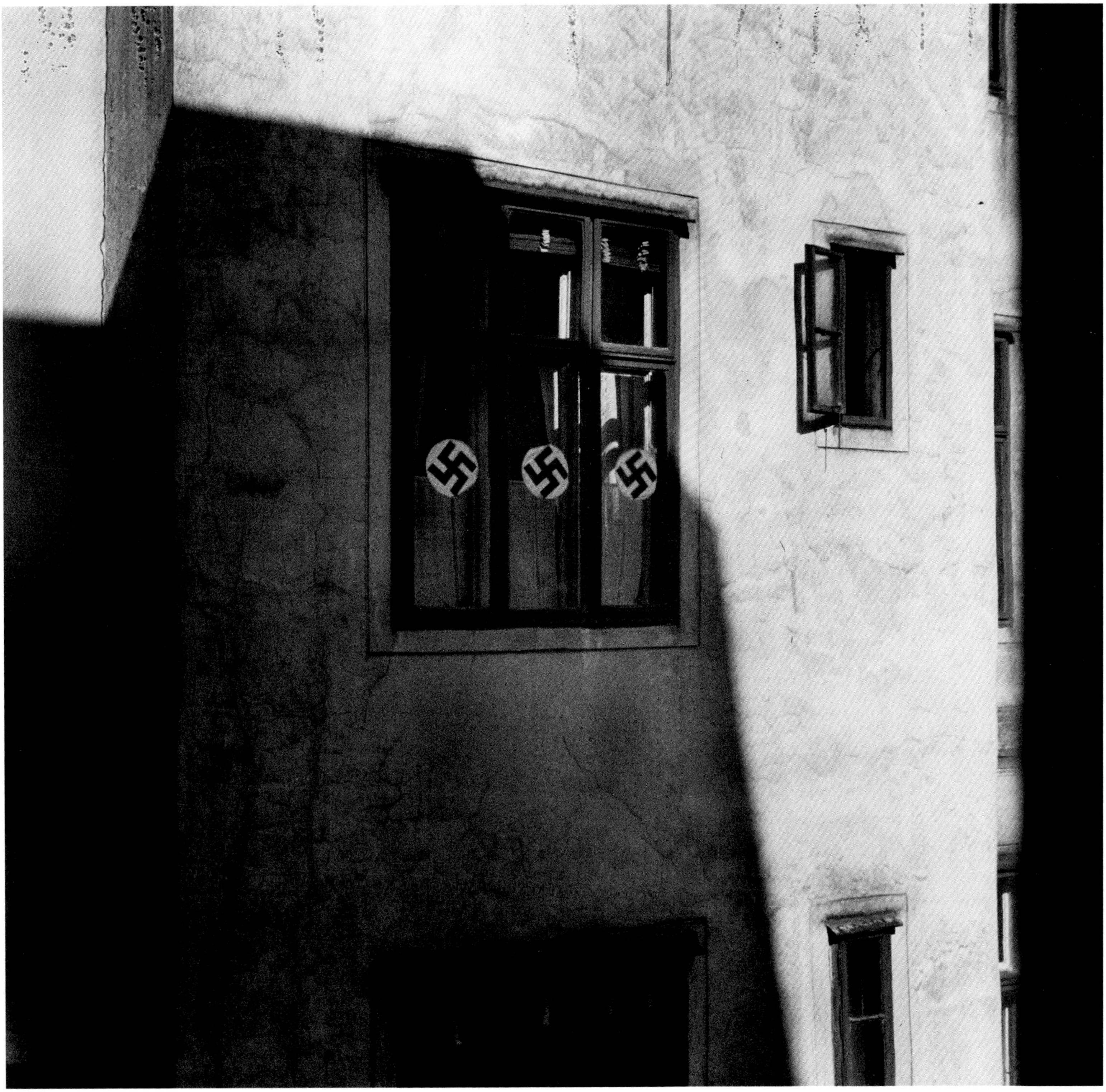

Edith Suschitzky
Swastikas in Shadow, Vienna, ca. 1932
Modern silver-gelatin print, 30.2 × 30 cm
National Galleries of Scotland, PGP 279.18

Edith Tudor-Hart in London

Duncan Forbes

Soon, however, the road to Moscow would cease to be a joke. Austrian socialists of all tendencies, particularly after their defeat at the hands of the Austro-Fascists in the street battles of February 1934, did head to Russia, sometimes via Spain, and often with tragic consequences.[29] Edith Suschitzky—now Tudor-Hart—was fortunate to head westward, from Vienna to London. Did she marry Alexander Tudor-Hart for reasons of political convenience as MI5 investigators, worried about the parallels with Kim Philby, later feared? Perhaps. But she also married for love, and her few surviving letters to Alexander from the nineteen-thirties reveal a disarming mix of anxiety and passion quite beyond simulation.

The British citizenship conferred on Edith Tudor-Hart was far from egalitarian: her claim as an unemployed woman of working age was on her husband, not the state. Earning an income was imperative; she worked hard and, until the outbreak of war, with some success to enter fields of photographic practice in which women in Britain struggled to participate.[30] A crucial early supporter of her career was the modernist designer and builder Jack Pritchard, with whom Beatrix Tudor-Hart had recently had a child. Pritchard, who had visited the Bauhaus at Dessau in March 1931, acted as a key contact in London for exile architects and designers, offering them accommodation in his Lawn Road flats and as much patronage as he could muster through his Isokon Furniture Company.[31] As in Vienna, Edith Tudor-Hart lived and worked on the fringes of a progressive fraction of bourgeois cultural workers. Their politics, played out through a commitment to modernist planning and welfare reform, attempted to redress the imbalance—so obvious during the slump of the thirties—between monopoly capitalism and state provision. United by a staunch opposition to Nazism, most of this group included supporters from the mid-thirties of the Popular Front, the Comintern-inspired alliance of leftist political forces mobilized against the rise of fascism. Some, like the Hungarian-born architect Ernö Goldfinger, a close friend of the Tudor-Harts, were also openly associated with the CPGB.[32] Although not of major political significance in Britain (the Labour Party kept a suspicious distance), the Popular Front formed the center of gravity of leftist cultural politics, particularly its literary forms. Showing due obeisance to the Comintern line, most of Tudor-Hart's photography from this period would also be framed by the Popular Front's undiscriminating politics of left "Unity."

One of Pritchard's earliest introductions was to R. S. Lambert, Germanophile and editor of *The Listener,* with the result that

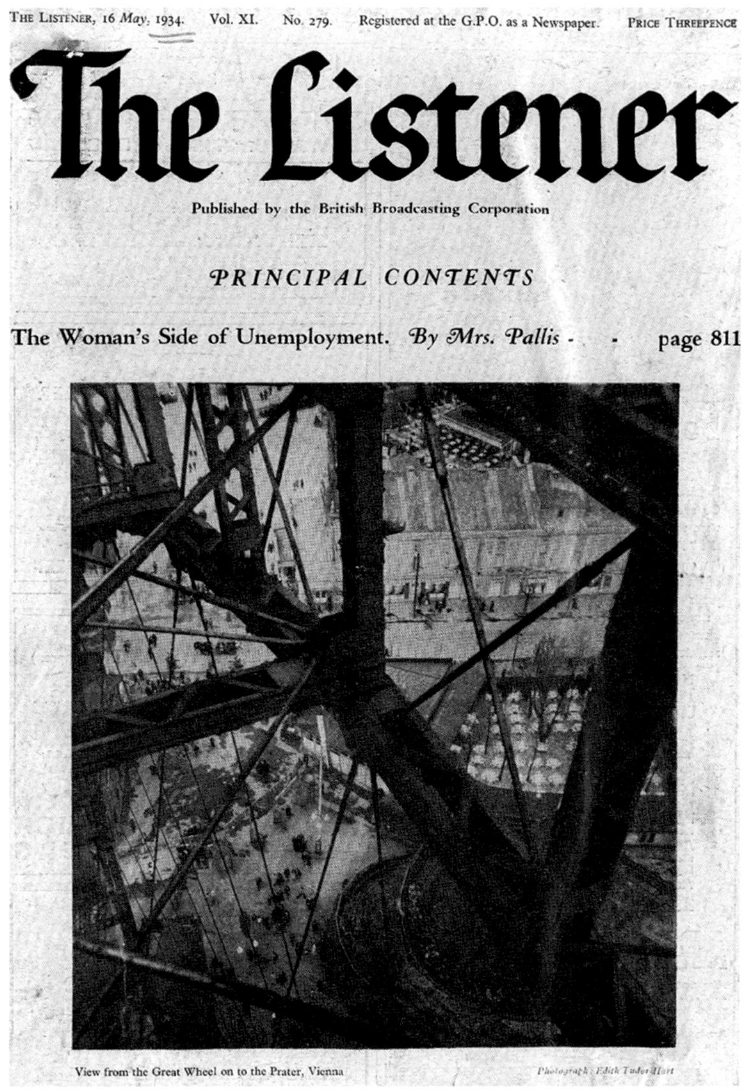
THE LISTENER, 16 May, 1934. Vol. XI. No. 279. Registered at the G.P.O. as a Newspaper. PRICE THREEPENCE

The Listener

Published by the British Broadcasting Corporation

PRINCIPAL CONTENTS

The Woman's Side of Unemployment. By Mrs. Pallis - - page 811

View from the Great Wheel on to the Prater, Vienna

Photograph: Edith Tudor-Hart

Fig. 16
Edith Tudor-Hart, front cover of *The Listener,* May 16, 1934, from Edith Tudor-Hart's scrapbook

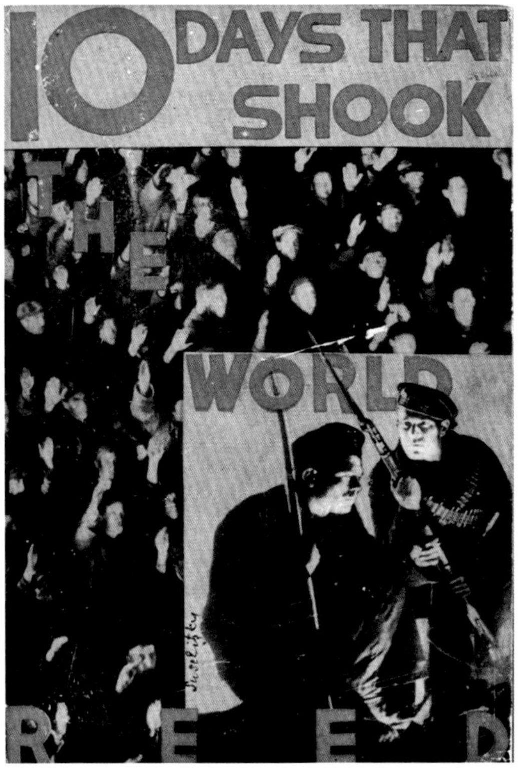

Fig. 17
Edith Suschitzky, front cover of *Ten Days That Shook the World* by John Reed (London, 1932)

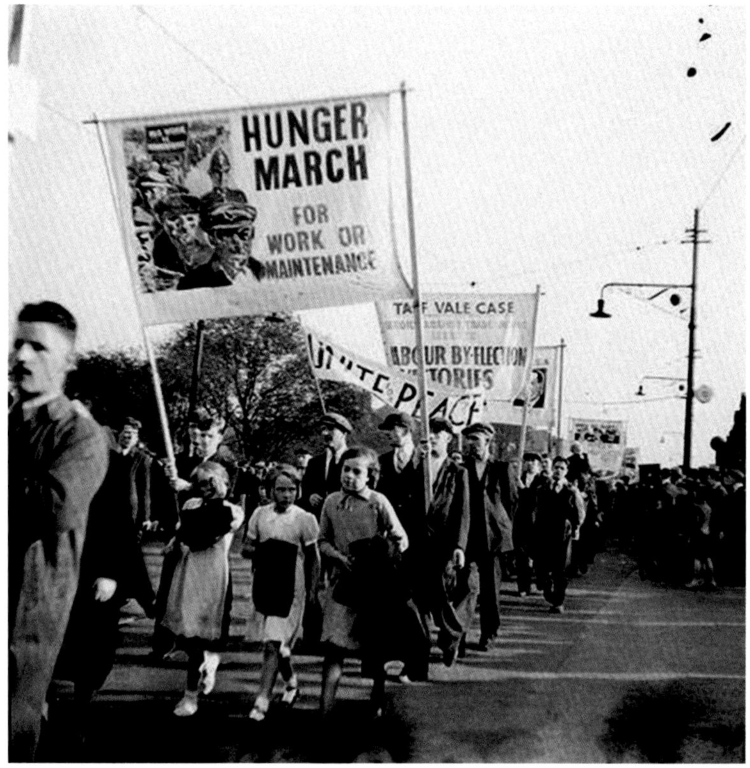

Fig. 18
Helen Muspratt, *Hunger Marchers, Liverpool,* 1938

Tudor-Hart's photographs, including magazine covers and montages, began to appear in the paper from late 1933 (fig. 16).[33] Published by the BBC, *The Listener* was far from a socialist journal, although it was one of the few nonspecialist outlets promoting modernist functionalism as a social project, the aim being to elevate the working classes into a bourgeois technocracy, mainly by means of municipal planning and architecture. It also staged a more tentative debate about the character of the New Photography, setting up readers' competitions in an attempt to incorporate them into the new way of seeing. This may have been at Tudor-Hart's behest—*Der Kuckuck* ran similar competitions during the early thirties—although, much to the frustration of *The Listener*'s editors, most entrants showed little interest in abandoning the pastoral subject-matter of the photographic clubs.[34] Edith Tudor-Hart's engagement with modernist aesthetics had been cursory, and the British domestication of a critical continental modernism—expressed most dynamically in commercial art—provided little encouragement. Although she photographed two of the high points of modernist architecture, the Kensal House and Lawn Road flats, and produced the occasional photomontage, Tudor-Hart's photography increasingly succumbed to that very British aesthetic form: naturalism, or the allure of surface appearances (fig. 17).[35]

Moving from south to north London in 1934, the Tudor-Harts were involved in social networks comprising members of the highest echelons of the CPGB, the Hampstead modernists, and, increasingly, refugees from Austria and Germany. Attempts by Special Branch to keep track of their movements did little to prevent a busy domestic environment in which Tudor-Hart offered what aid she could to impoverished exiles. The experience of Lotte Moos, a German exile and fellow traveler, was not untypical, although under the pressures of internment, probably disingenuous:

> I was introduced to Edith Tudor-Hart by Edith Bone, a casual acquaintance of my husband's from Berlin, who thought Mrs. T. H. might give me some work in her darkroom. This was in the summer of 1934. I went there hoping to find some work. However, there was hardly any work to be done, and later . . . we went there mainly to take a bath . . . and I to wash and to iron my things, and to print photos, also sometimes to have a good meal, for Mrs. T. H. had a very good cook. Many refugees did that, as a matter of fact. There were always two plain-clothes men standing at the corner, far away visible [*sic*]. I only mention this to say that our purpose in going there was most harmless and that we did not mind them. Mrs. T. H. knew our political affinities, but neither I nor my

husband had anything politically to do with her, nor really personally. When she went away to Cornwall, she allowed me to live there for one week. She was very hospitable.[36]

Largely isolated from the photographic mainstream, Edith Tudor-Hart did what she could to work alongside and support other women photographers (most of them sympathetic to the Communist cause), including Helen Muspratt, Margaret Monck, Grete Stern, and the South African-born photographer and filmmaker Vera Elkan, with whom she shared a central London studio for a while from 1937 (figs. 18 and 19). Tudor-Hart also photographed in collaboration with her brother, who arrived in London as a student in 1934 and joined Paul Rotha's film unit as a cameraman later in the decade.[37] With the modest economic recovery of the mid-nineteen-thirties, Tudor-Hart's portrait business began to flourish and she was able to pick up advertising work, most notably for the progressive toy manufacturer Abbatt Toys. In domestic and commercial form, her sensitivity to the processes of childhood play lent her imagery a liveliness that broke the mold of the more static studio portrait. It is also tempting to read a feminist challenge encoded in her letterhead: "Edith Tudor-Hart—Modern Photography."

Documentary photography played only a minor role in British visual culture during the thirties, dwarfed by the documentary film movement and subject to the limitations of a Communist Party that showed scant interest in photography as a political weapon. Photography played almost no role in the propaganda culture of the CPGB, and its effort in 1929 to establish an illustrated journal along continental lines was short-lived (fig. 20).[38] The venality of a popular press kept afloat on a swelling wave of commercial advertising was a common theme on the left, and Tudor-Hart never attempted a career as a photojournalist amongst the patriarchs of Fleet Street.[39] With a few exceptions, she confined her published work in Britain before the war to smaller circulation journals and magazines, often with a campaigning emphasis. These included *The Geographical Magazine, Design for To-Day, Sun Bathing Review,* and the satirical magazine *Lilliput.* Later publications included *Mother and Child, Child Education,* and *The Times Educational Supplement.* In December 1944, *Picture Post* applied to the Ministry of Information for a photographer's permit for Tudor-Hart, and she produced a handful of significant photo essays for the journal in the postwar period. However, as the Cold War intensified, Tudor-Hart's career was hampered by her earlier political activity. In early 1945, an MI5 officer suggested that the Ministry of Information be made fully aware of her "long association with the Communist Party."[40]

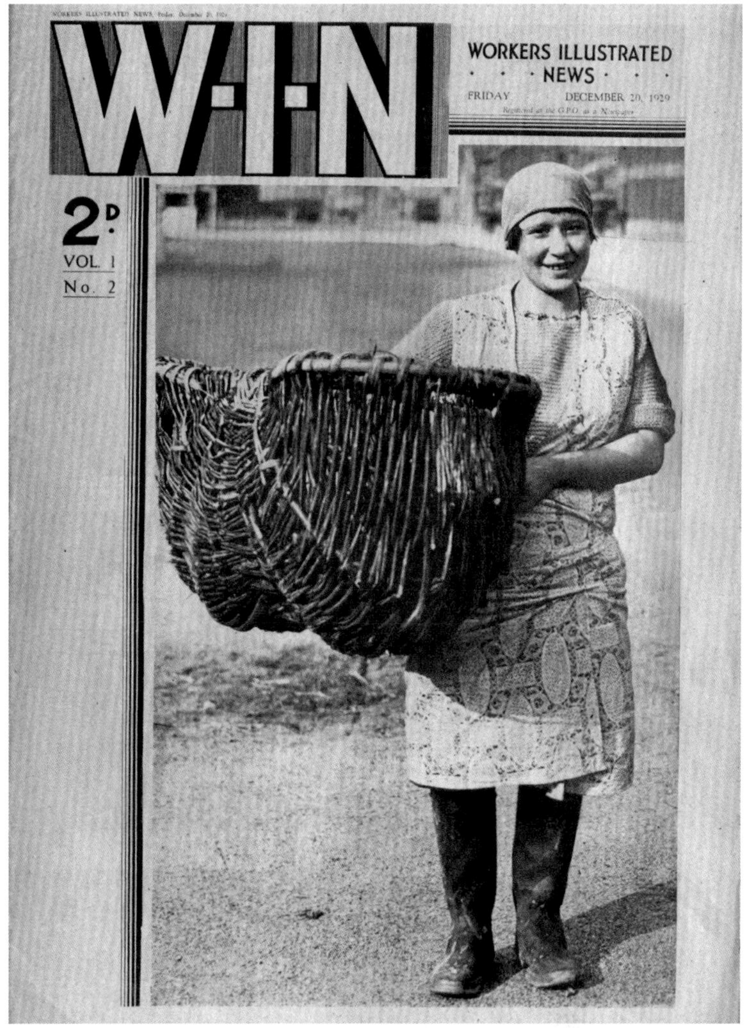

Fig. 20
Photographer unknown, front cover of *Workers' Illustrated News,* December 29, 1929

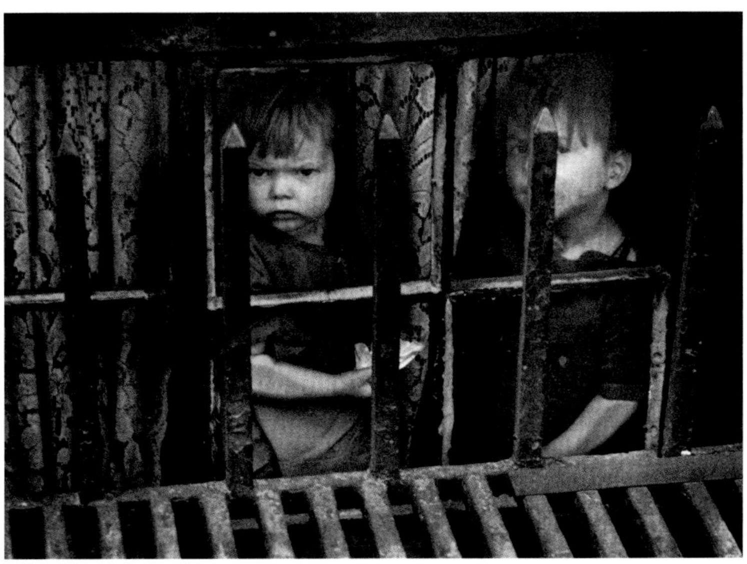

Fig. 19
Margaret Monck, *Children at Shadwell, East London,* 1937

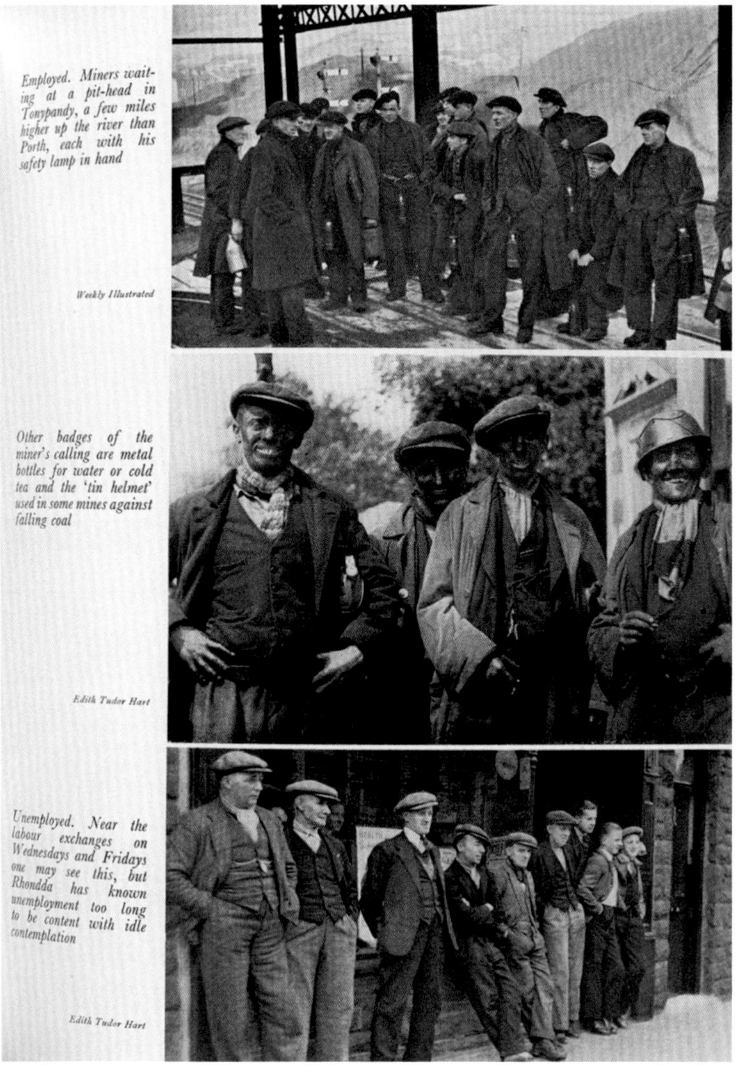

Fig. 21
Edith Tudor-Hart, "The Rhondda Valley," *Geographical Magazine,* March 1936, p. 377

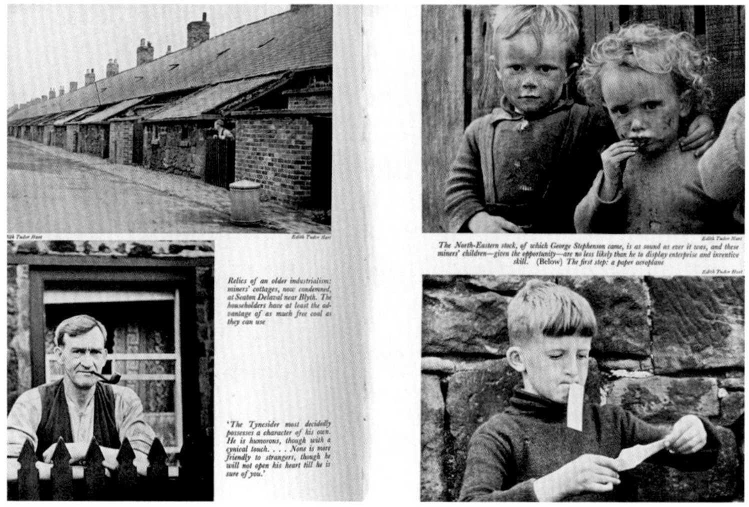

Fig. 22
Edith Tudor-Hart, "Tyneside," *Geographical Magazine,* November 1937, pp. 56–57

Distanced from its Bolshevik origins, the cultural politics of the Popular Front promoted the visibility of the working class, but it did so in terms that starkly delimited its political agency. Furthermore, Edith Tudor-Hart's nuanced representation of class relations was usually subject to an editorial combination of text and image out of her control, rarely contradicting the reform-minded tenor of Popular Front politics. Thus, *The Geographical Magazine* published photographs by Tudor-Hart in articles about the Rhondda Valley and Tyneside in 1936 and 1937 respectively, two industrial areas of Britain suffering cruel hardship.[41] Her images supported through illustration a narrative of piecemeal economic reform and pragmatic rehabilitation of the unemployed under the impact of the British national government's Special Areas Commission, a program of state intervention which largely failed. The articles articulate a pastoral conception of working-class survival, celebrating communal rather than political strength, in the face of adversity. Nonetheless, Tudor-Hart's photographs are strikingly different from the stock photography used: taken for the most part in close proximity to her subjects, they suggest a quality of dialogue and exchange absent from the more distanced images of the photojournalists (figs. 21 and 22). The women, children, and workers she photographed appear less objectified and more enabled—if only partially—to represent themselves.

Similar problems of contextual re-presentation afflicted Tudor-Hart's contribution to Margery Spring Rice's important book *Working-Class Wives,* published in 1939.[42] Based on a fact-finding survey of over 1,200 working women, Spring Rice issued a ringing critique of the failings of public health provisions for married women, arguing for many of the reforms later introduced by the National Health Service. But in tune with the subpolitical character of interwar British feminism, the book expresses little desire to confront patriarchy and is authoritarian in its direction of the lives of young working-class mothers. In this context, Tudor-Hart's photographs are used to provide an illustration of the problem ("The Abiding Maternal Personality") or a portrayal of the solution ("The Travelling Clinic of the Country"), rather than an articulation of working-class subjectivity (fig. 23). In these and similar examples, the editorial context and the cultural politics of the Popular Front worked to diminish the political agency of photographer and subject alike.

Throughout the nineteen-thirties, the quality of Edith Tudor-Hart's photography consistently exceeded the contexts of its re-presentation, a supplement that owed everything to her grasp, perhaps more intuitive than theoretical, of the conditions of photographic

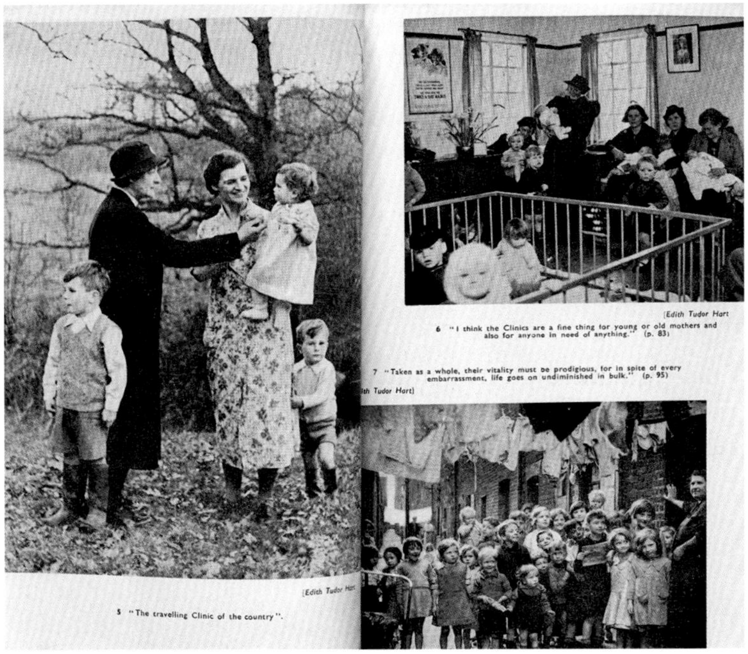

Fig. 23
Edith Tudor-Hart in *Working-Class Wives: Their Health and Conditions* by Margery Spring Rice (Harmondsworth, 1939), unpaginated

realism. Occasionally, however, realist articulation was made more explicit. Along with the photographer John Maltby, Tudor-Hart was involved in the production of the pamphlet, *"Jubilee" Chimp,* published by the National Unemployed Workers' Movement in 1935 in order to protest the excesses of the Silver Jubilee of George V (fig. 24).[43] Jubilee was the first chimpanzee born in the London Zoo, and the pamphlet provided a clear indictment of the capitalist system through the simple expedient of comparing Jubilee's privileged conditions in terms of nutrition and built environment with the poor diet, slum housing, and high mortality rates of sections of the British working class (fig. 25). Designed to stimulate a questioning of the social whole, this was a strategy derived from continental illustrated journals—*Der Kuckuck* had published a similar story in September 1931, comparing the living conditions of the Berlin poor with the more salubrious accommodation of the city's dog home.[44] This suasive technique, an echo of the awesome task of revolutionary mobilization from the previous decade, foundered in Britain under the political pragmatism of the Popular Front. At best it found form as a mode of satirical expression, rejuvenating one of the few subversive strands of British visual culture. Thus, in April 1939, the Hungarian exile Stefan Lorant printed a pair of Tudor-Hart photographs in *Lilliput* juxtaposing a poodle parlor with an East End slum (fig. 26); and in 1936 Bill Brandt published his book *The English at Home* to little commercial success, a wry view by a German exile of the antinomies of the English class system.[45]

Edith Tudor-Hart appears also to have been involved in efforts to promote the worker photography movement in Britain. She was associated, albeit briefly, with two Popular Front formations: the Workers' Film and Photo League, founded in 1934, and what may have been a counter organization that met in her studio, the Progressive Photography Group. But neither association flourished, and Britain never came close to forging the extensive networks of worker photographers that challenged the prevailing conditions of photographic production in Germany or the Soviet Union in the late nineteen-twenties. Tudor-Hart also attempted to exhibit her photography in contexts that would rouse the political cognition of her audience. At an Artists' International Exhibition in late 1934 she showed an image entitled *Sedition,* depicting three plain-clothes policemen at a political

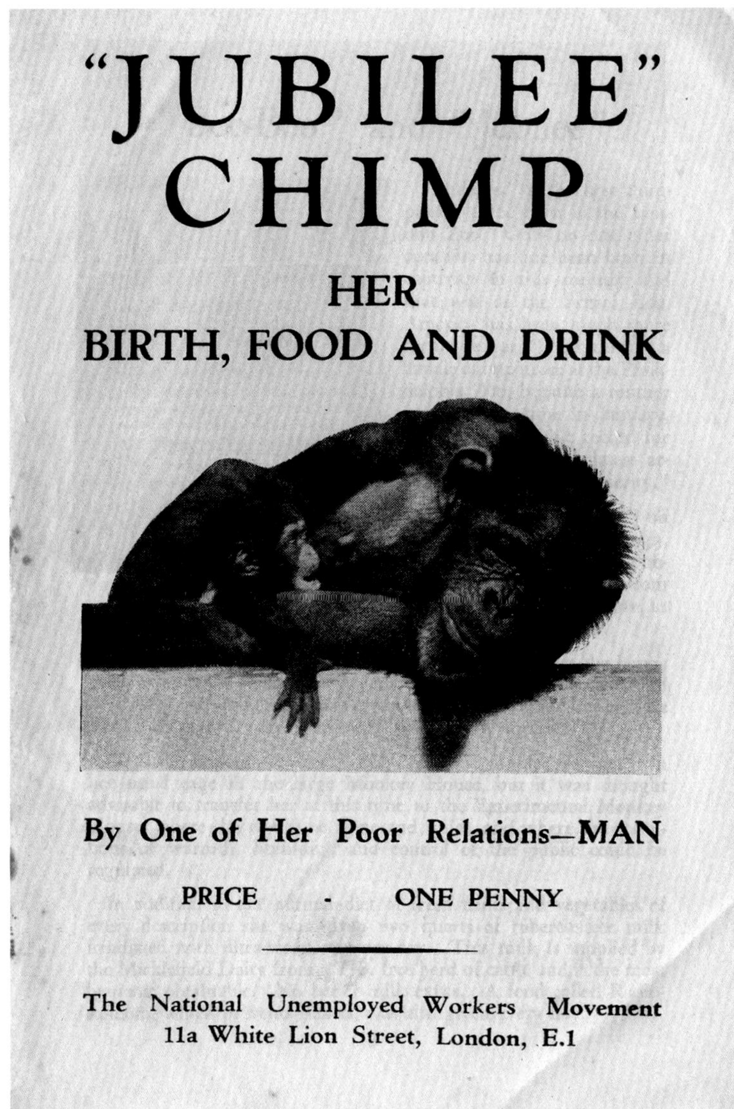

Fig. 24
John Maltby, front cover of the pamphlet *"Jubilee" Chimp: Her Birth, Food and Drink by One of Her Poor Relations—MAN* (London, 1935)

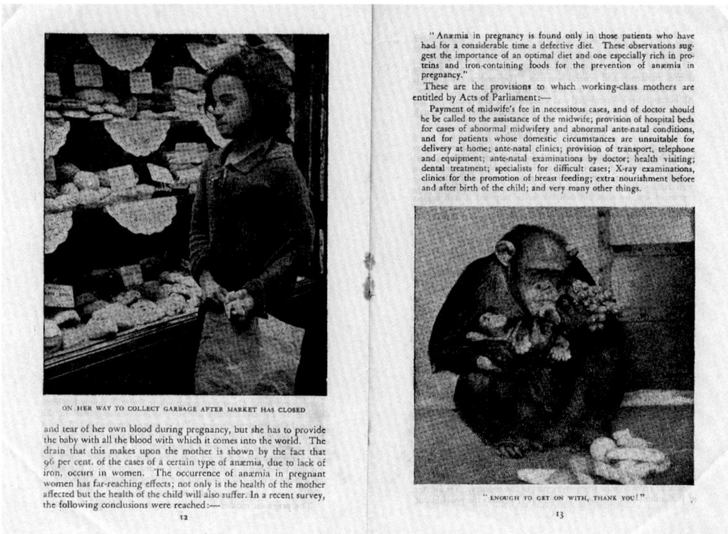
ON HER WAY TO COLLECT GARBAGE AFTER MARKET HAS CLOSED

and tear of her own blood during pregnancy, but she has to provide the baby with all the blood with which it comes into the world. The drain that this makes upon the mother is shown by the fact that 96 per cent. of the cases of a certain type of anæmia, due to lack of iron, occurs in women. The occurrence of anæmia in pregnant women has far-reaching effects; not only is the health of the mother affected but the health of the child will also suffer. In a recent survey, the following conclusions were reached:—

12

"Anæmia in pregnancy is found only in those patients who have had for a considerable time a defective diet. These observations suggest the importance of an optimal diet and one especially rich in proteins and iron-containing foods for the prevention of anæmia in pregnancy."

These are the provisions to which working-class mothers are entitled by Acts of Parliament:—

Payment of midwife's fee in necessitous cases, and of doctor should he be called to the assistance of the midwife; provision of hospital beds for cases of abnormal midwifery and abnormal ante-natal conditions, and for patients whose domestic circumstances are unsuitable for delivery at home; ante-natal clinics; provision of transport, telephone and equipment; ante-natal examinations by doctor; health visiting; dental treatment; specialists for difficult cases; X-ray examinations, clinics for the promotion of breast feeding; extra nourishment before and after birth of the child; and very many other things.

"ENOUGH TO GET ON WITH, THANK YOU!"

13

Fig. 25
Edith Tudor-Hart (left) and John Maltby (right) in the pamphlet *"Jubilee" Chimp: Her Birth, Food and Drink by One of Her Poor Relations—MAN* (London, 1935), pp. 12–13

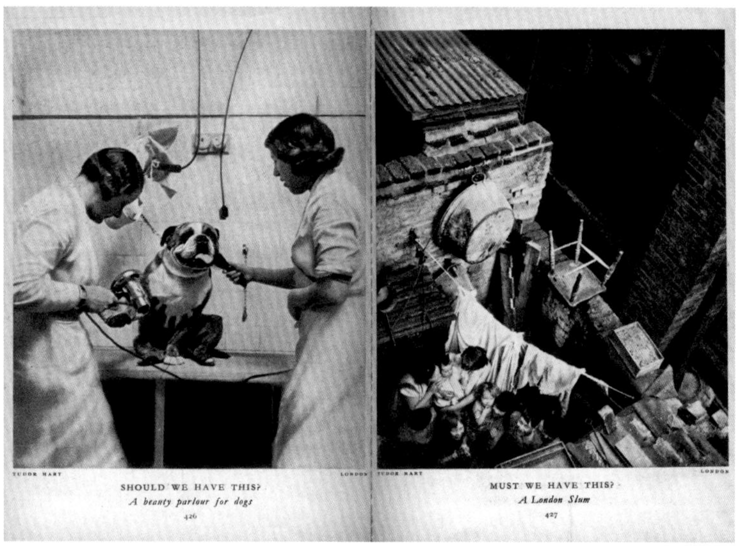

Fig. 26
Edith Tudor-Hart in *Lilliput,* April 1939, pp. 426–27

demonstration, one taking furious notes (fig. 27). The direct gaze of another officer immediately implicates the viewer in the "seditious" act, encouraging a questioning of the Sedition Bill—extending, amongst other things, police powers of search—then opposed by a broad section of the left.[46] Critics sometimes noted this responsive function of Tudor-Hart's photography. As late as July 1940, in an otherwise dilettantish review of an exhibition of "Modern Photography" at Marx House, one writer picked up on the antagonistic character of the dialectical photograph. Brandt's and Tudor-Hart's imagery was "photography with a vengeance in every sense of the word."[47]

However, on the whole the conservative populism of the Popular Front closed down the potential of photography as an agitational tool, enervating its organizational forms and reinstating high cultural norms against more radical aesthetic strategies. In Britain from the mid-thirties we witness a renewed privileging of artistic expression in photography, a cementing of forms of bourgeois identification (often sentimental), and an enhanced objectification of class. Something of all this can be seen in the work of Howard Coster, a portrait photographer and, for a while at least, enthusiastic fellow traveler. Little of his documentary work from this period now survives, although one print of a working-class mother and child, now hidden in the bowels of the National Portrait Gallery in London, includes some revealing instructions to his printer (fig. 28):

> (2) Print it on something a little more contrasty. (I don't want a very 'NAICE' studio picture. I want grim REALITY. This child was starving! & they were so poor—the mother was down & out!. Give me facts & give me LIFE in the print!
> Now use your Emotional side of thought.
> Print by Tuesday please.[48]

Similar strategies aimed at aestheticizing, rather than politicizing, everyday life were adopted by the CPGB, which in 1938 began to stage photographic competitions in its paper, the *Daily Worker.* Its initial judging received 298 entries, but the winning images were overwhelmingly sentimental and contained no political content (fig. 29).[49] Although photography was occasionally utilized in May Day brochures (reflecting perhaps the increased resources generated by the British Aid Spain movement), under the Popular Front the British left largely ignored the propaganda potential of the medium (fig. 30).

In this cloying atmosphere, Edith Tudor-Hart never succeeded in publishing her definitive testimony, a book variously titled *Rich Man, Poor Man* or *East End, West End* and planned in collaboration with the illustrators Pearl Binder and James Fitton. Her project survives today, unreconstructed, in what remains of her negative archive. However, in the context of British photography during the nineteen-thirties, Tudor-Hart's practice is highly significant. Its quality of exchange with her subjects, its interest in the analytical power of the dialectical photograph, and its effort to articulate the social whole all mark a qualitative break with the bourgeois tourist gaze that informed photographic imagery of the British working class throughout much of the interwar period (fig. 31). For the first time, and in a hostile climate, photography in Britain began to develop a rendition of class relations, both nuanced and combative. This was substantially the achievement of exile photographers and publishers.

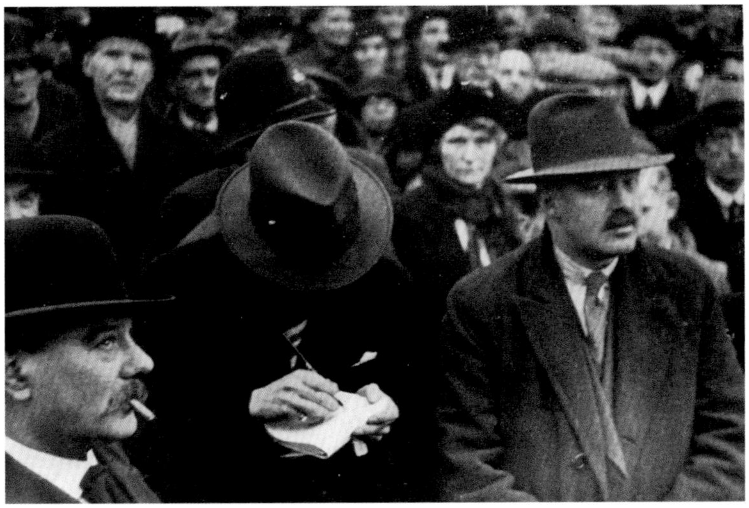

Fig. 27
Edith Tudor-Hart, "Sedition," *Left Review,* March 1935, p. 191

By the outbreak of World War Two, Tudor-Hart's revolutionary idealism lay in tatters, lacerated by the CPGB's somersaulting political strategy, by the distortions perpetuated by some in her circle in defense of the Moscow trials, and by the betrayal of the Nazi-Soviet pact signed in August 1939. Whatever her loyalties to comrades and party, her considerable risk-taking in support of the Soviet cause must have seemed, in moments of reflection, ever more futile. Since arriving in London, Tudor-Hart had continued to operate as a low-level Comintern agent undetected by British authorities. Occasionally she had come close to arrest, not least when she was implicated in the case of Percy Glading, one of the very few British spies to be captured during this period.[50] Harassed until her death by investigators obsessed with the high-level Soviet infiltration of British security services, it is perhaps ironic that MI5 were broadly correct about Tudor-Hart's activities at the time of Philby's initial interrogation in 1951:

> There is no firm evidence, beyond her own admissions to [obliterated], of Edith TUDOR-HART's work for the Russian Intelligence Service, either in Austria or in the United Kingdom. The diversity and character of her contacts in this country, however, can only serve to raise her above the mass of unimportant rank and file aliens [*sic*] communists and to set her into a special category. Exactly what her work in the United Kingdom for the communist cause has amounted to is difficult to assess, but there is the possibility that she has been a Russian Intelligence Service contact, possibly a talent-spotter or a cut-out and means of communication between the British Communist Party and Austrian Communist Party in exile during the war years. At all events, she has been a convinced communist in touch with top-ranking communists and known Russian spies for the past twenty-five years.[51]

Tudor-Hart worked as a courier under the code-name "Edith," introducing contacts—most notoriously Philby—to agents further up the Soviets' illegal *rezidentura* hierarchy. Her knowledge of tradecraft made her useful for carrying information securely within Britain and occasionally Western Europe. In September 1937, in the wake of Stalin's purges, Arnold Deutsch—credited by the KGB with recruiting twenty British agents—was recalled to Moscow. The London *rezidentura* closed down and Tudor-Hart became an important conduit between operatives and the Communist activist Bob Stewart, who reported to the Soviet embassy.[52] She also played a key role during the war in maintaining contacts between the CPGB and the well-organized network of Austrian Communists in exile, a link of some strategic significance for Moscow. Although Tudor-Hart suffered sporadic surveillance during the war years, and by 1945 was clearly being informed upon by someone close to her, the British authorities never reconstructed a precise chronicle of her activities.

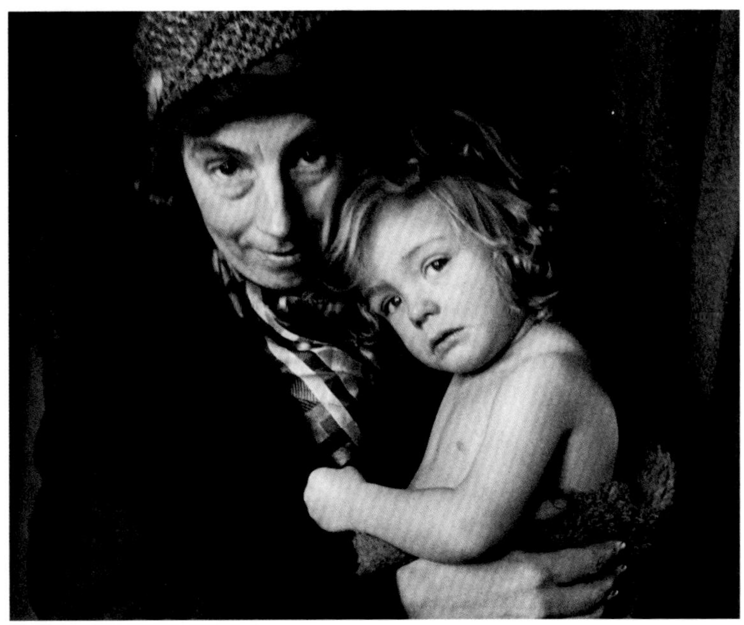

Fig. 28
Howard Coster, *Untitled Portrait,* ca. 1935

As a British citizen, Tudor-Hart escaped internment, but the coming of war brought growing hardship. Pritchard's patronage had run dry and in July 1940, in response to a plea for work, he suggested that she move to Canada. His colleague, the design historian John Gloag, was still less encouraging, noting that photography was "a very dangerous occupation for somebody who has got Austrian parents."[53] Now a single mother, Tudor-Hart coped with a young child whose severe autism was becoming increasingly obvious. She lost her studio during the Blitz, was forced to find a position with a photographic printer, and worked for a while as a housekeeper. In May 1942, a Special Branch watcher, ever attuned to appearances, noted that "from her dress and habits she does not seem to be in affluent circumstances."[54] Tudor-Hart also aided, as best she could, her two exiled cousins Josef and Wilhelm, released from Australian internment in 1941, and supported her mother Adele, whom she had brought to England in 1938. Fragmentary evidence from her security service files suggests that from the end of the war she slowly extricated herself from Communist activism, a situation probably exacerbated by splits in the Austrian party. Although Tudor-Hart remained a CPGB member under the name "Betty Gray" and continued to concern MI5 because of her relationship with the Austrian atom physicist Engelbert Broda, the pressures of a secret life and the politics of the Stalin era closed in on her.[55] In October 1951, worried about possible police raids after the interrogation of Philby, she destroyed her photographic records as well as some negatives. One eager informer described her as "a sick woman, highly neurotic and suffering from a persecution mania."[56] Defeated and demoralized, her life as a partisan of the Soviet cause was over.

Although Tudor-Hart's CPGB associations were known, her activity for the Comintern was never made public and she continued to work as a photographer until the mid-nineteen-fifties, running a portrait studio and publishing intermittently in specialist magazines and in the mass circulation *Picture Post* (fig. 32).[57] However, the marginalization in the postwar period of a progressive cultural politics—expressed in photography by an increasingly subjective documentary humanism—worked to negate the potential of the dialectical image fought for by worker photographers during the nineteen-twenties. Instead, Tudor-Hart concentrated on documenting issues of child welfare, health, and education, working for cam-

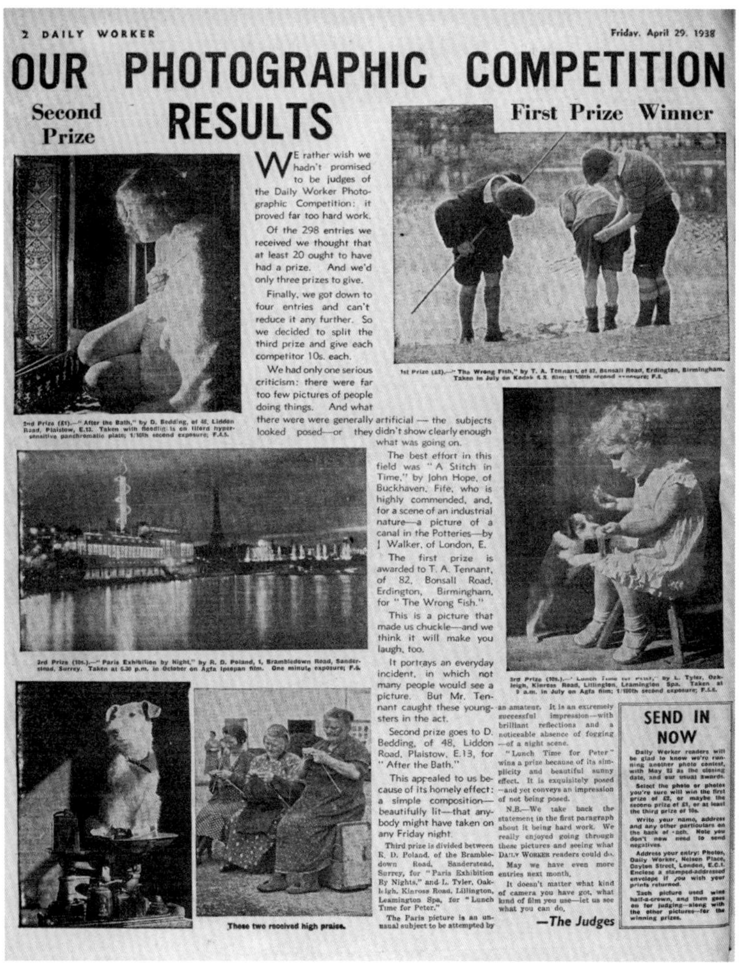
2 DAILY WORKER — Friday, April 29, 1938

OUR PHOTOGRAPHIC COMPETITION RESULTS

Second Prize

First Prize Winner

WE rather wish we hadn't promised to be judges of the Daily Worker Photographic Competition: it proved far too hard work.

Of the 298 entries we received we thought that at least 20 ought to have had a prize. And we'd only three prizes to give.

Finally, we got down to four entries and can't reduce it any further. So we decided to split the third prize and give each competitor 10s. each.

We had only one serious criticism: there were far too few pictures of people doing things. And what there were were generally artificial — the subjects looked posed—or they didn't show clearly enough what was going on.

The best effort in this field was "A Stitch in Time," by John Hope, of Buckhaven, Fife, who is highly commended, and, for a scene of an industrial nature—a picture of a canal in the Potteries—by J. Walker, of London, E.

The first prize is awarded to T. A. Tennant, of 82, Bonsall Road, Erdington, Birmingham, for "The Wrong Fish."

This is a picture that made us chuckle—and we think it will make you laugh, too.

It portrays an everyday incident, in which not many people would see a picture. But Mr. Tennant caught these youngsters in the act.

Second prize goes to D. Bedding, of 48, Liddon Road, Plaistow, E.13, for "After the Bath."

This appealed to us because of its homely effect: a simple composition—beautifully lit—that anybody might have taken on any Friday night.

Third prize is divided between R. D. Poland, of the Brambledown Road, Sanderstead, Surrey, for "Paris Exhibition By Nights," and L. Tyler, Oakleigh, Kinross Road, Lillington, Leamington Spa, for "Lunch Time for Peter."

The Paris picture is an unusual subject to be attempted by an amateur. It is an extremely successful impression—with brilliant reflections and a noticeable absence of fogging—of a night scene.

"Lunch Time for Peter" wins a prize because of its simplicity and beautiful sunny effect. It is exquisitely posed—and yet conveys an impression of not being posed.

N.B.—We take back the statement in the first paragraph about it being hard work. We really enjoyed going through these pictures and seeing what DAILY WORKER readers could do.

May we have even more entries next month.

It doesn't matter what kind of camera you have got, what kind of film you use—let us see what you can do.

—The Judges

1st Prize (£2).—"The Wrong Fish," by T. A. Tennant, of 82, Bonsall Road, Erdington, Birmingham. Taken in July on Kodak S.S. film; 1/100th second exposure; F.8.

2nd Prize (£1).—"After the Bath," by D. Bedding, of 48, Liddon Road, Plaistow, E.13. Taken with floodlight on Ilford hypersensitive panchromatic plate; 1/10th second exposure; F.4.5.

3rd Prize (10s.).—"Paris Exhibition by Night," by R. D. Poland, 1, Brambledown Road, Sanderstead, Surrey. Taken at 6.30 p.m. in October on Agfa Ipsopan film. One minute exposure; F.6.

3rd Prize (10s.).—"Lunch Time for Peter," by L. Tyler, Oakleigh, Kinross Road, Lillington, Leamington Spa. Taken at 9 a.m. in July on Agfa film; 1/100th second exposure; F.5.6.

These two received high praise.

SEND IN NOW

Daily Worker readers will be glad to know we're running another photo contest, with May 13 as the closing date, and our usual awards.

Select the photo or photos you're sure will win the first prize of £2, or maybe the second prize of £1, or at least the third prize of 10s.

Write your name, address and any other particulars on the back of each. Note you don't now need to send negatives.

Address your entry: Photos, Daily Worker, Nelson Place, Cayton Street, London, E.C.1. Enclose a stamped-addressed envelope if you wish your prints returned.

Each picture used wins half-a-crown, and then goes on for judging—along with the other pictures—for the winning prizes.

Fig. 29
"Our Photographic Competition Results," *Daily Worker,* April 29, 1938, p. 2

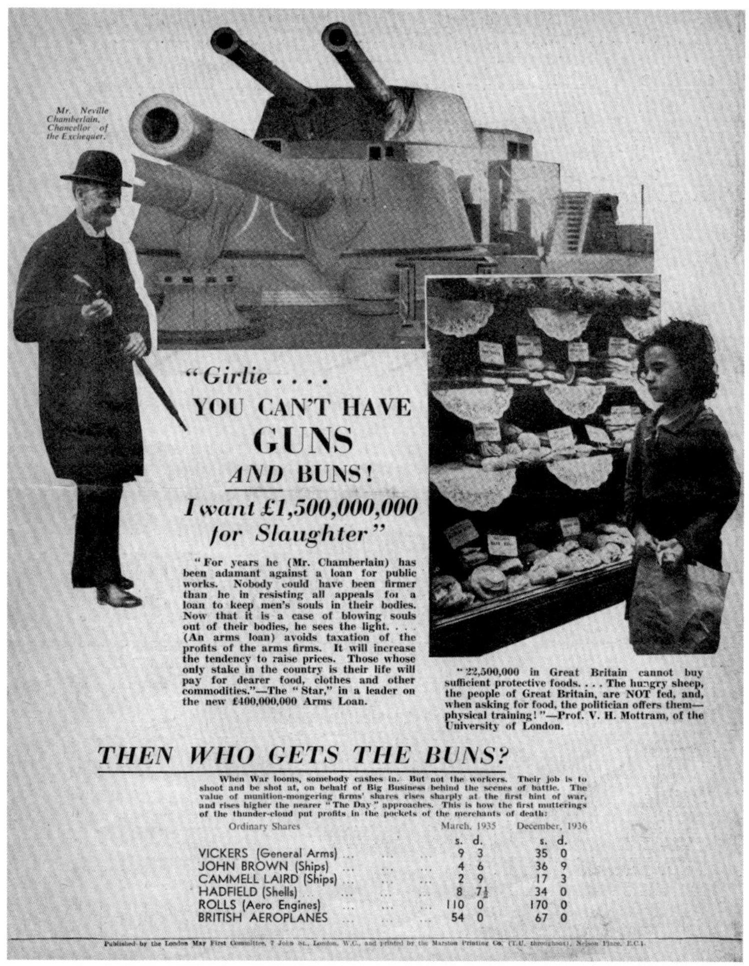
Mr. Neville Chamberlain, Chancellor of the Exchequer.

"Girlie . . . .
YOU CAN'T HAVE GUNS AND BUNS!
I want £1,500,000,000 for Slaughter"

"For years he (Mr. Chamberlain) has been adamant against a loan for public works. Nobody could have been firmer than he in resisting all appeals for a loan to keep men's souls in their bodies. Now that it is a case of blowing souls out of their bodies, he sees the light. . . . (An arms loan) avoids taxation of the profits of the arms firms. It will increase the tendency to raise prices. Those whose only stake in the country is their life will pay for dearer food, clothes and other commodities."—The "Star," in a leader on the new £400,000,000 Arms Loan.

"22,500,000 in Great Britain cannot buy sufficient protective foods. . . . The hungry sheep, the people of Great Britain, are NOT fed, and, when asking for food, the politician offers them—physical training!"—Prof. V. H. Mottram, of the University of London.

THEN WHO GETS THE BUNS?

When War looms, somebody cashes in. But not the workers. Their job is to shoot and be shot at, on behalf of Big Business behind the scenes of battle. The value of munition-mongering firms' shares rises sharply at the first hint of war, and rises higher the nearer "The Day" approaches. This is how the first mutterings of the thunder-cloud put profits in the pockets of the merchants of death:

Ordinary Shares	March, 1935		December, 1936	
	s.	d.	s.	d.
VICKERS (General Arms)	9	3	35	0
JOHN BROWN (Ships)	4	6	36	9
CAMMELL LAIRD (Ships)	2	9	17	3
HADFIELD (Shells)	8	7½	34	0
ROLLS (Aero Engines)	110	0	170	0
BRITISH AEROPLANES	54	0	67	0

Published by the London May First Committee, 7 John St., London, W.C., and printed by the Marston Printing Co. (T.U. throughout), Nelson Place, E.C.1.

Fig. 30
Edith Tudor-Hart, *May Day 1937,* p. 10

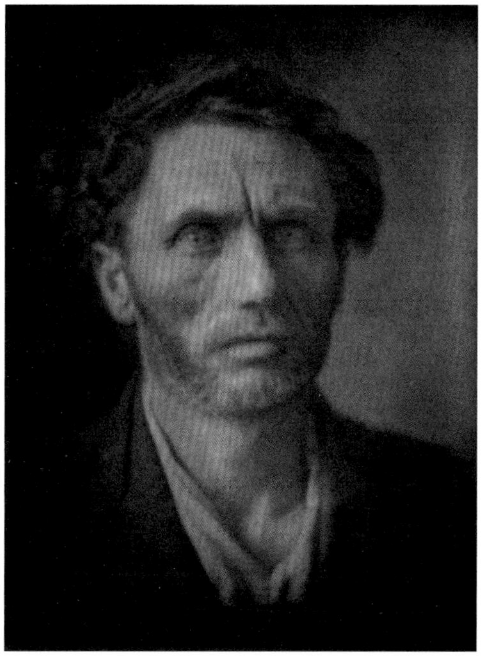

Fig. 31
Emil Otto Hoppé, "Franz," in J. D. Beresford and E. O. Hoppé, *Taken from Life* (London, 1922), opposite p. 83

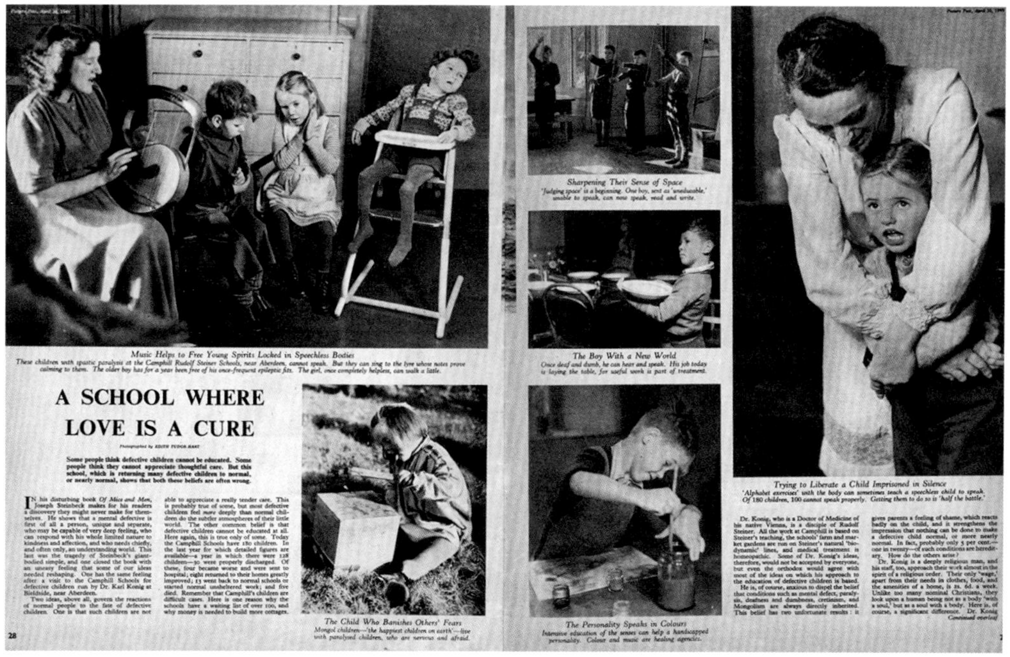

Music Helps to Free Young Spirits Locked in Speechless Bodies
These children with spastic paralysis at the Camphill Rudolf Steiner Schools, near Aberdeen, cannot speak. But they can sing to the lyre whose notes prove calming to them. The older boy has for a year been free of his once-frequent epileptic fits. The girl, once completely helpless, can walk a little.

A SCHOOL WHERE LOVE IS A CURE

Photographed by EDITH TUDOR-HART

Some people think defective children cannot be educated. Some people think they cannot appreciate thoughtful care. But this school, which is returning many defective children to normal, or nearly normal, shows that both these beliefs are often wrong.

In his disturbing book *Of Mice and Men*, Joseph Steinbeck makes for his readers a discovery they might never make for themselves. He shows that a mental defective is first of all a person, unique and separate, who may be capable of very deep feeling, who can respond with his whole limited nature to kindness and affection, and who needs chiefly, and often only, an understanding world. This last was the tragedy of Steinbeck's giant-bodied simple, and one closed the book with an uneasy feeling that some of our ideas needed reshaping. One has the same feeling after a visit to the Camphill Schools for defective children run by Dr. Karl Konig at Bieldside, near Aberdeen.

Two ideas, above all, govern the reactions of normal people to the fate of defective children. One is that such children are not able to appreciate a really tender care. This is probably true of some, but most defective children feel *more* deeply than normal children do the subtler atmospheres of their little world. The other common belief is that defective children cannot be educated at all. Here again, this is true only of some. Today the Camphill Schools have 180 children. In the last year for which detailed figures are available—a year in which there were 128 children—30 were properly discharged. Of these, four became worse and were sent to hospital; eight returned to their homes greatly improved; 13 went back to normal schools or started normal unsheltered work; and five died. Remember that Camphill's children are difficult cases. Here is one reason why the schools have a waiting list of over 100, and why money is needed to build more cottages.

28

The Child Who Banishes Others' Fears
Mongol children—'the happiest children on earth'—live with paralysed children, who are nervous and afraid.

Sharpening Their Sense of Space
'Judging space' is a beginning. One boy, sent as 'uneducable,' unable to speak, can now speak, read and write.

The Boy With a New World
Once deaf and dumb, he can hear and speak. His job today is laying the table, for useful work is part of treatment.

The Personality Speaks in Colours
Intensive education of the senses can help a handicapped personality. Colour and music are healing agencies.

Trying to Liberate a Child Imprisoned in Silence
'Alphabet exercises' with the body can sometimes teach a speechless child to speak. Of 180 children, 100 cannot speak properly. Getting them to do so is 'half the battle.'

Dr. Konig, who is a Doctor of Medicine of his native Vienna, is a disciple of Rudolf Steiner. All the work at Camphill is based on Steiner's teaching, the schools' farm and market gardens are run on Steiner's natural 'bio-dynamic' lines, and medical treatment is homeopathic. Some of Dr. Konig's ideas, therefore, would not be accepted by everyone, but even the orthodox would agree with most of the ideas on which his approach to the education of defective children is based.

He is, of course, anxious to dispel the belief that conditions such as mental defect, paralysis, deafness and dumbness, cretinism, and Mongolism are always directly inherited. This belief has two unfortunate results: it gives parents a feeling of shame, which reacts badly on the child, and it strengthens the impression that nothing can be done to make a defective child normal, or more nearly normal. In fact, probably only 5 per cent.—one in twenty—of such conditions are hereditary. How do the others arise?

Dr. Konig is a deeply religious man, and his staff, too, approach their work almost in the spirit of a religious order. Their only 'wage,' apart from their needs in clothes, food, and the amenities of a home, is 2s. 6d. a week. Unlike too many nominal Christians, they look upon a human being not as a body 'with a soul,' but as a soul with a body. Here is, of course, a significant difference. Dr. Konig

Continued overleaf

Fig. 32
Edith Tudor-Hart, "A School Where Love is a Cure," *Picture Post,* April 30, 1949, pp. 28–29

paigning journals put out by agencies like the British Medical Association, Mencap, and the National Baby Welfare Council.[58] These projects embodied a lifelong concern with the processes of childhood development and might—cautiously—be read as a rationalized, public expression of anguish over her son's illness. Tudor-Hart's thinking continued to be influenced by contacts first made in Vienna during the twenties, including the exiled Anna Freud and the founder of the Camphill movement, Karl König. From her arrival in London, the photographer had collaborated with women excluded from professional discussions of public health and housing; their agitation helped achieve what one writer has described as the liberal "feminization of the state."[59] However, her postwar documentary projects reflect the growing limitations of that process as the emphasis on rebuilding family life negated feminist advances and the welfare state was constructed to tempt women to return to the home. Similarly, whilst women were encouraged to consume photography within the domestic environment, their postwar opportunities as professional photographers remained severely constrained. It proved increasingly impossible for Tudor-Hart to use her camera to engage critically with social policies that offered piecemeal reform but contained little emancipatory logic.

Nonetheless, the photography from this period is compelling, expressing a utopian investment in the figure of the socialized child that is more complex than the mass of its humdrum competitors. Tudor-Hart's observational skills were acute, the Viennese legacy of a progressive pedagogy still active. However, if, as Fredric Jameson has argued, "utopia emerges at the moment of the suspension of the political," perhaps also its "excision," then the quality of this work derives from a greater absence.[60] The child as a metaphor of futurity is overwhelming in Tudor-Hart's documentary, a displacement and narrowing of an encompassing and defeated collective aspiration. For her, children represent the subversive potential of socialization through self-government *and* mutual discovery, through individualism *and* collectivity, a sociality at odds with the imposition of a competitive egoism. However, within the image, the contradictions are acute: Tudor-Hart's children appear in adult-managed institutions, their human presence often diminished by the context of normalizing medical and educational discourses, as well as by a documentary regime of surface appearances. It is doubtful, too, that the slender hope they represent worked in any effective way to counteract Tudor-Hart's personal dystopias, let alone the loss of political possibility heralded by the Cold War. But despite their contingency, her images of children striving to remake their environments reveal something of Edith Tudor-Hart's own passage into adulthood, charged by a radical optimism and determined to prevail against a brutal world.

Notes continued from page 18.

29 See Barry McLoughlin et al., *Aufbruch, Hoffnung, Endstation: Österreicherinnen und Österreicher in der Sowjetunion 1925–1945* (Vienna, 1997).
30 For a contemporary comment on the question, see Carine Cadby, "Photography as a Career for Women," *Photographic Review* 1, no. 2 (Summer 1930), pp. 19–20.
31 Jack Pritchard's circle included Ernö Goldfinger, Walter Gropius, Marcel Breuer, Arthur Korn, Jacques and Jacqueline Groag, Naum Slutsky, and Egon Riss. See his autobiographical work *View from a Long Chair: The Memoirs of Jack Pritchard* (London, 1984). A number of Comintern agents, including Arnold Deutsch, found a home in the Lawn Road flats. See Christopher Andrew and Vasili Mitrokhin, *The Mitrokhin Archive: The KGB in Europe and the West* (London, 2000), pp. 74–75.
32 For Edith Tudor-Hart's links to Ernö Goldfinger, who never actually joined the CPGB, see Nigel Warburton, *Ernö Goldfinger: The Life of an Architect* (London, 2004).
33 See *The Listener,* November 29, 1933, December 13, 1933, January 10, 1934, May 16, 1934, June 13, 1934, and January 2, 1935.
34 See P. Morton Shand, "The First Hundred Years of Photography," *The Listener,* December 19, 1934, pp. 1029–33. For the photographic competitions, see *The Listener,* June 13, 1934, pp. 989 and 1002–3, July 18, 1934, pp. 120–21, and July 25, 1934, pp. 160–61.
35 For Tudor-Hart's montages, see G. T. Grinko, *The Five-Year Plan of the Soviet Union: A Political Interpretation* (London, 1930), John Reed, *Ten Days that Shook the World* (London, 1932), and *New Homes for Old* (September 1934).
36 Charlotte Moos, statement to the Governess of Holloway Prison, April 27, 1940, TNA KV 2/1241. Moos's husband was Brian Goold-Verschoyle, a Comintern agent who later disappeared in the Soviet Union.
37 See Duncan Forbes, "Wolf Suschitzky in Vienna and London: Photographic Exchange and Continuity," in Michael Omasta et al., *Wolf Suschitzky: Photos* (Vienna, 2006), pp. 16–29.
38 See Duncan Forbes, "The Worker Photography Movement in Britain, 1934–1939," in *The Worker Photography Movement [1926–1939]: Essays and Documents,* ed. Jorge Ribalta, exh. cat. Museo Nacional Centro de Arte Reina Sofia (Madrid, 2011), pp. 206–17.
39 Although Tudor-Hart was clearly interested in the idea of photojournalism as a profession, publishing two articles on the subject. See "More Freedom for the Photo-Reporters," *Photography* (February 1934) and "Photography as a Profession," *Miniature Camera Magazine* (December 1936).
40 See the Ministry of Information vetting inquiry, December 26, 1944, and the memo from W. Ogilvie, January 6, 1945, TNA KV 2/1013.
41 Miles Davies, "The Rhondda Valley," *The Geographical Magazine* (March 1936), pp. 372–86, and G. H. J. Daysh, "Tyneside," *The Geographical Magazine* (November 1937), pp. 51–66. Some of Edith Tudor-Hart's photographs were also published in Wal Hannington's important assessment of this question, *The Problem of the Distressed Areas* (London, 1937).
42 Margery Spring Rice, *Working-Class Wives: Their Health and Conditions* (Harmondsworth, 1939).
43 *"Jubilee" Chimp: Her Birth, Food and Drink by One of Her Poor Relations—MAN* (London, 1935).
44 "Hundeleben," *Der Kuckuck,* no. 39, September 27, 1931, p. 15.
45 Bill Brandt, *The English at Home* (London, 1936). Stefan Lorant (1901–1997), who arrived in Britain in 1934, established *Lilliput* in 1937. He had previously worked as a film director and newspaper editor in Berlin, Munich, and Vienna. In 1938, he became editor-in-chief of the newly founded *Picture Post.*
46 *Sedition* appears to be one of a number of negatives destroyed by Tudor-Hart. The image was subsequently reproduced in the Popular Front journal *Left Review* (March 1935), p. 191.
47 "Modern Photography at Marx House," *New Statesman and Nation,* July 27, 1940, pp. 87–88.
48 Untitled photograph, National Portrait Gallery, London, x136837.
49 *Daily Worker,* April 29, 1938, p. 2.
50 Percy Glading was a leading member of a spy ring operating inside the Woolwich Arsenal. He was arrested in January 1938 and subsequently imprisoned along with two coconspirators. Edith Tudor-Hart was suspected of having supplied a Leica camera to Glading and was questioned by Special Branch officers in March 1938. However, due to insufficient evidence she was never arrested. For further information on Glading, see Nigel West and Oleg Tsarev, *The Crown Jewels: The British Secrets at the Heart of the KGB Archives* (London, 1998), pp. 124–26.
51 MI5 narrative history for Edith Tudor-Hart, December 1, 1951, TNA KV 2/1604. The MI5 officer Peter Wright describes an interrogation of Tudor-Hart during the sixties in his *Spycatcher: The Candid Autobiography of a Senior Intelligence Officer* (New York, 1987), p. 249.
52 For information on Bob Stewart, see Nigel West and Oleg Tsarev, *The Crown Jewels: The British Secrets at the Heart of the KGB Archives* (London, 1998), pp. 131 and 182. Stewart's MI5 files are available at TNA KV 2/1180–3.
53 Jack Pritchard to Edith Tudor-Hart, July 18, 1940, University of East Anglia, Pritchard Papers, PP/8/65/2, and John Gloag to Jack Pritchard, August 26, 1940, PP/8/17/5.
54 Special Branch memo, May 11, 1942, TNA KV 2/1013.
55 Paul Broda, *Scientist Spies: A Memoir of My Three Parents and the Atom Bomb* (Leicester, 2011).
56 Interview with unnamed source, October 3, 1951, TNA KV 2/1014.
57 See especially Edith Tudor-Hart, "Making a Mess Cleanly," *Picture Post,* June 9, 1945, pp. 22–23; "A School Where Love Is a Cure," *Picture Post,* April 30, 1949, pp. 28–31; and "Where Youth Has Its Fling," *Picture Post,* November 24, 1951, pp. 34–35.
58 See, among others, Edith Tudor-Hart, "The Mentally Handicapped Child," *Mother and Child* 22, no. 7 (October 1951), pp. 166–67 (a journal of the National Baby Welfare Council); "Children of the Fountain," *Family Doctor* 5, no. 6 (June 1955), pp. 424–25 (published by the British Medical Association); and *Moving and Growing: Physical Education in the Primary School Part One* by the Ministry of Education (London, 1952).
59 Robert Colls, *Identity of England* (Oxford, 2002), p. 118. Edith Tudor-Hart completed documentary commissions for the South London Hospital for Women and Children (in collaboration with Grete Stern, 1935) and the London Women's Parliament (1943).
60 Fredric Jameson, "The Politics of Utopia," *New Left Review* 25 (January/February 2004), p. 43. There are intriguing parallels here with the career of the Austrian exile photographer Margaret Michaelis. See Helen Ennis, *Margaret Michaelis: Love, Loss and Photography* (Melbourne, 2005).

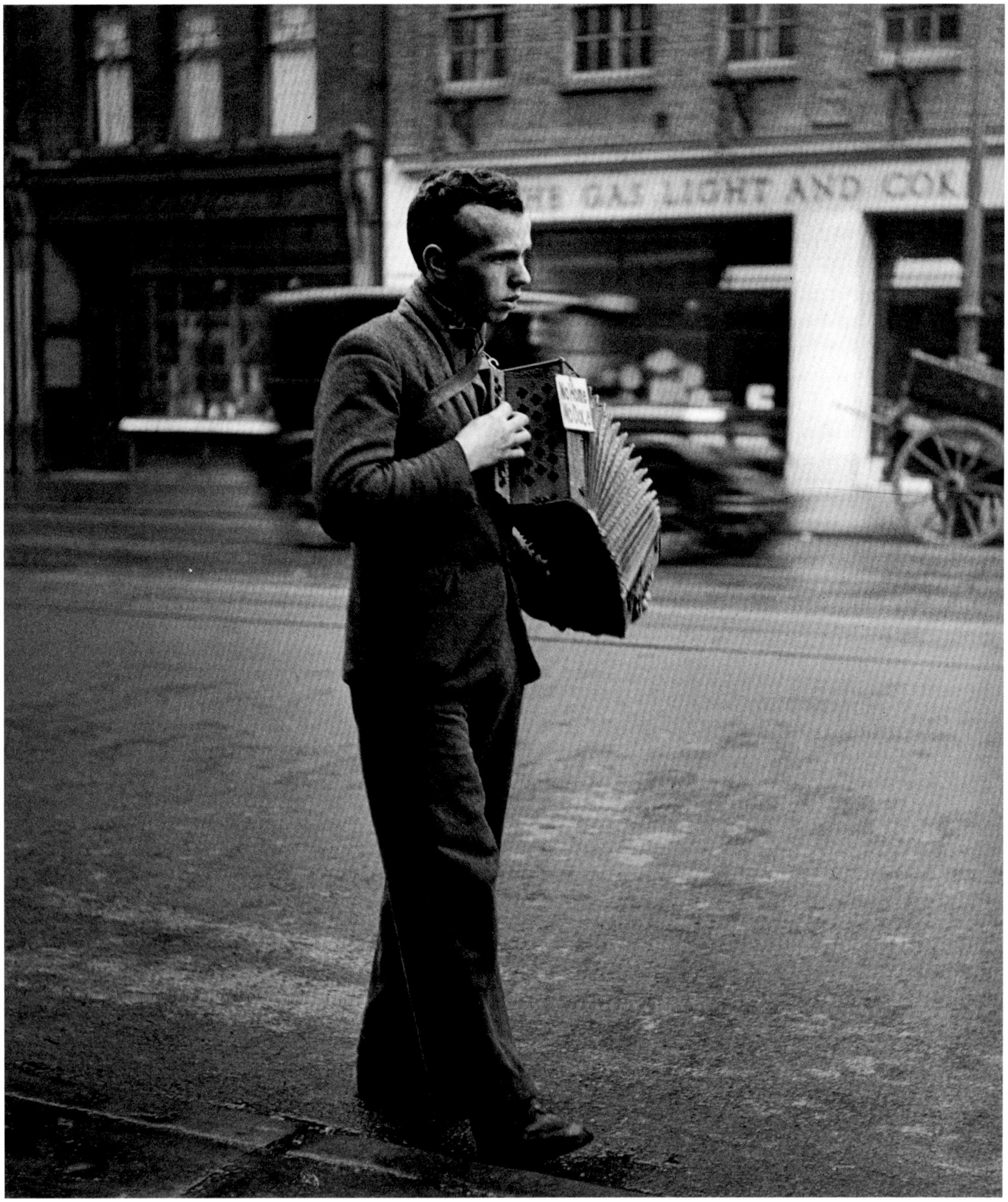

Edith Suschitzky
No Home, No Dole, London, ca. 1931
Modern silver-gelatin print, 33.4 × 27.5 cm
National Galleries of Scotland, PGP 279.2

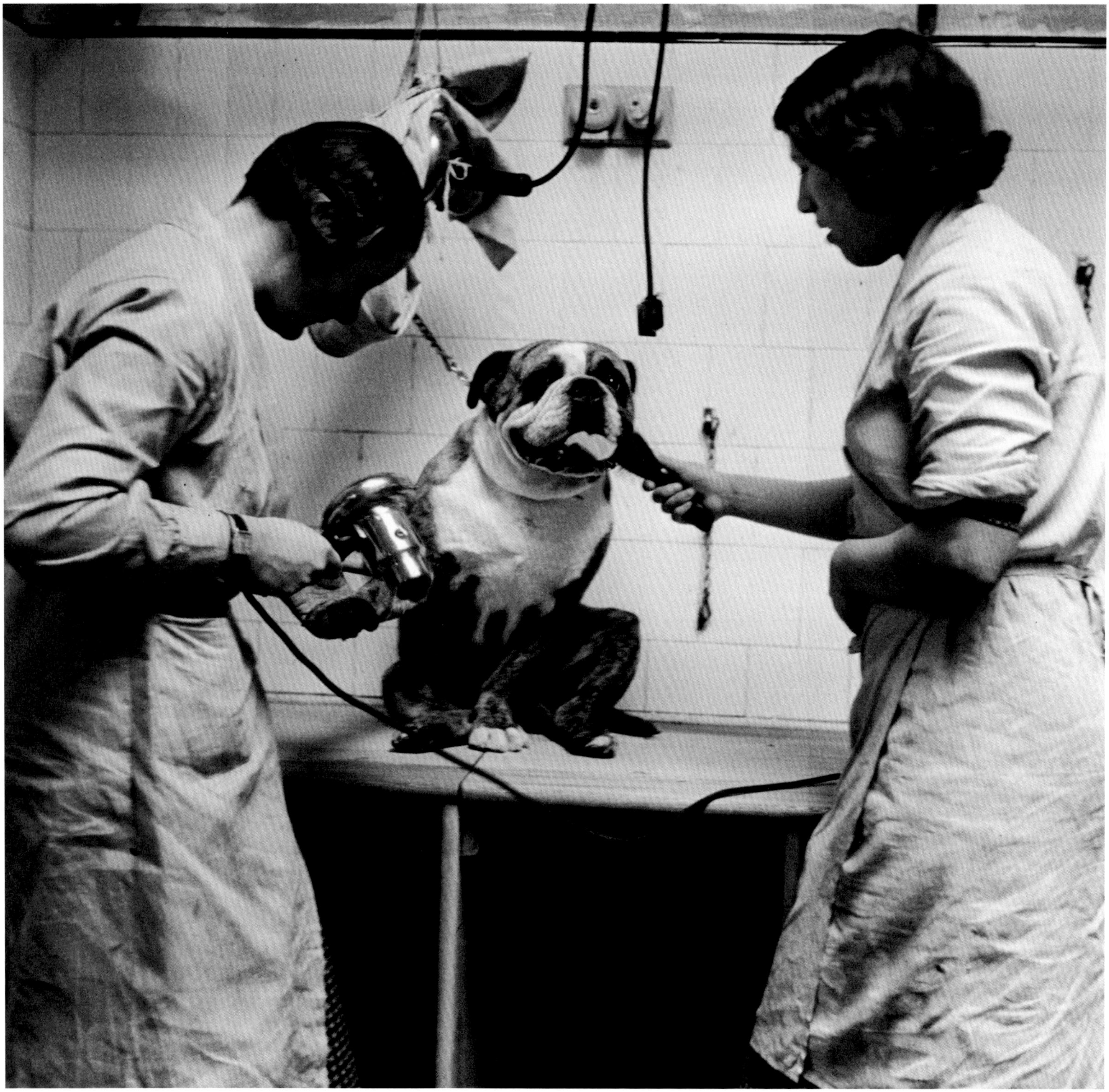

Edith Tudor-Hart
Poodle Parlour, London, ca. 1937
Modern silver-gelatin print, 30.2 × 30.1 cm
National Galleries of Scotland, PGP 279.33

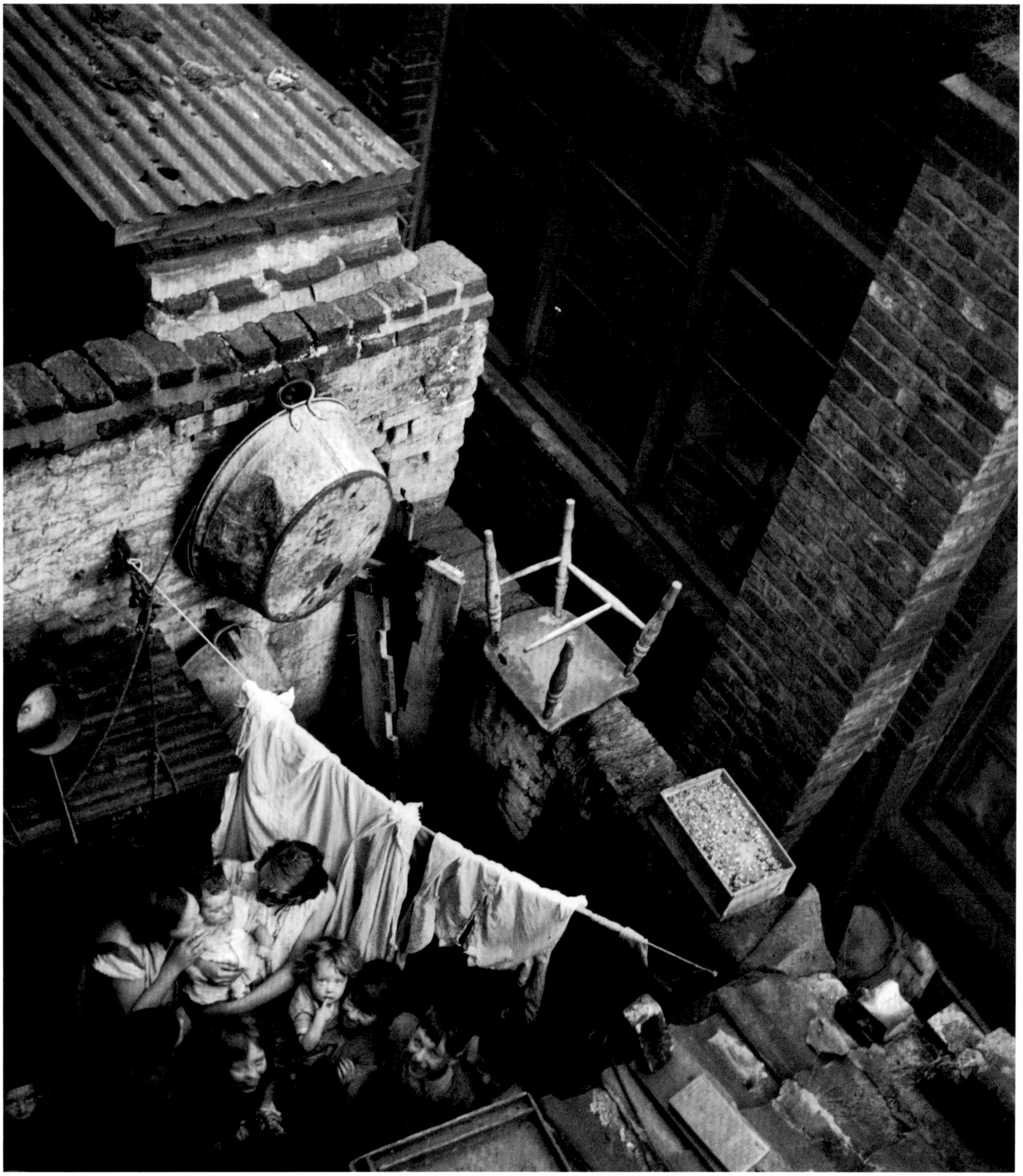

Edith Tudor-Hart
Gee Street, Finsbury, London, ca. 1936
Modern silver-gelatin print, 34.1 × 29 cm
National Galleries of Scotland, PGP 279.32

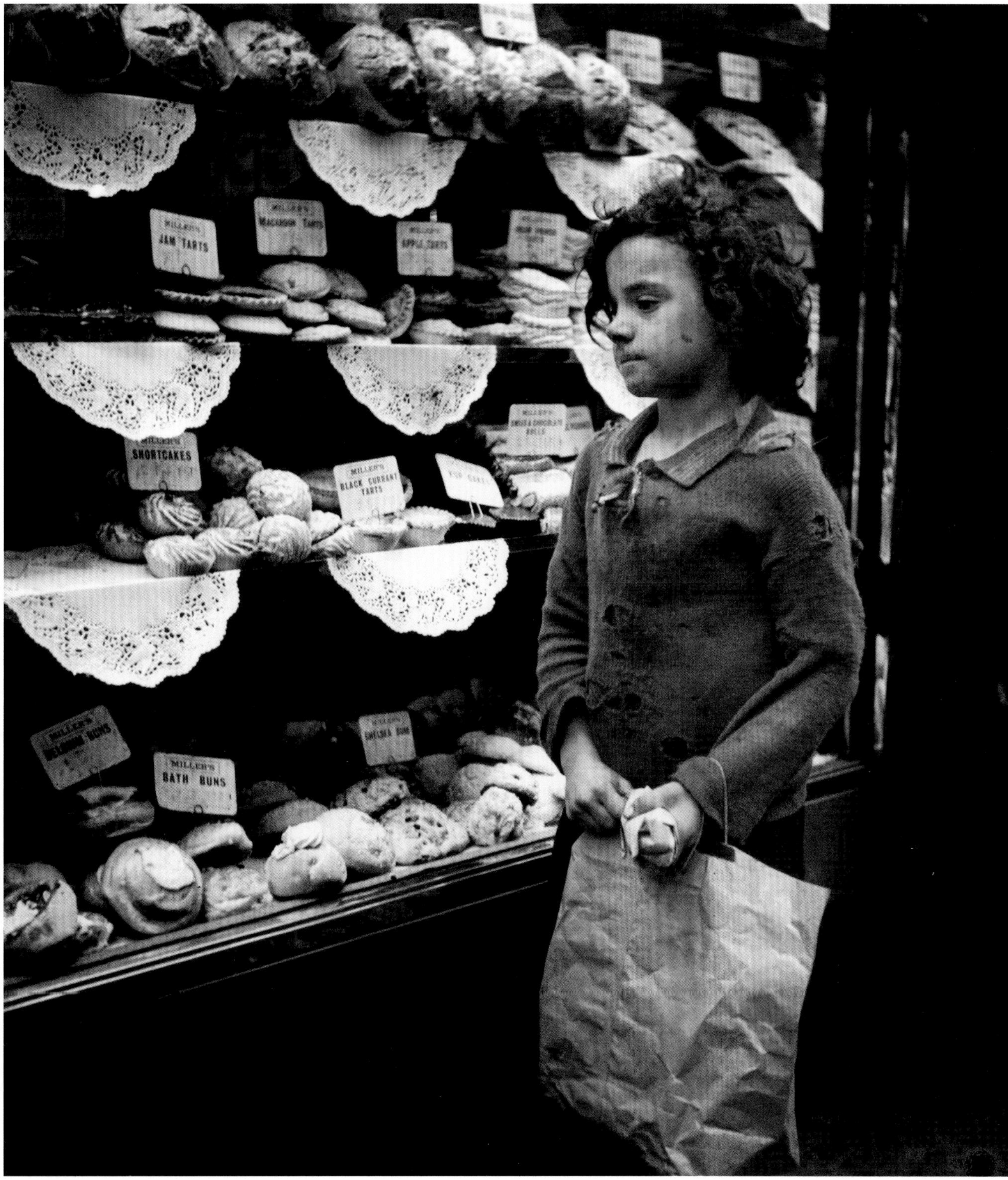

Edith Tudor-Hart
Girl Staring into Bakery Window, London, ca. 1935
Modern silver-gelatin print, 35.3 × 30 cm
National Galleries of Scotland, PGP 279.31

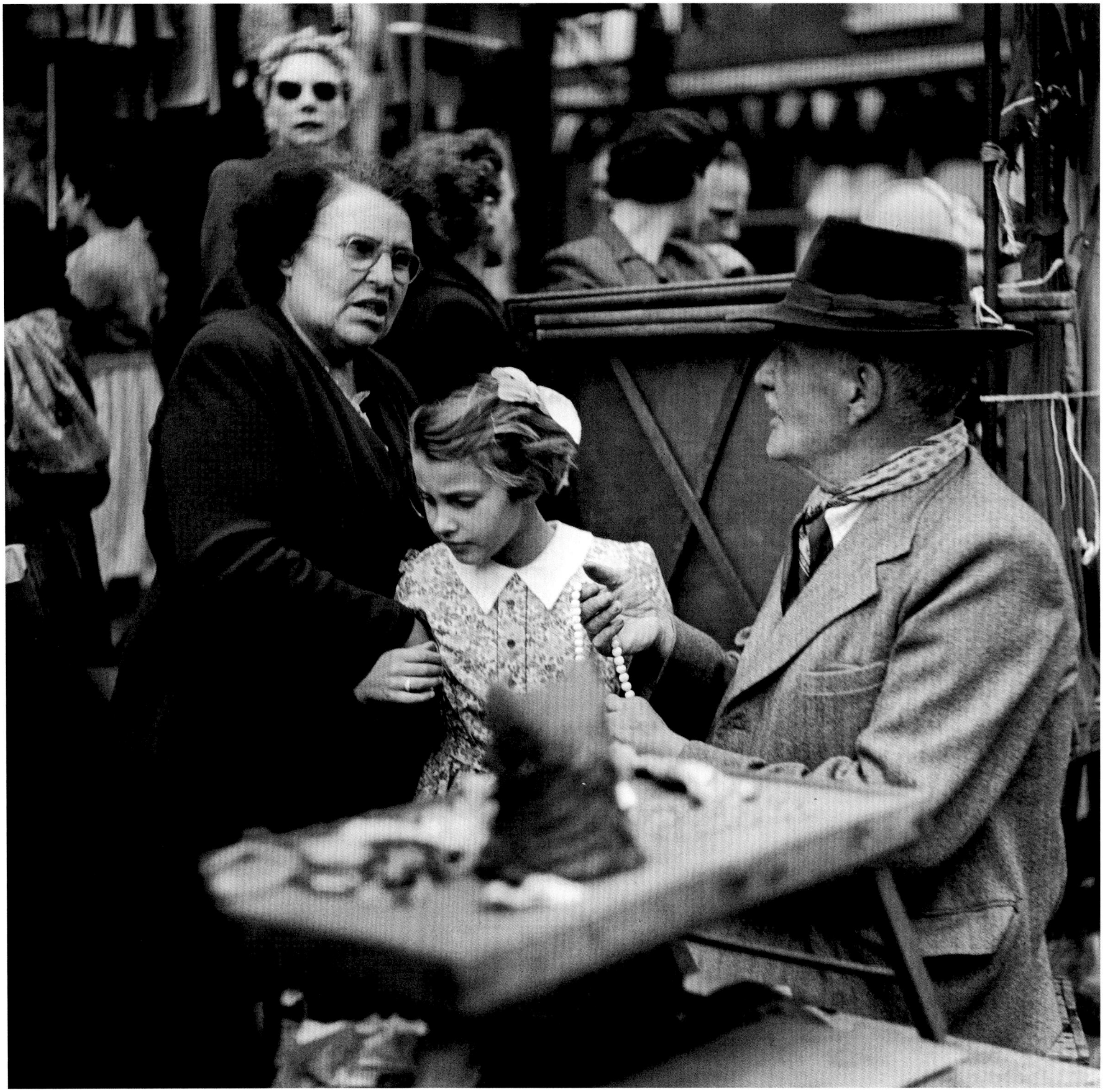

Edith Suschitzky
Caledonian Market, London, ca. 1931
Modern silver-gelatin print, 27.7 × 27.5 cm
National Galleries of Scotland, PGP 279.29

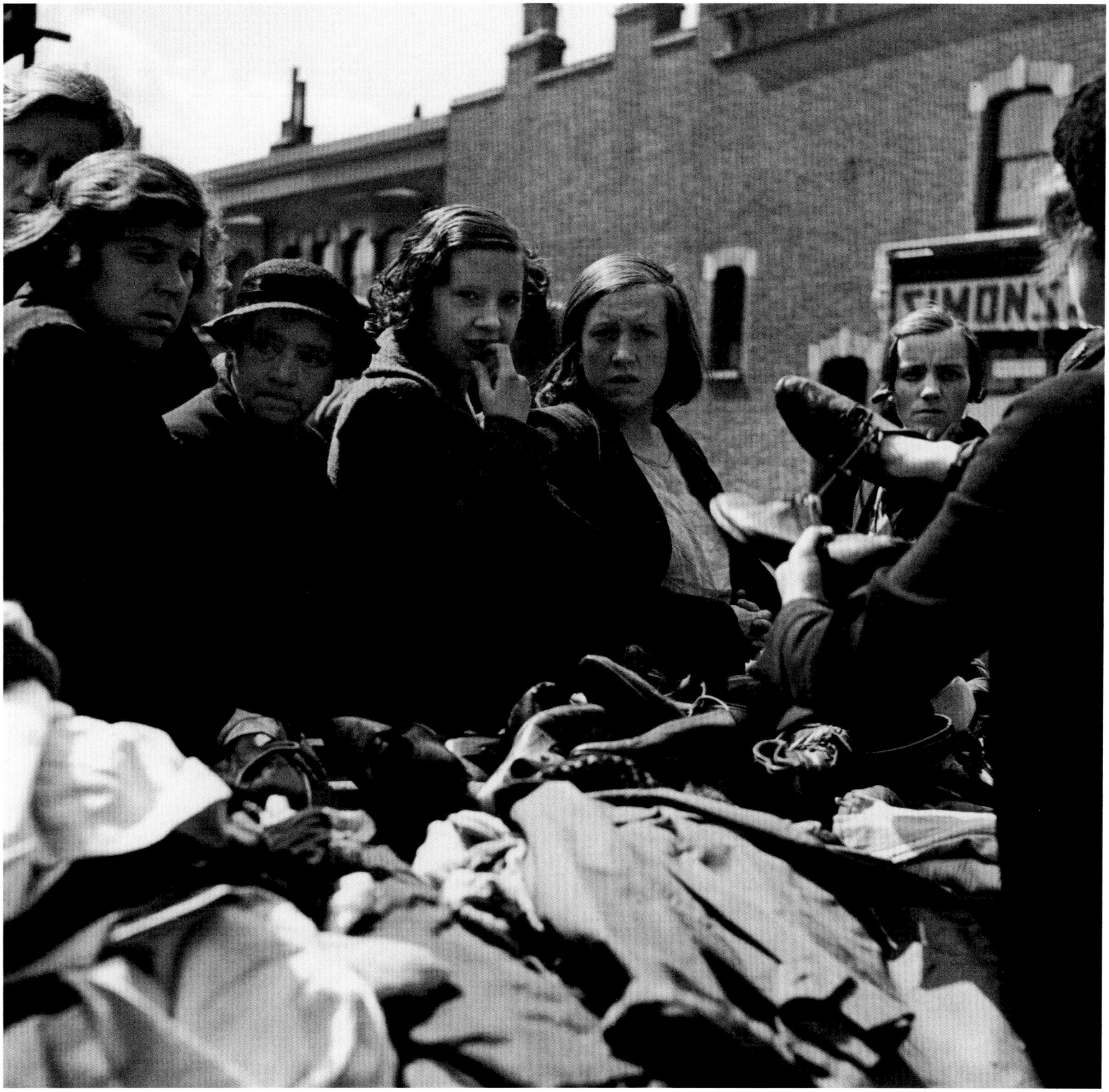

Edith Suschitzky
Caledonian Market, London, ca. 1931
Modern silver-gelatin print, 30.1 × 30 cm
National Galleries of Scotland, PGP 279.62

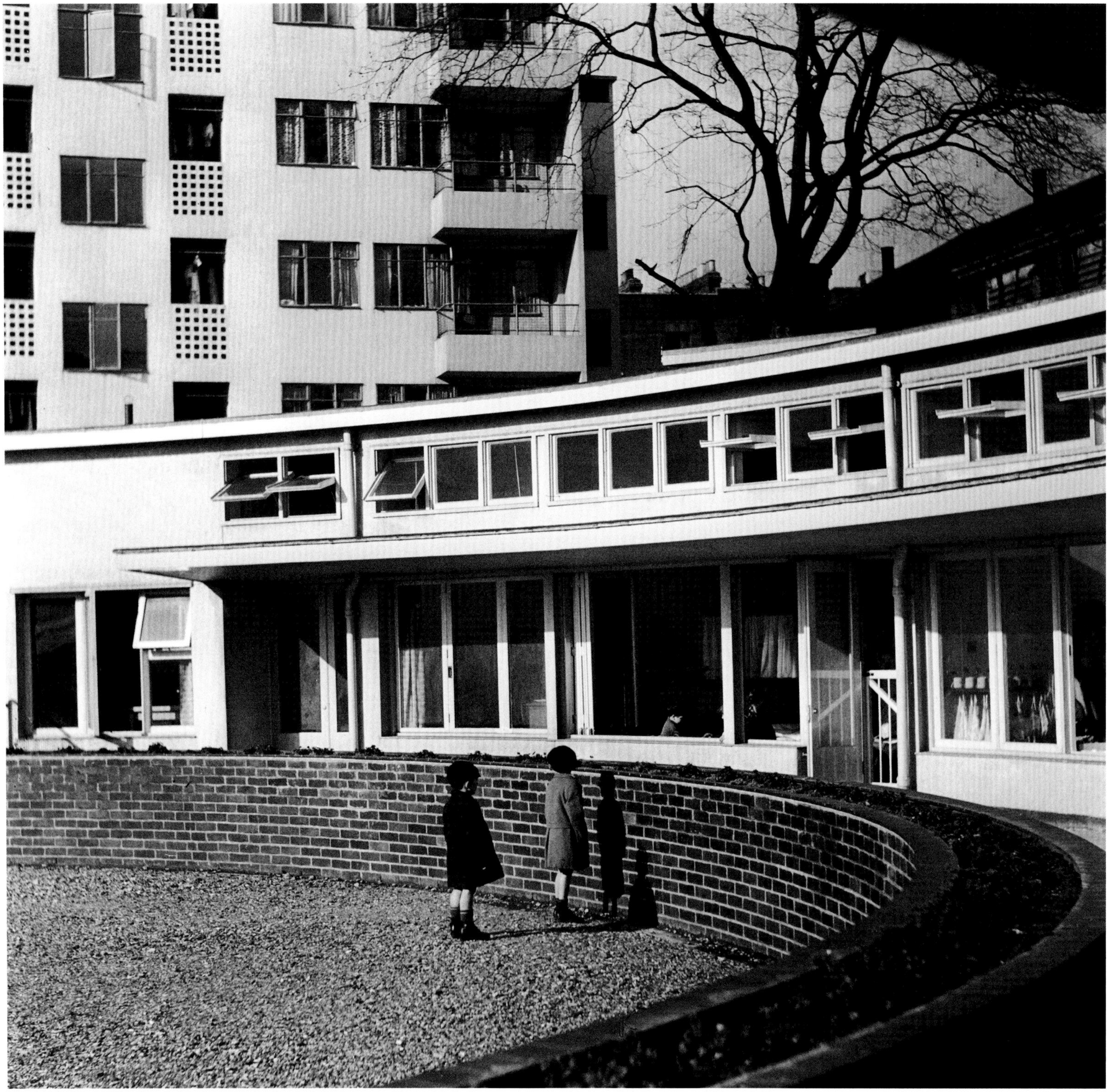

Edith Tudor-Hart
Kensal House, London, ca. 1938
Modern silver-gelatin print, 30.3 × 29.9 cm
National Galleries of Scotland, PGP 279.69

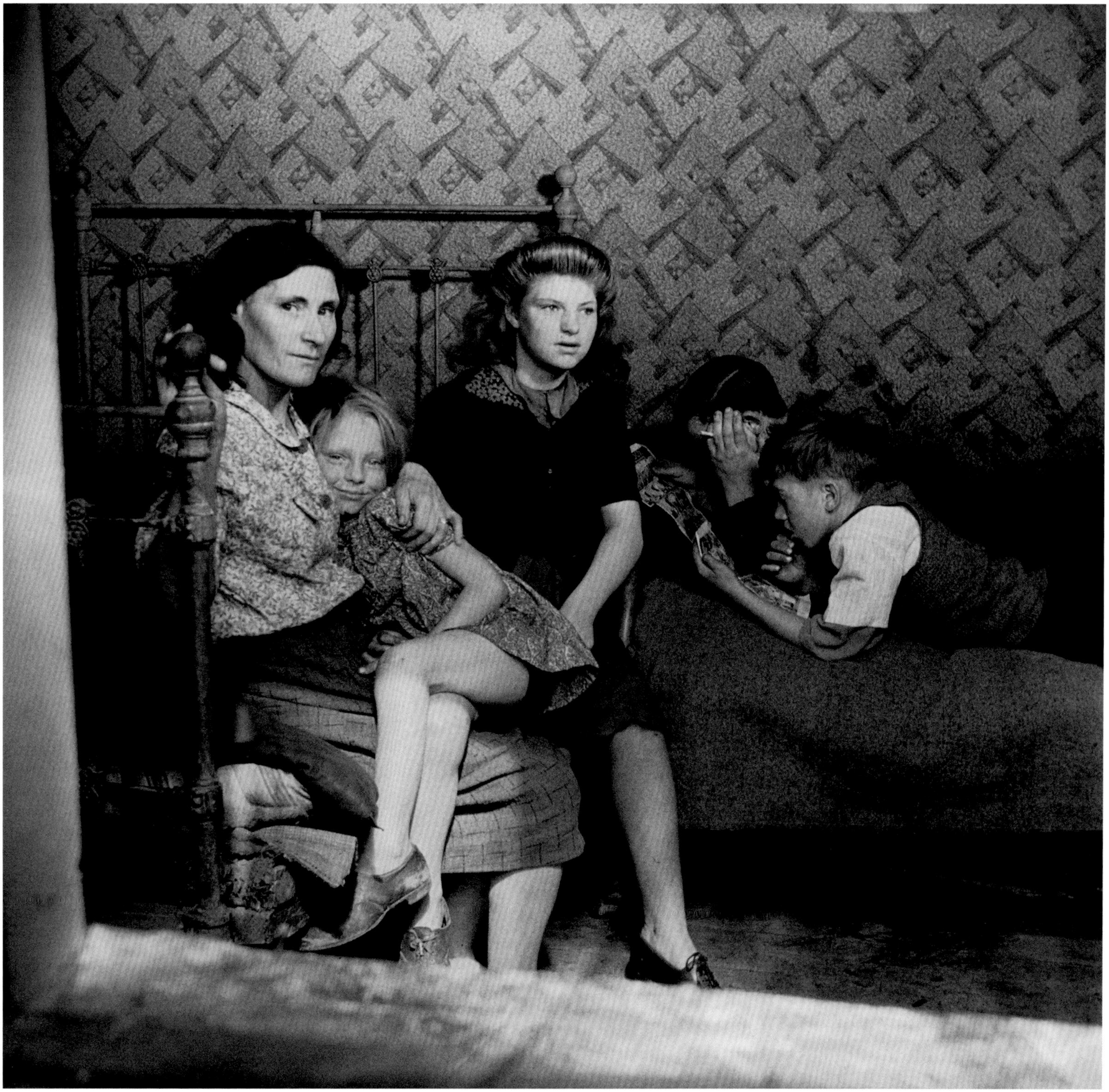

Edith Suschitzky
Family, Stepney, London, ca. 1932
Modern silver-gelatin print, 30.2 × 30.1 cm
National Galleries of Scotland, PGP 279.3

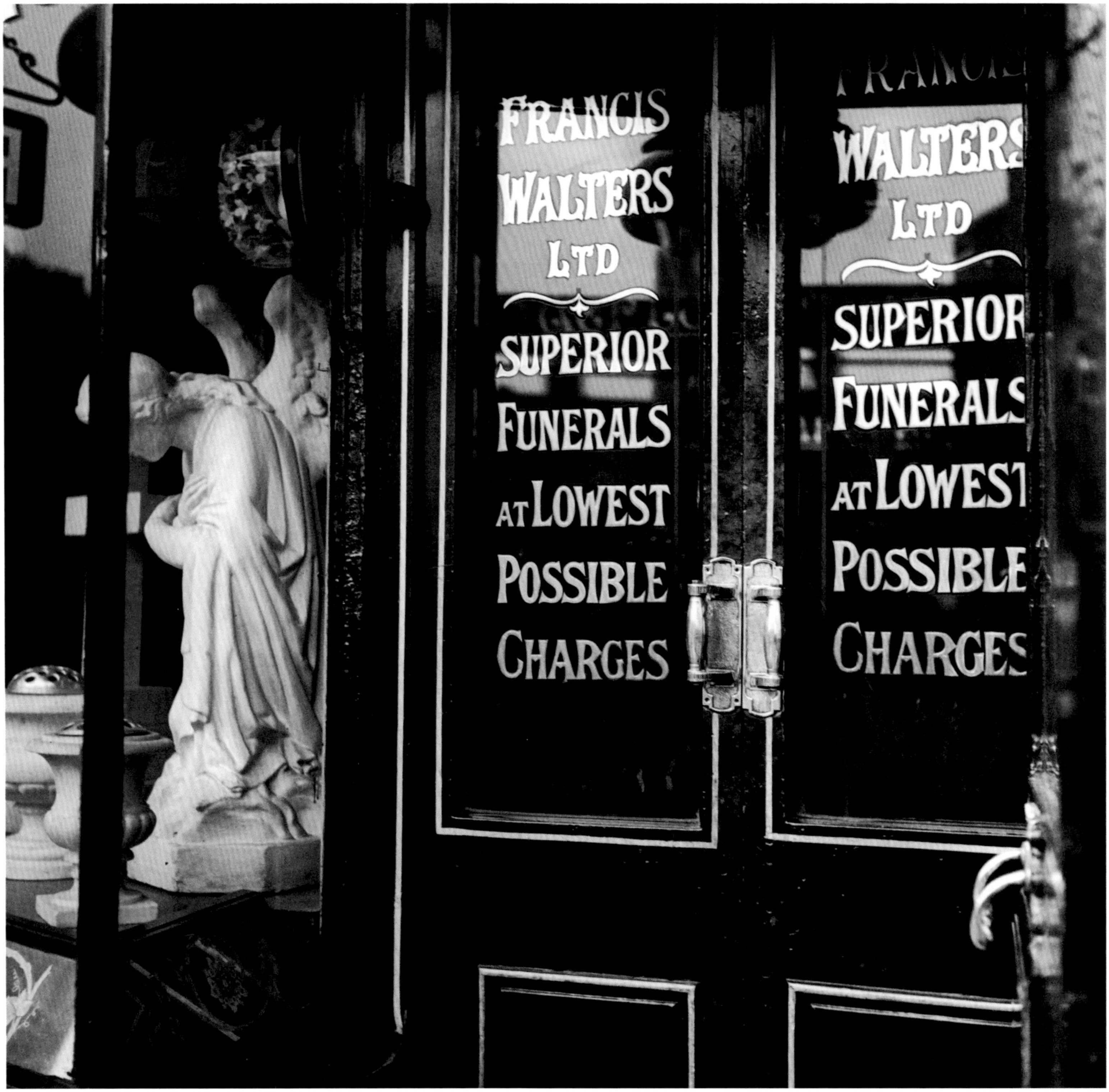

Edith Tudor-Hart
Funeral Parlour, London, ca. 1935
Modern silver-gelatin print, 30.2 × 30.1 cm
National Galleries of Scotland, PGP 279.65

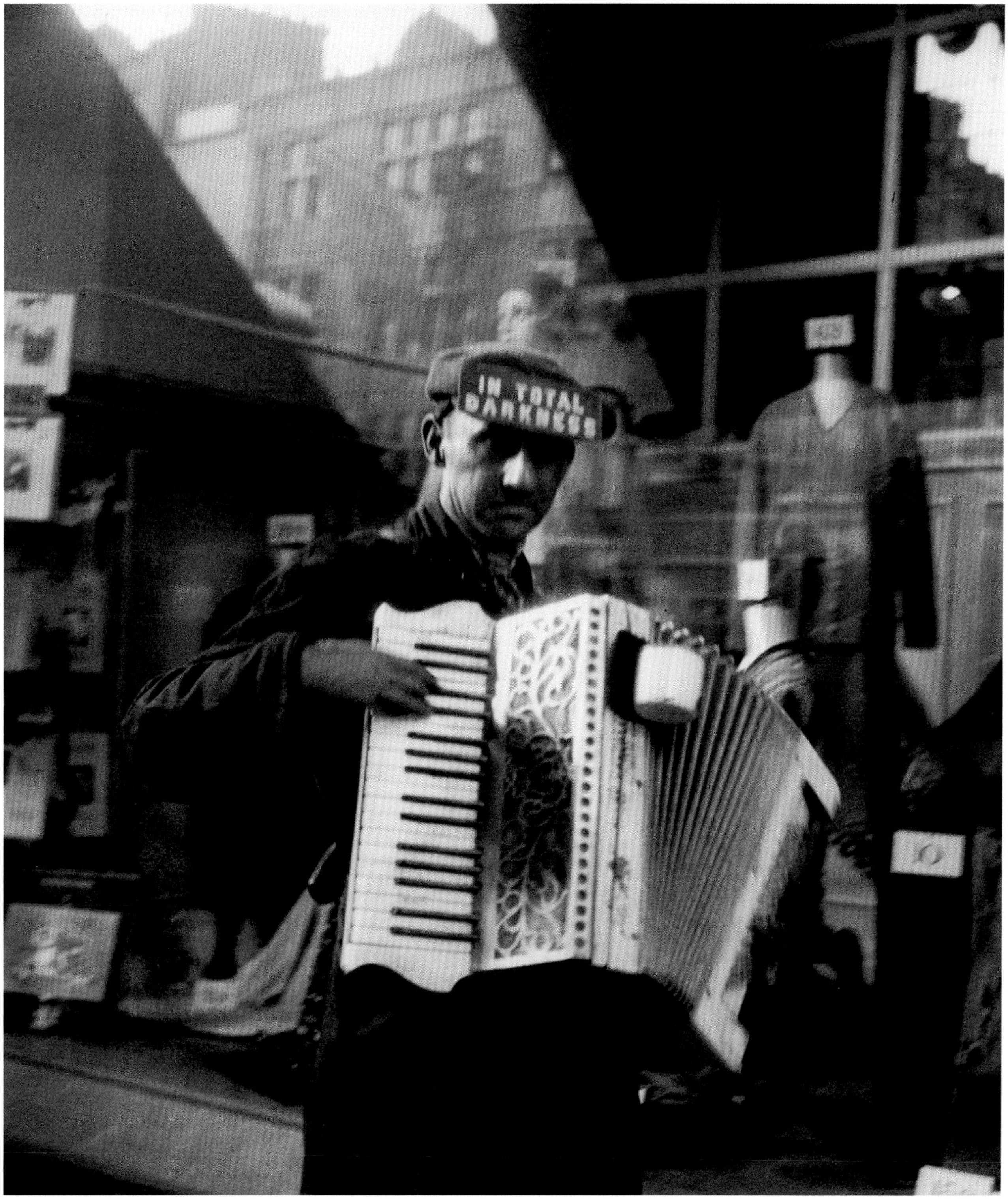

Edith Tudor-Hart
In Total Darkness, London, ca. 1936
Modern silver-gelatin print, 32.4 × 26.5 cm
National Galleries of Scotland, PGP 279.66

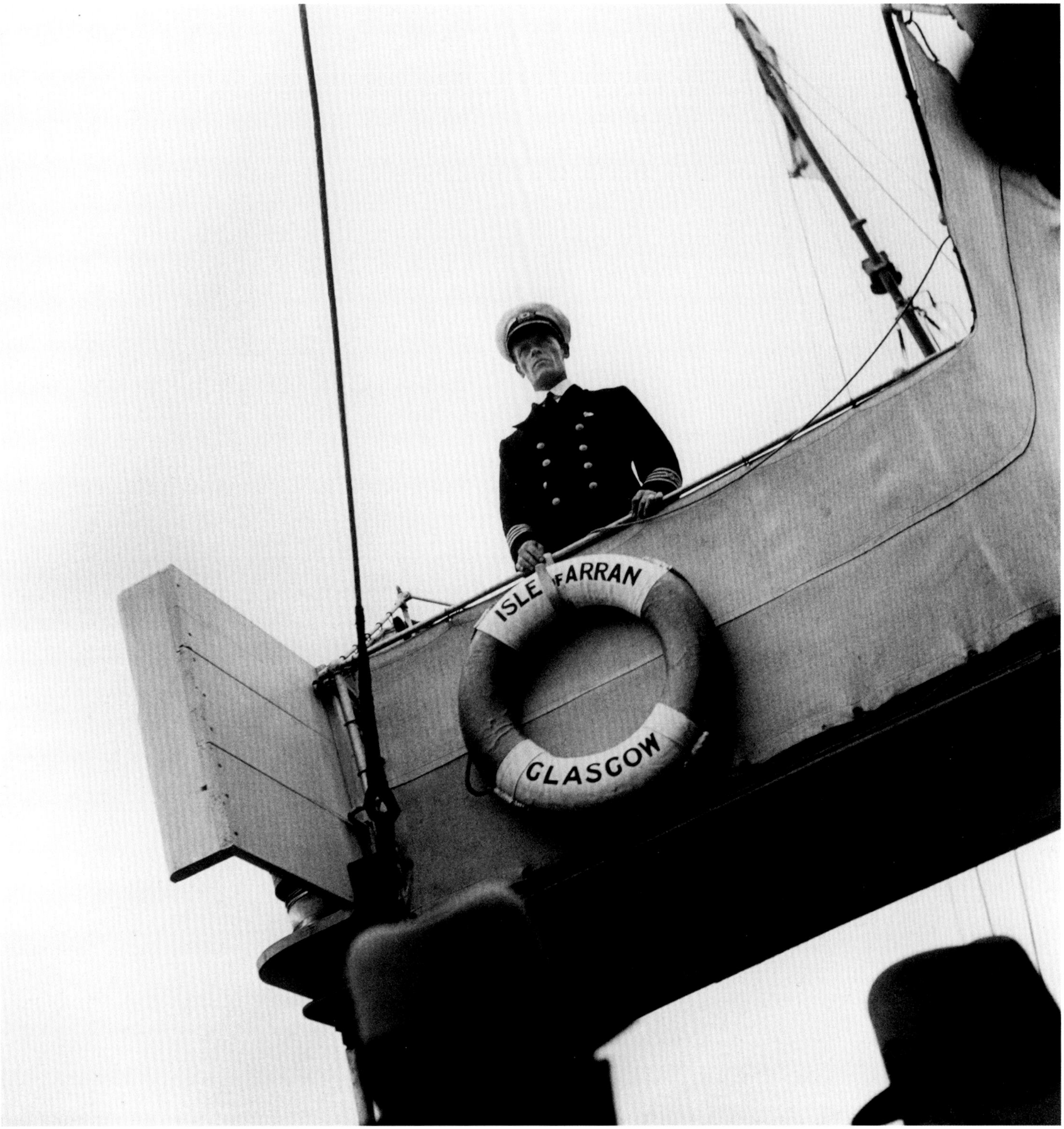

Edith Tudor-Hart
Isle of Arran Ferry, London, ca. 1935
Modern silver-gelatin print, 30.2 × 28.3 cm
National Galleries of Scotland, PGP 279.59

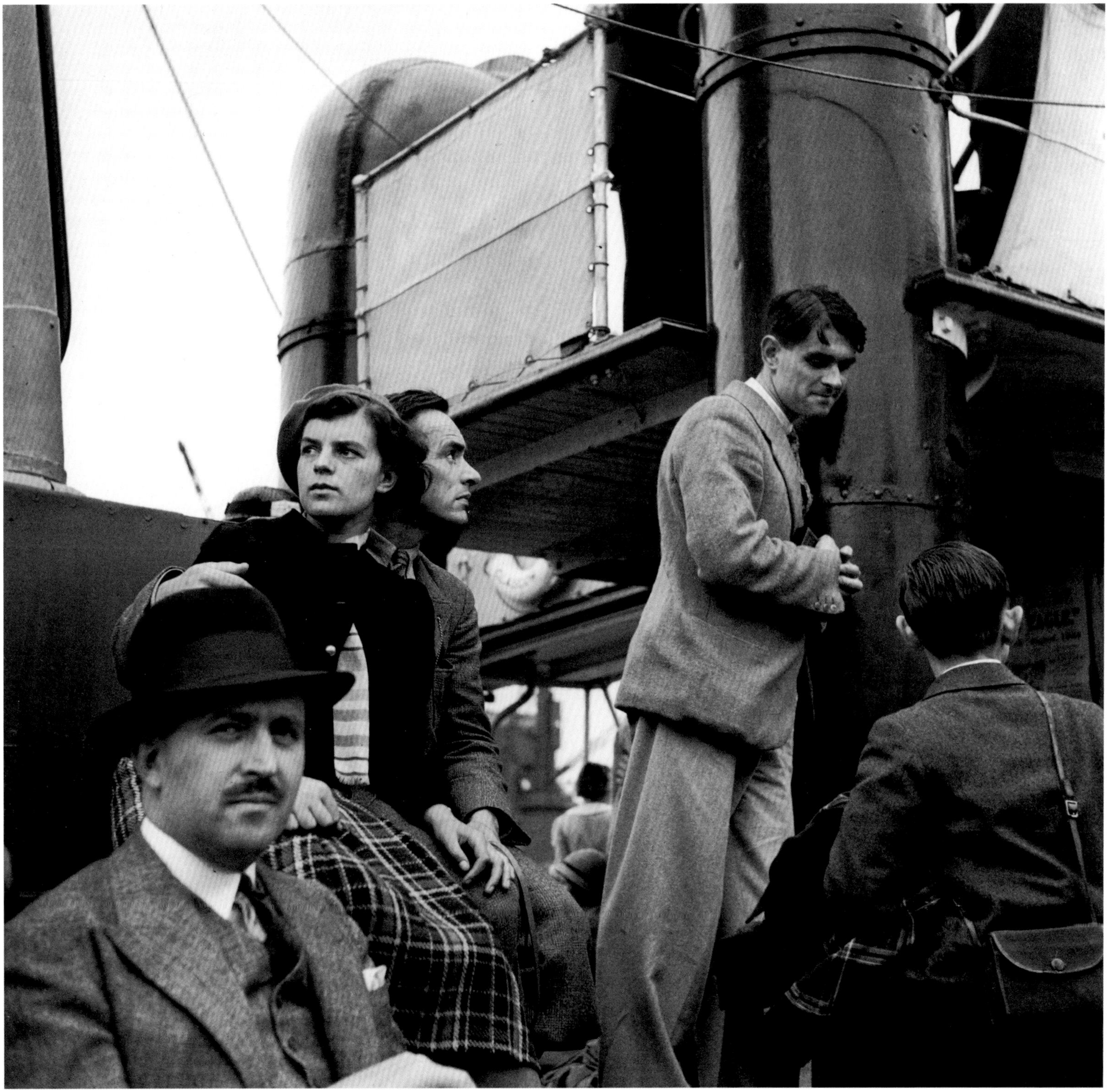

Edith Tudor-Hart
Isle of Arran Ferry, London, ca. 1935
Modern silver-gelatin print, 30.2 × 30.1 cm
National Galleries of Scotland, PGP 279.60

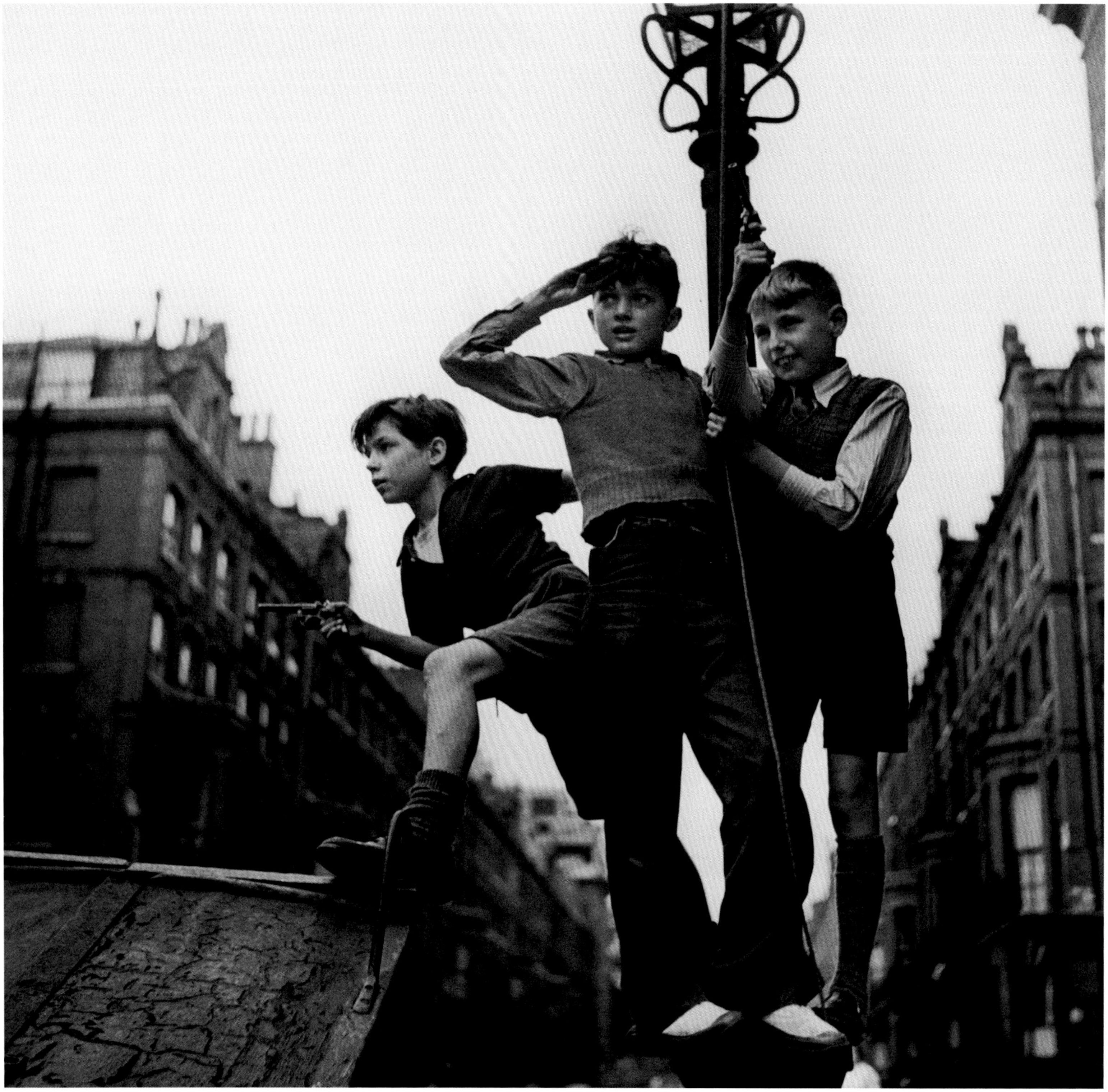

Edith Tudor-Hart
Boys in the Street, London, ca. 1935
Modern silver-gelatin print, 30.2 × 30 cm
National Galleries of Scotland, PGP 279.61

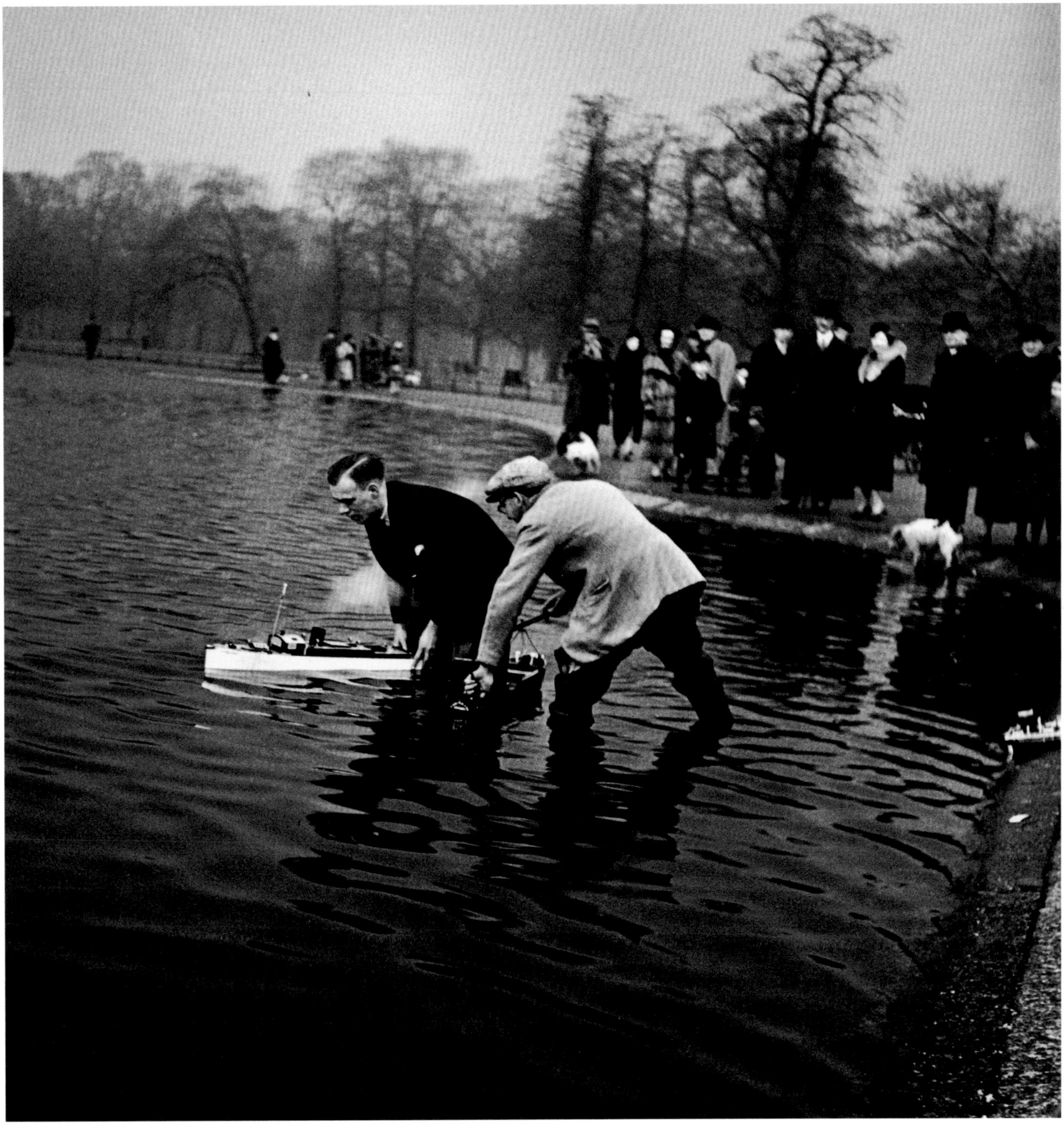

Edith Tudor-Hart
The Serpentine, Hyde Park, London, ca. 1937
Modern silver-gelatin print, 30.2 × 28.2 cm
National Galleries of Scotland, PGP 279.54

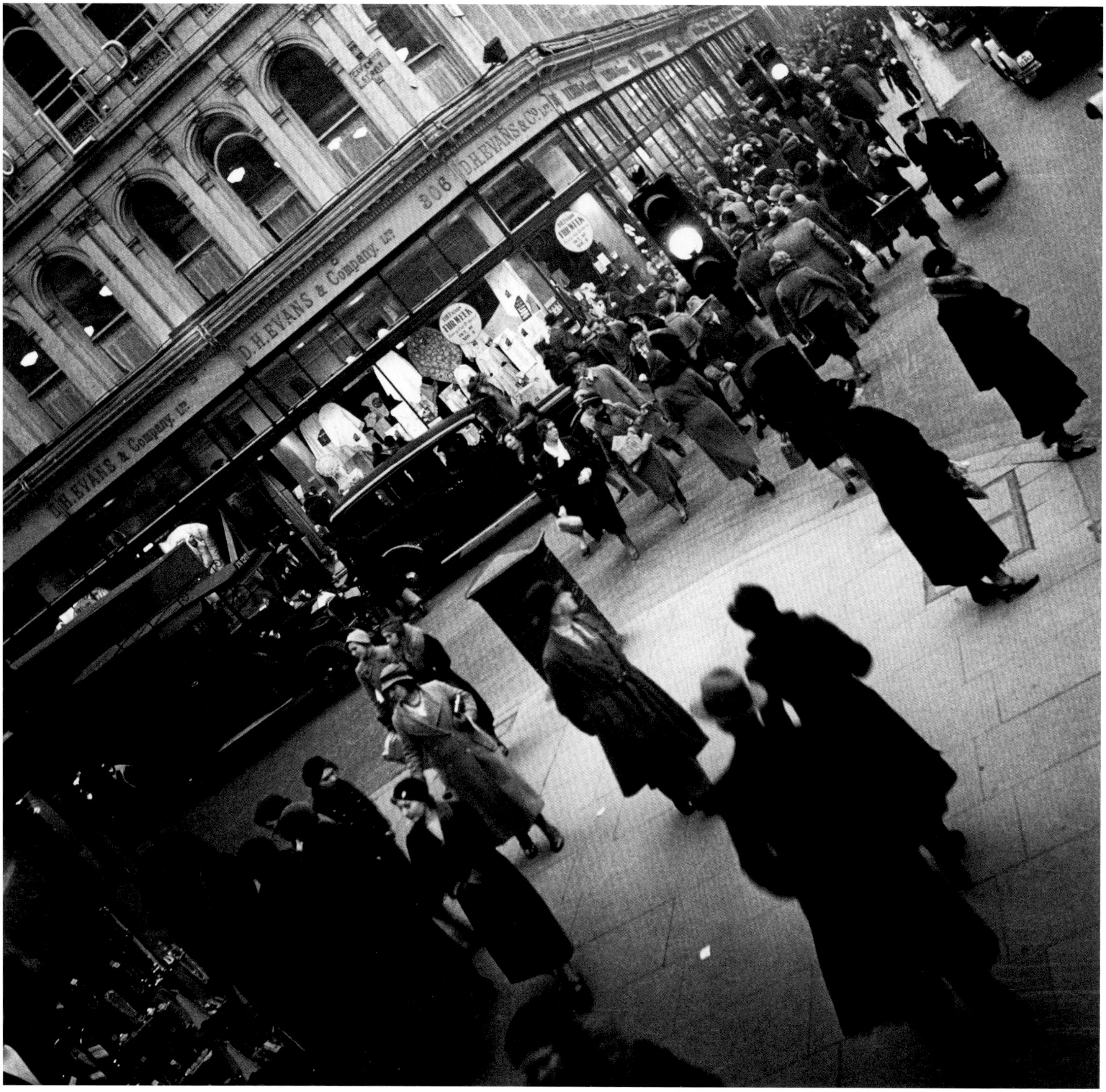

Edith Tudor-Hart
Oxford Street, London, ca. 1936
Modern silver-gelatin print, 30.2 × 30 cm
National Galleries of Scotland, PGP 279.55

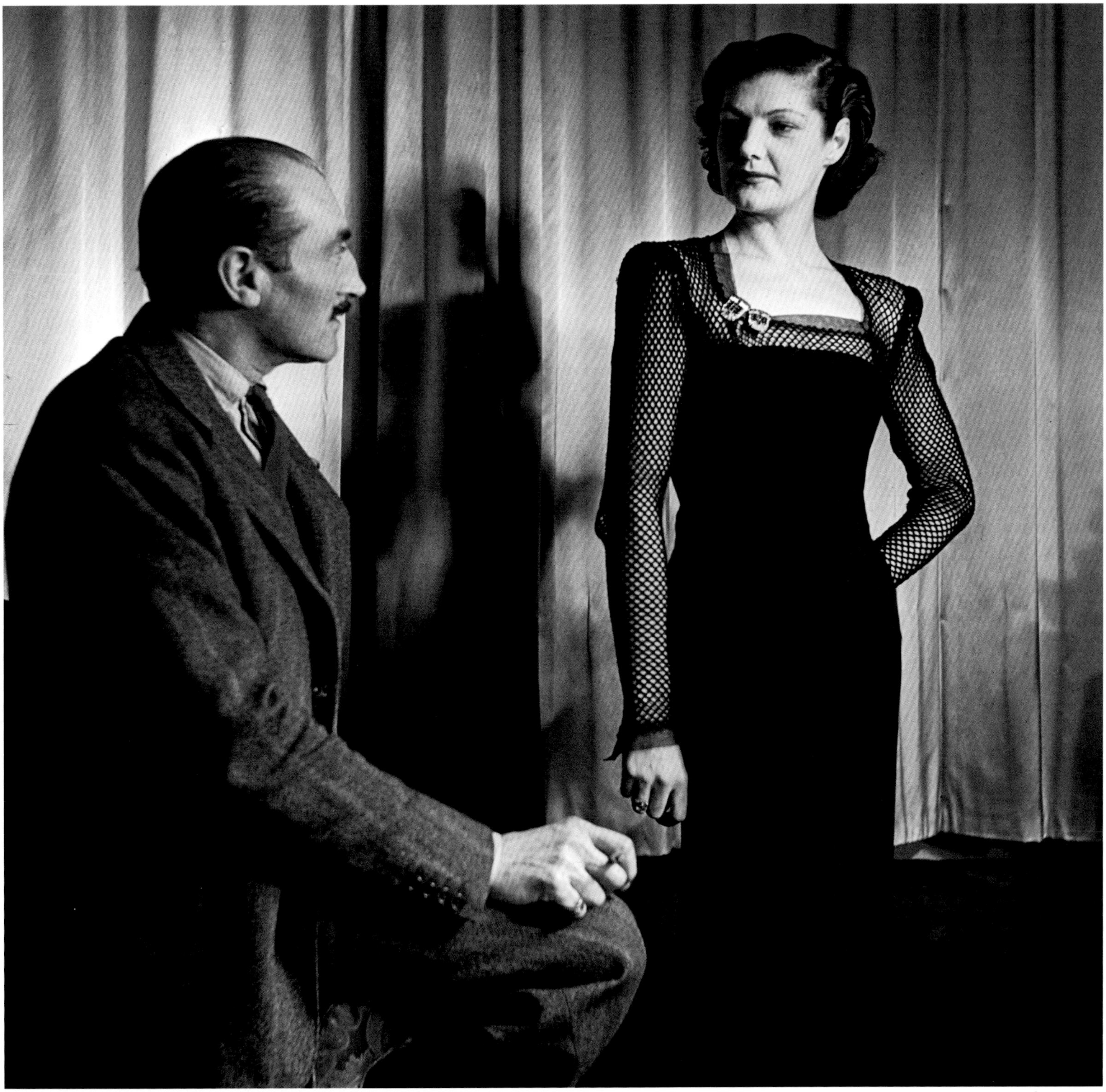

Edith Tudor-Hart
Untitled Fashion Shot, London, ca. 1940
Modern silver-gelatin print, 30.2 × 30.1 cm
National Galleries of Scotland, PGP 279.68

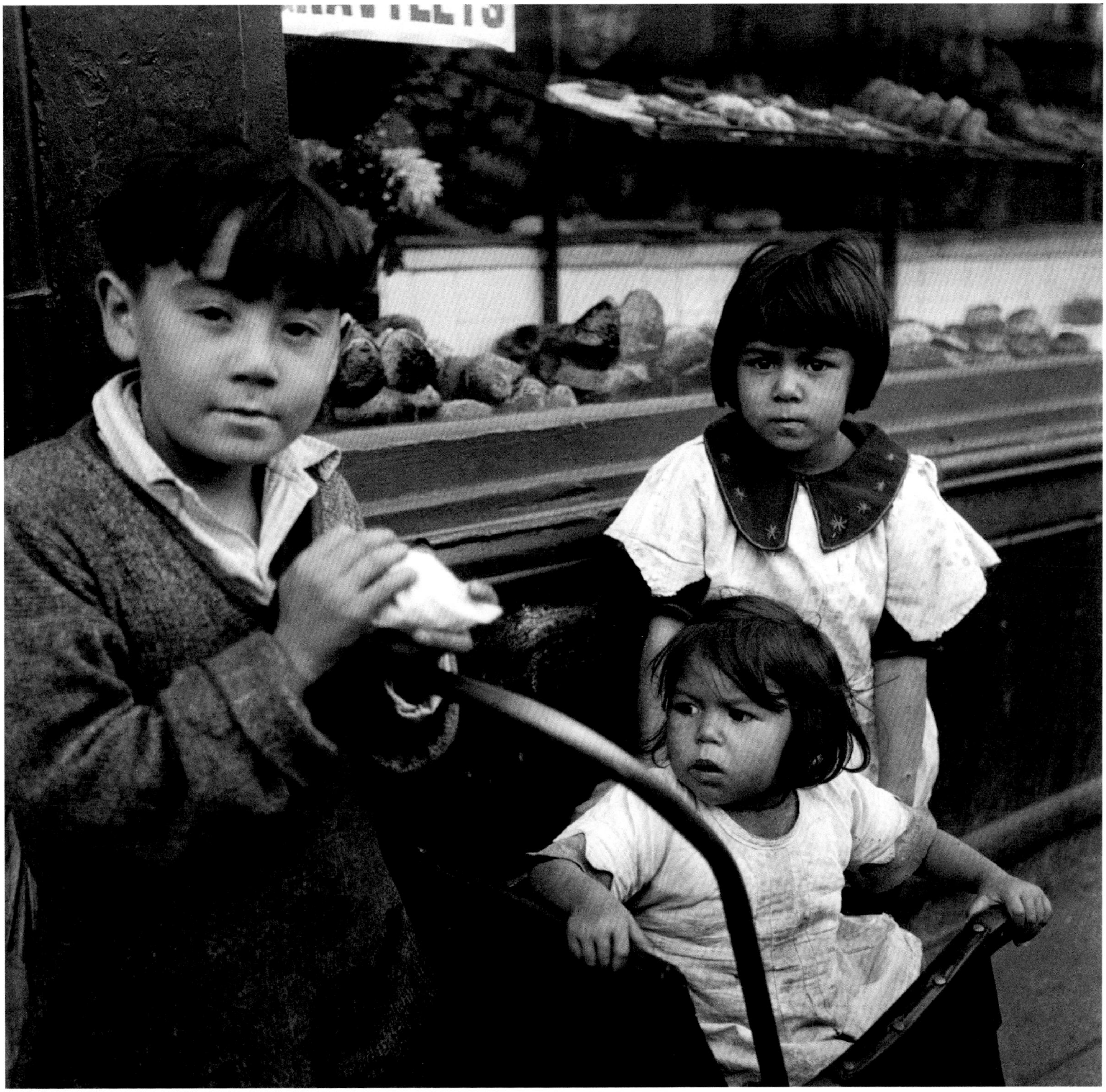

Edith Tudor-Hart
Children, Whitechapel, London, ca. 1931
Digital inkjet print, 29.9 × 30 cm
National Galleries of Scotland, PGP 279.89

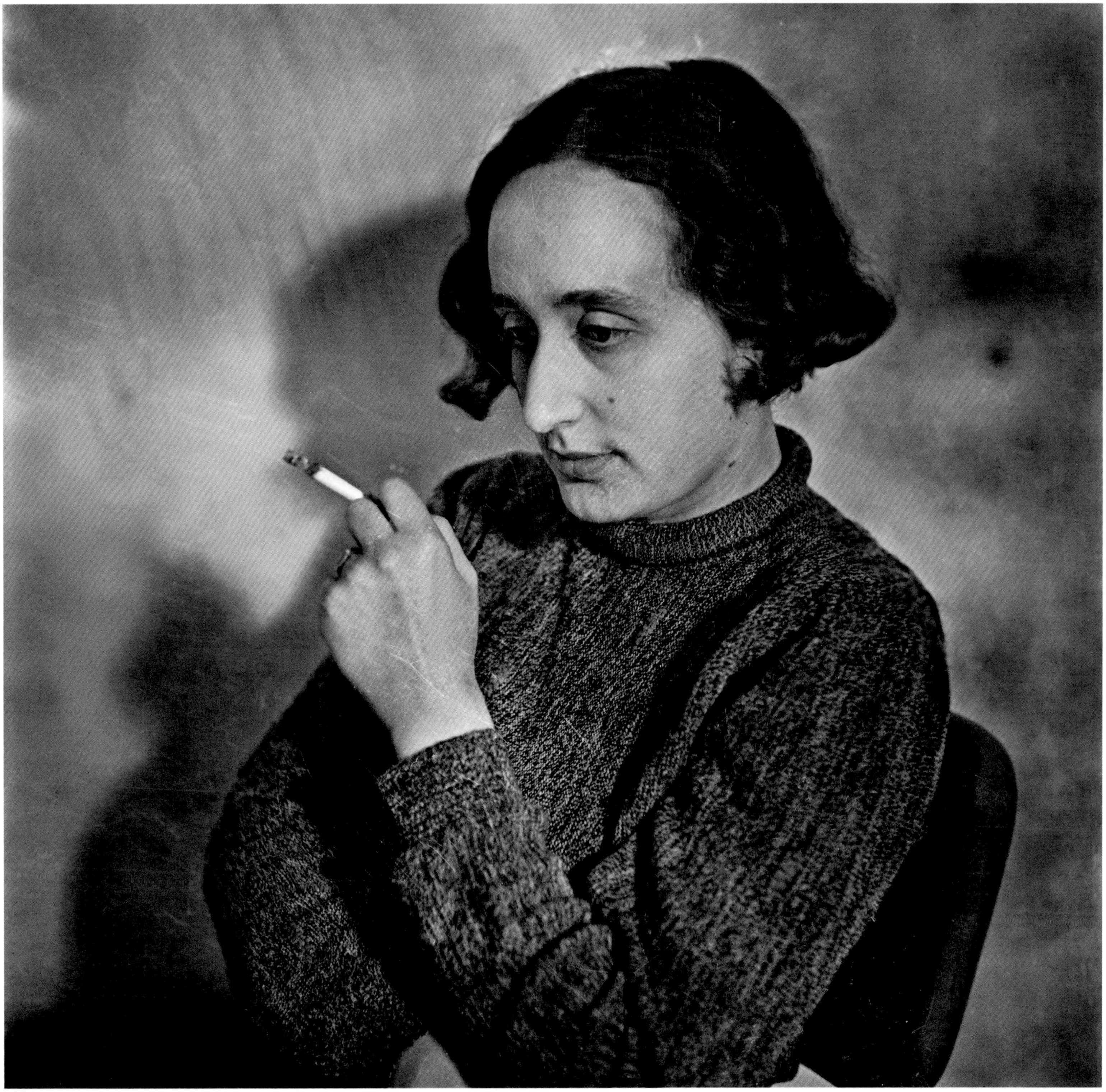

Edith Tudor-Hart
Self-Portrait, London, ca. 1936
Digital inkjet print, 30.4 × 30 cm
National Galleries of Scotland, PGP 279.73

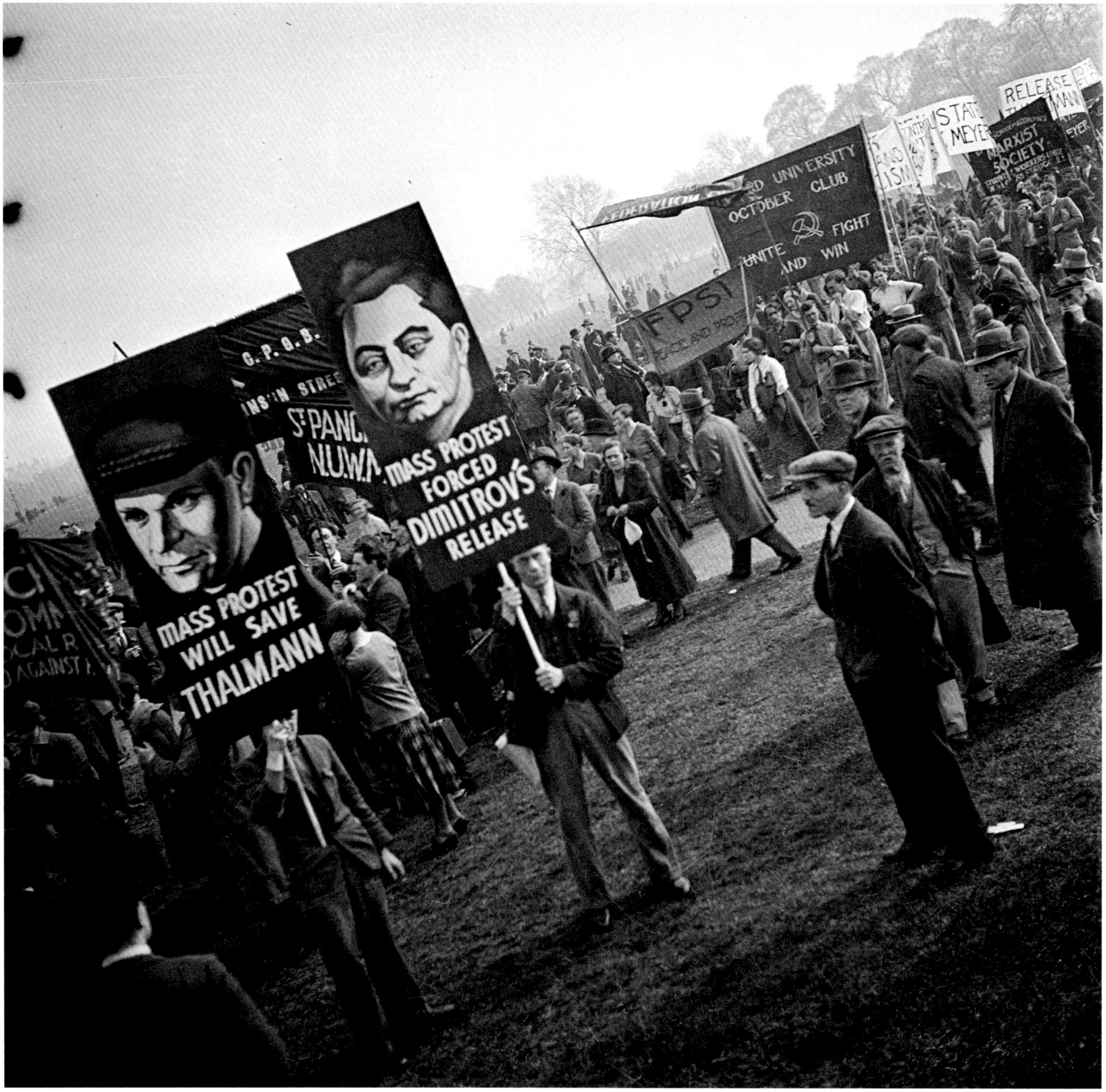

Edith Tudor-Hart
Communist Demonstration, London, ca. 1934
Digital inkjet print, 30.1 × 30 cm
National Galleries of Scotland, PGP 279.74

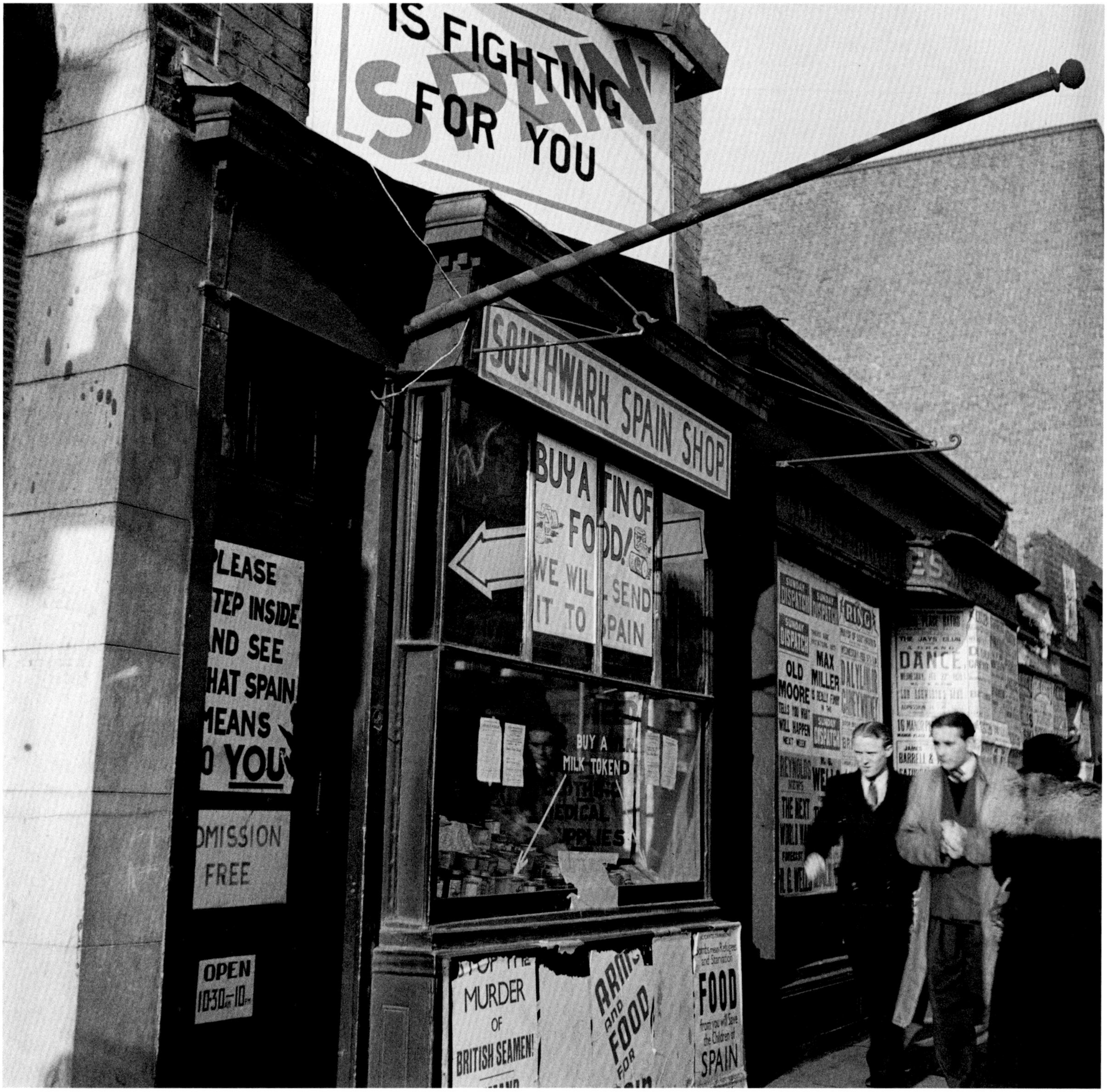

Edith Tudor-Hart
Southwark Spain Shop, London, ca. 1937
Digital inkjet print, 30 × 30 cm
National Galleries of Scotland, PGP 279.75

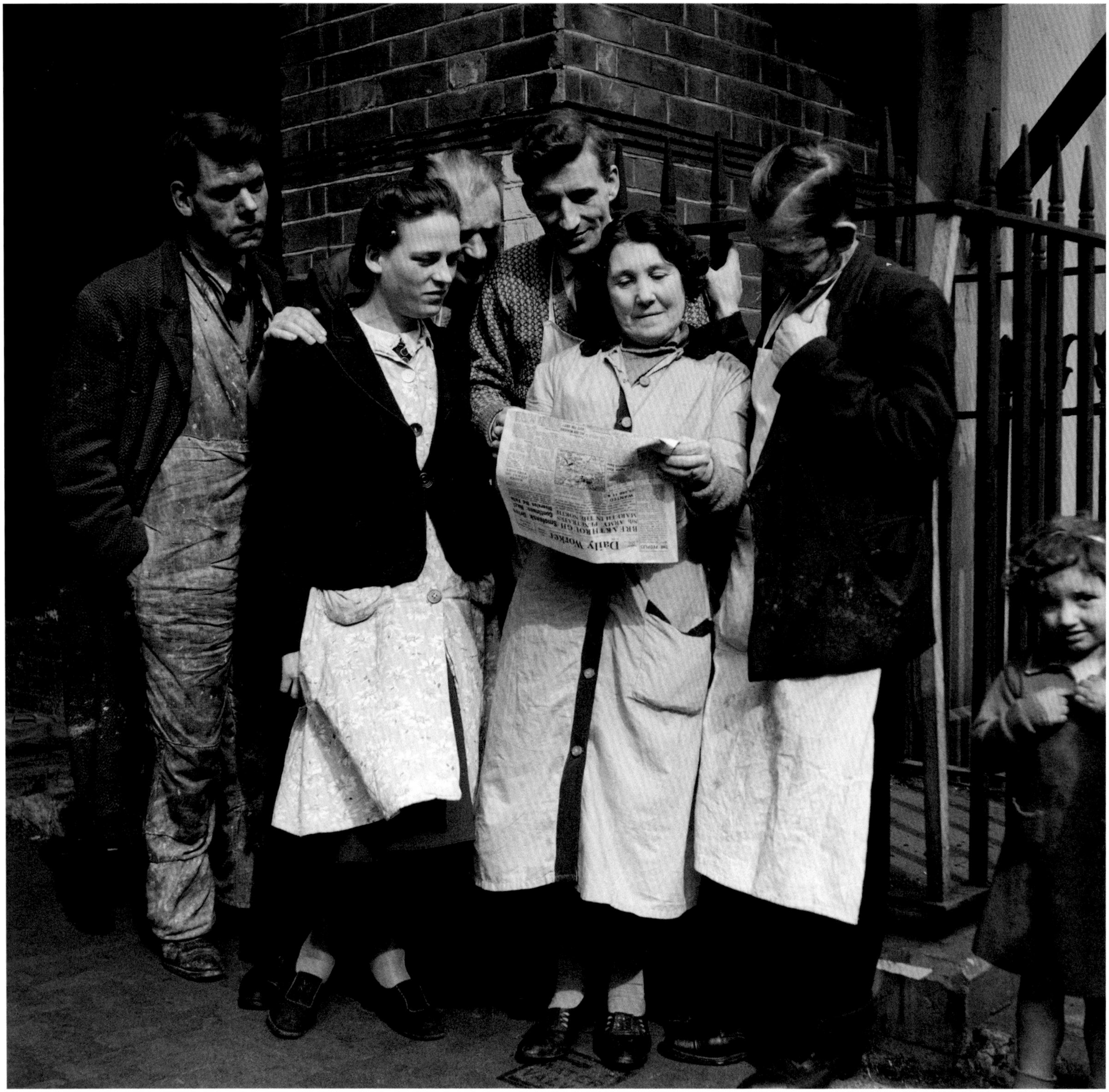

Edith Tudor-Hart
Group Reading the Daily Worker, London, ca. 1943
Digital inkjet print, 30.1 × 30 cm
National Galleries of Scotland, PGP 279.76

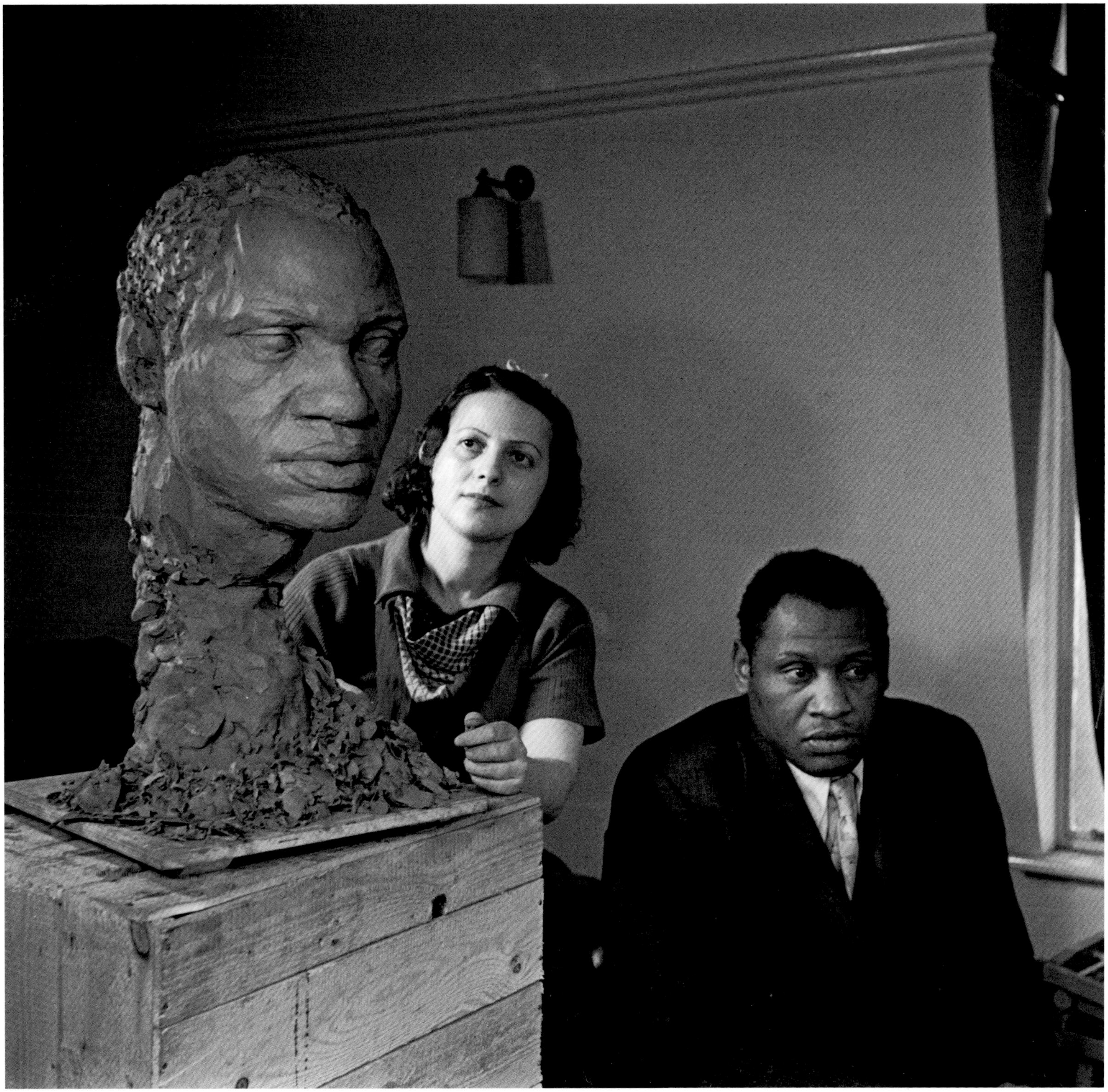

Edith Tudor-Hart
Alfredda Brilliant Sculpting Paul Robeson, London, ca. 1939
Modern silver-gelatin print, 32.8 × 32.5 cm
National Galleries of Scotland, PGP 279.40

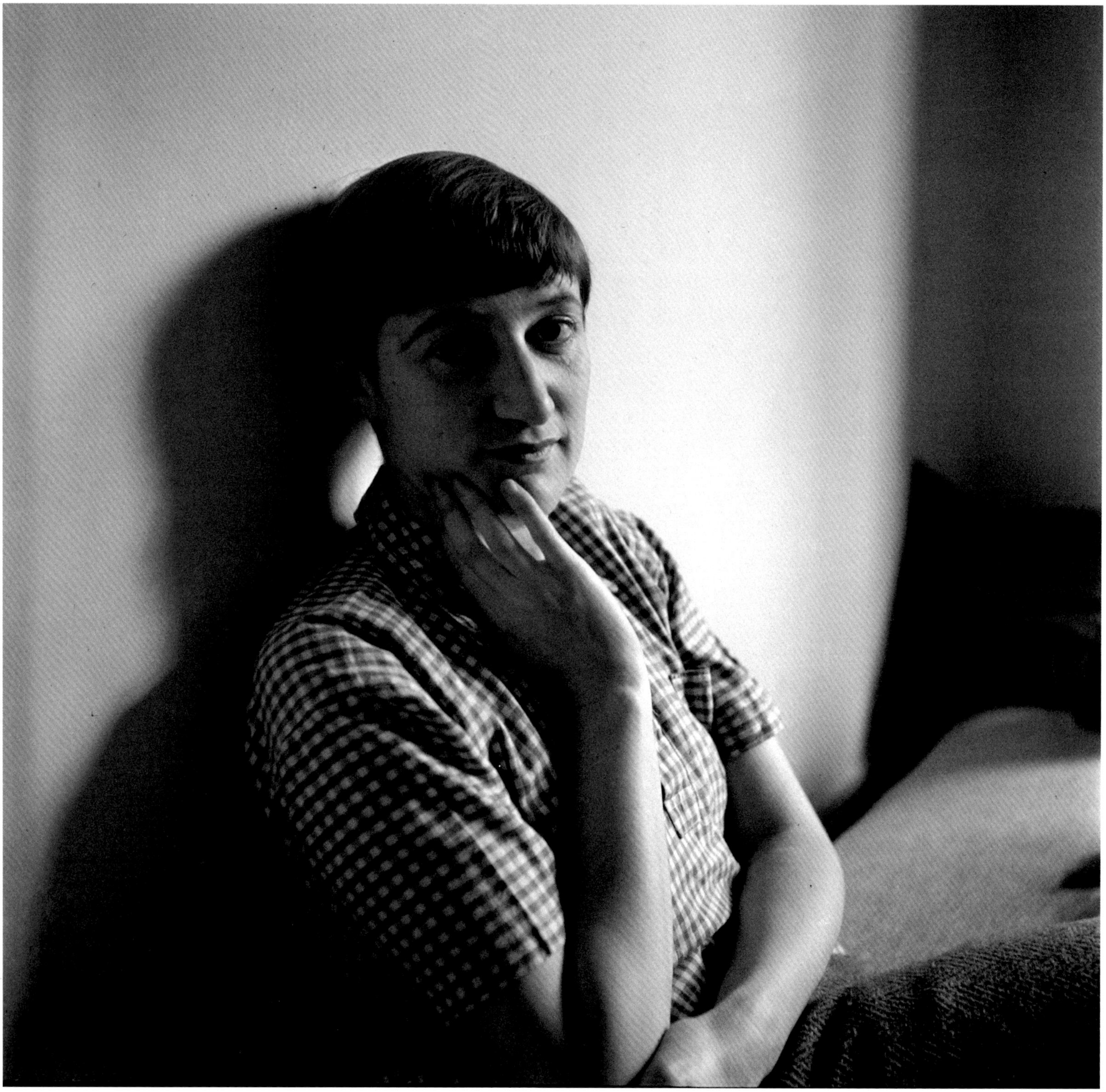

Edith Tudor-Hart
Pearl ("Polly") Binder, London, ca. 1935
Digital inkjet print, 30.2 × 30 cm
National Galleries of Scotland, PGP 279.77

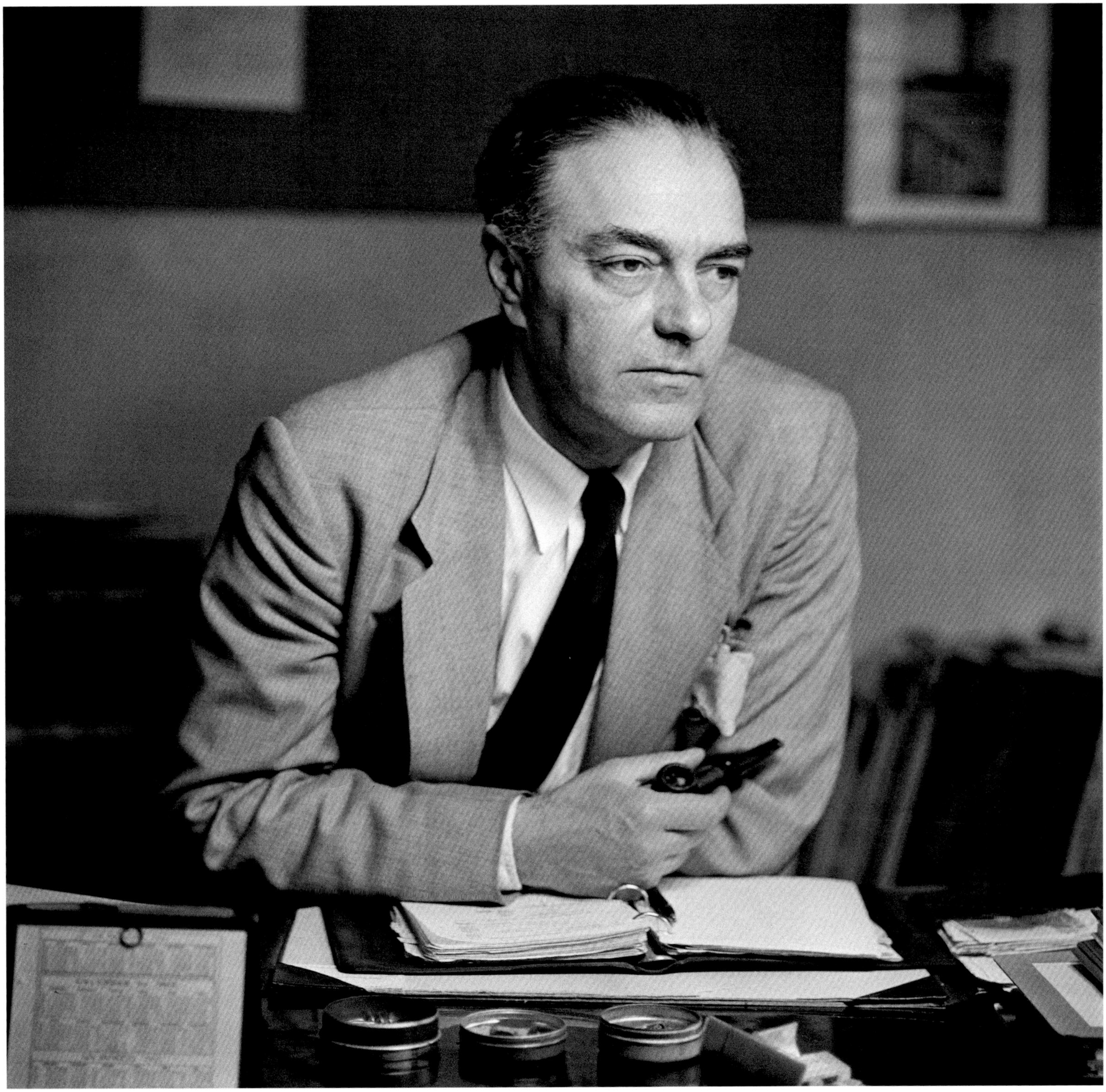

Edith Tudor-Hart
Ernö Goldfinger, London, ca. 1945
Digital inkjet print, 30.1 × 30 cm
National Galleries of Scotland, PGP 279.78

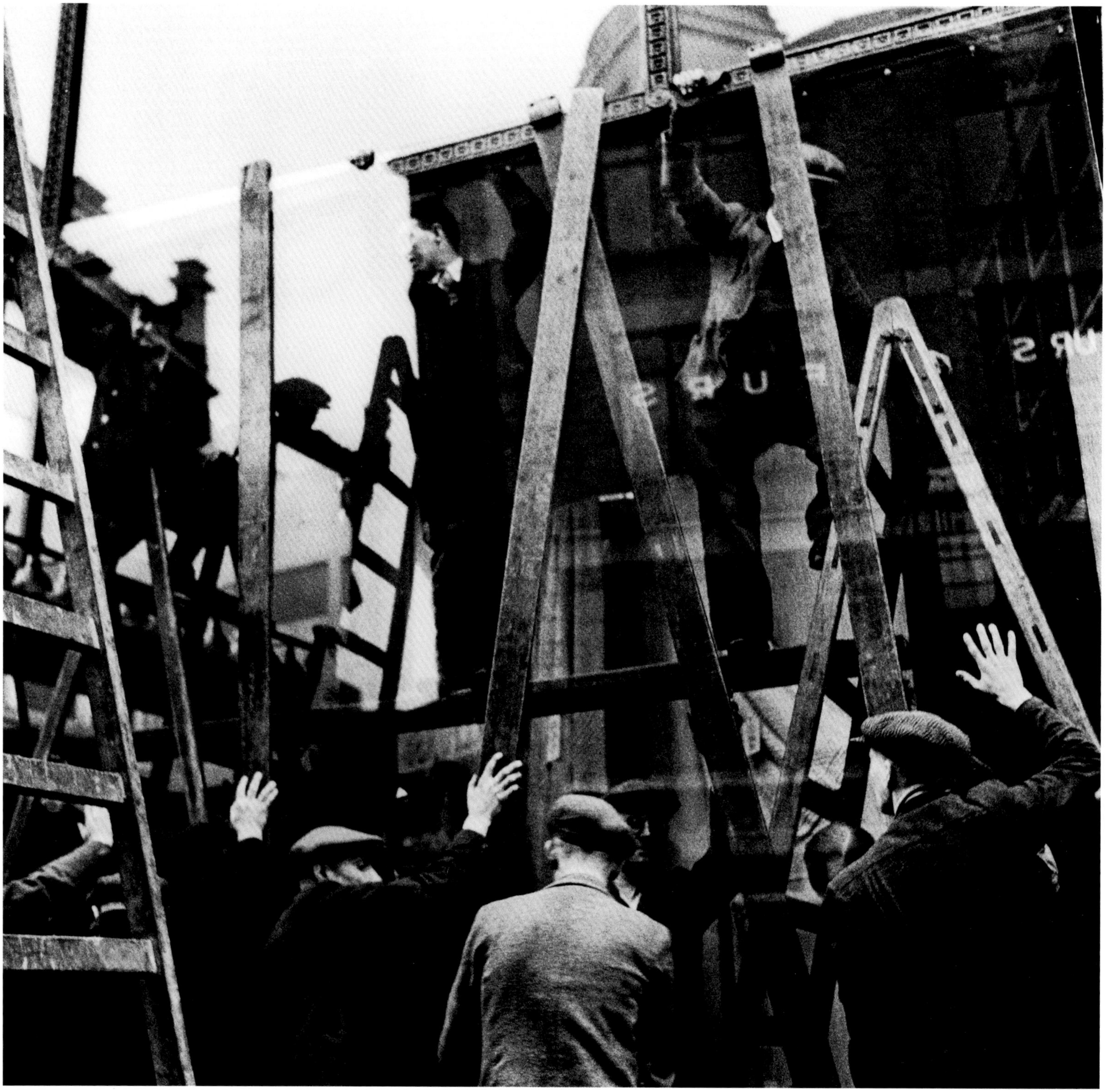

Edith Tudor-Hart
Window Fitters, London, ca. 1936
Modern silver-gelatin print, 28.3 × 27.8 cm
National Galleries of Scotland, PGP 279.64

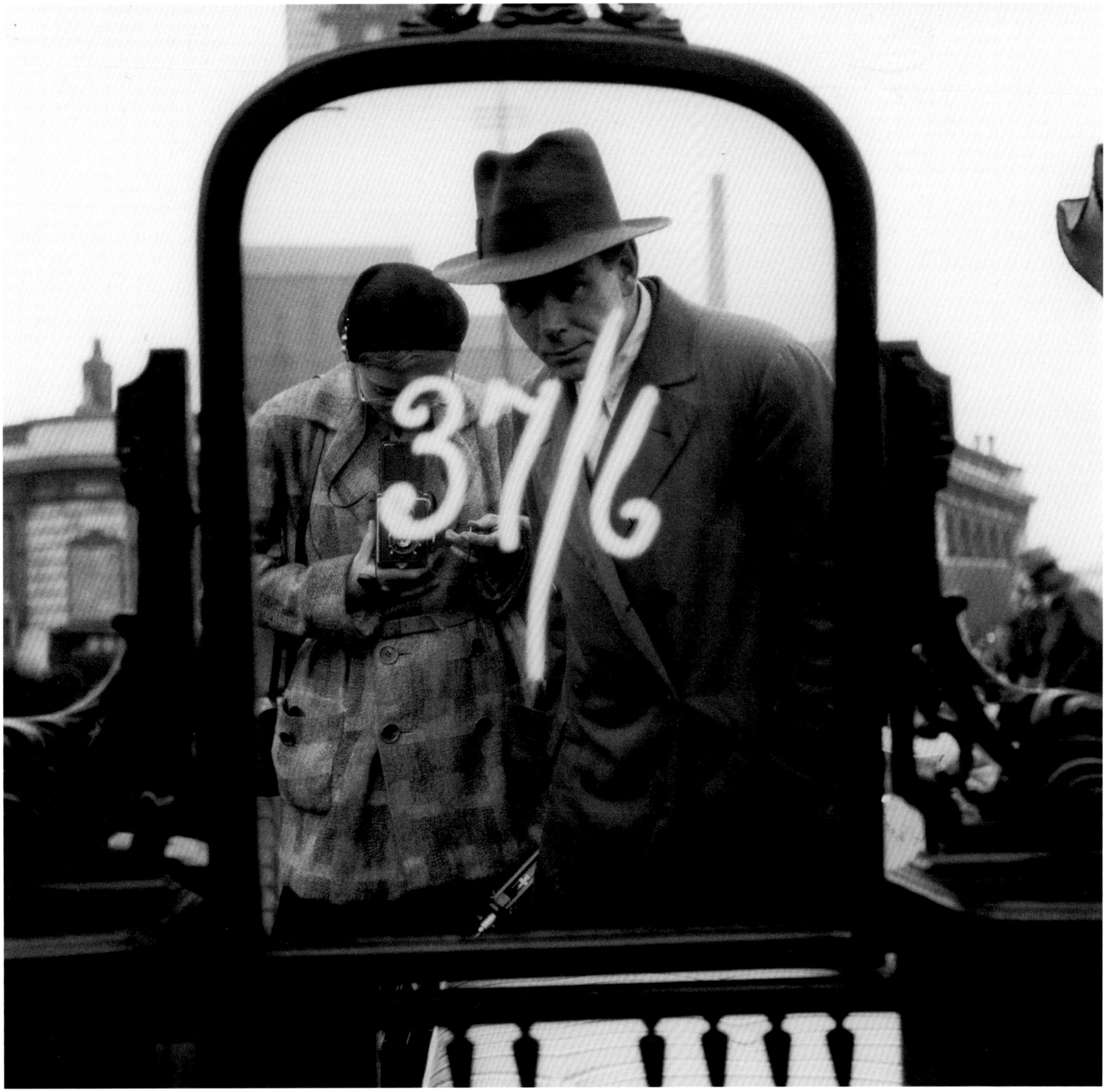

Edith Tudor-Hart
Self-Portrait with Unknown Man, Caledonian Market, London, ca. 1931
Modern silver-gelatin print, 22.8 × 22.6 cm
National Galleries of Scotland, PGP 279.70

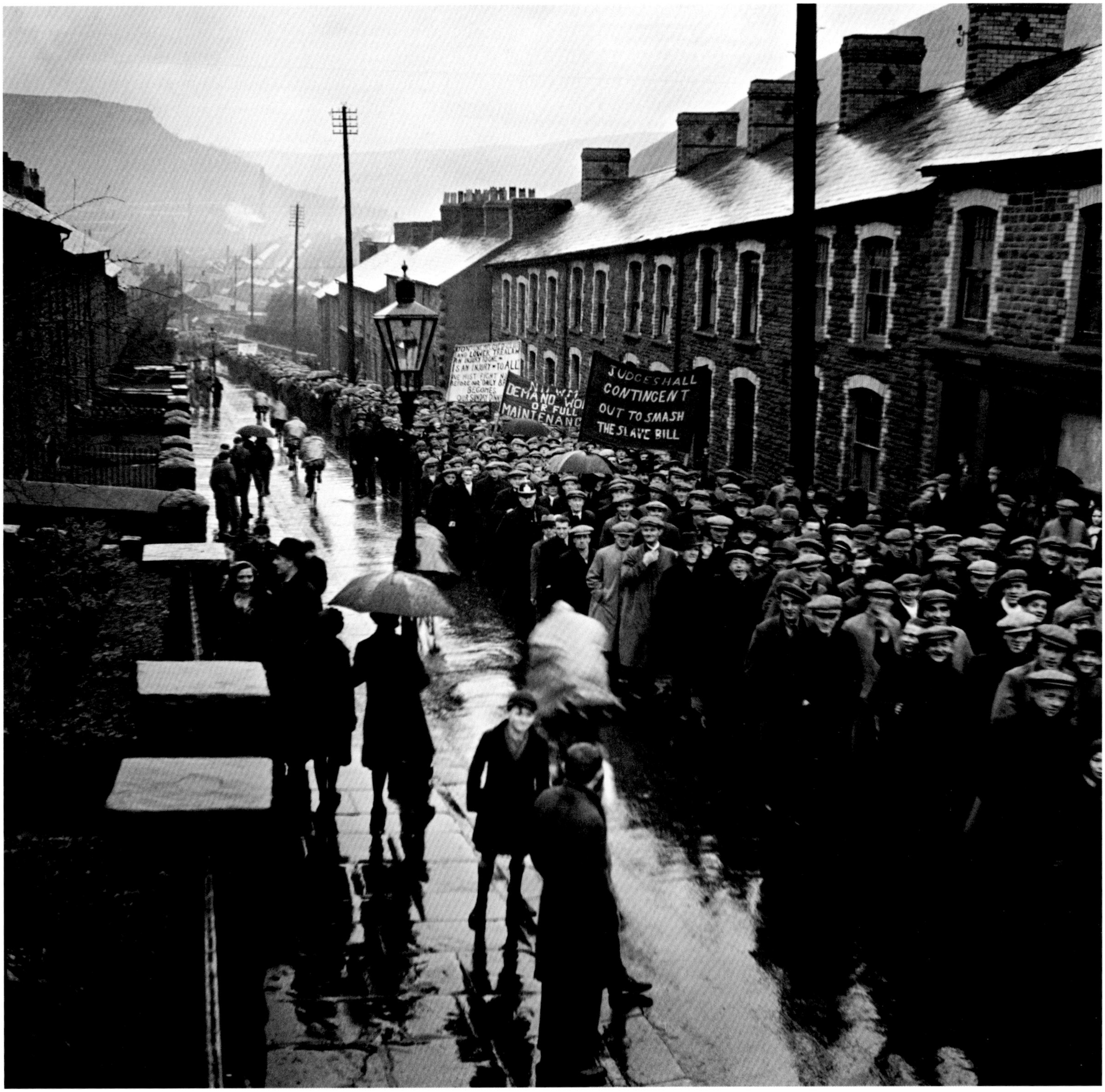

Edith Tudor-Hart
Unemployed Workers' Demonstration, Trealaw, South Wales, 1935
Modern silver-gelatin print, 30.3 × 30 cm
National Galleries of Scotland, PGP 279.4

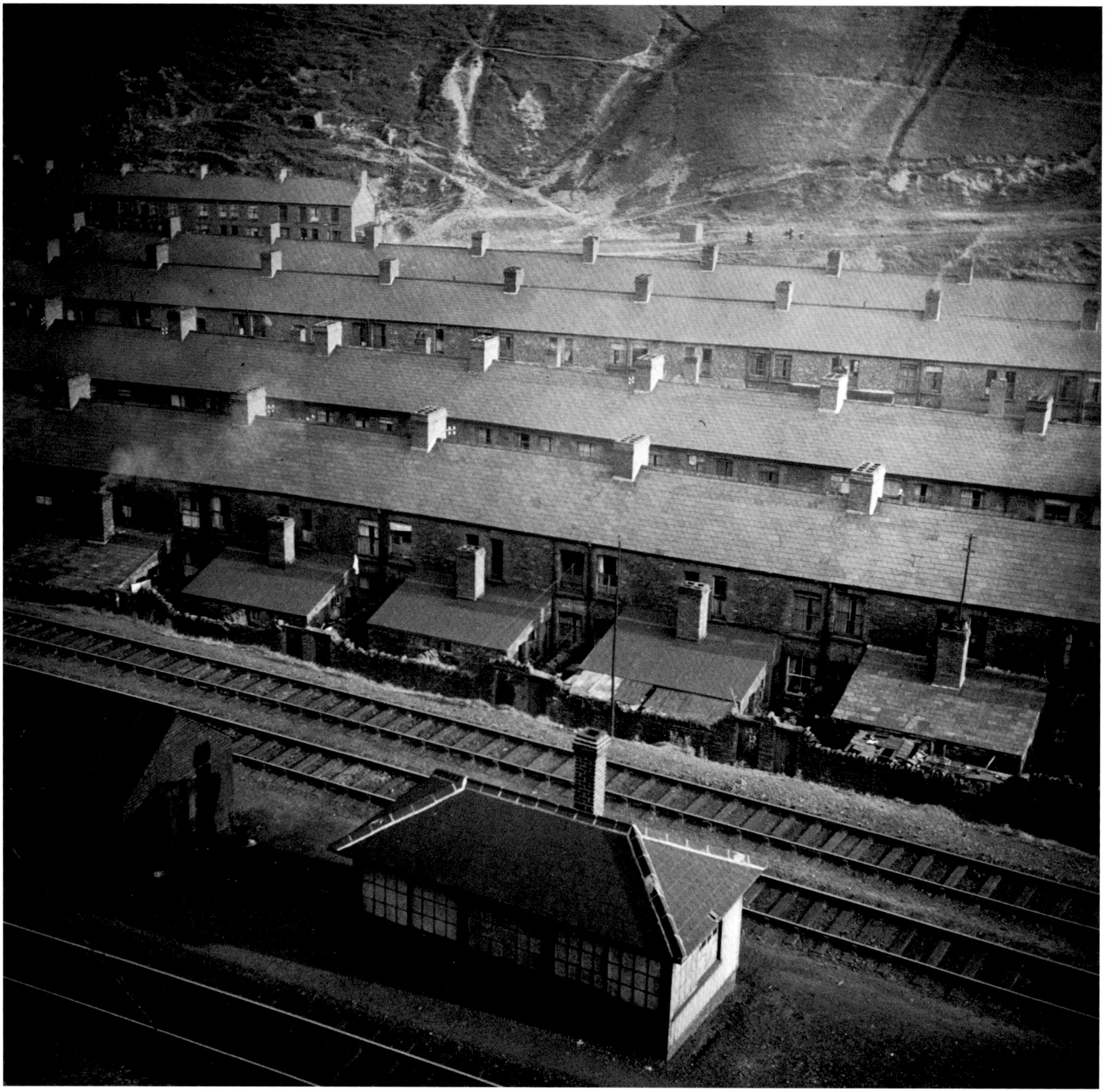

Edith Tudor-Hart
Miners' Cottages, Rhondda Valley, South Wales, ca. 1936
Modern silver-gelatin print, 30.2 × 30.1 cm
National Galleries of Scotland, PGP 279.47

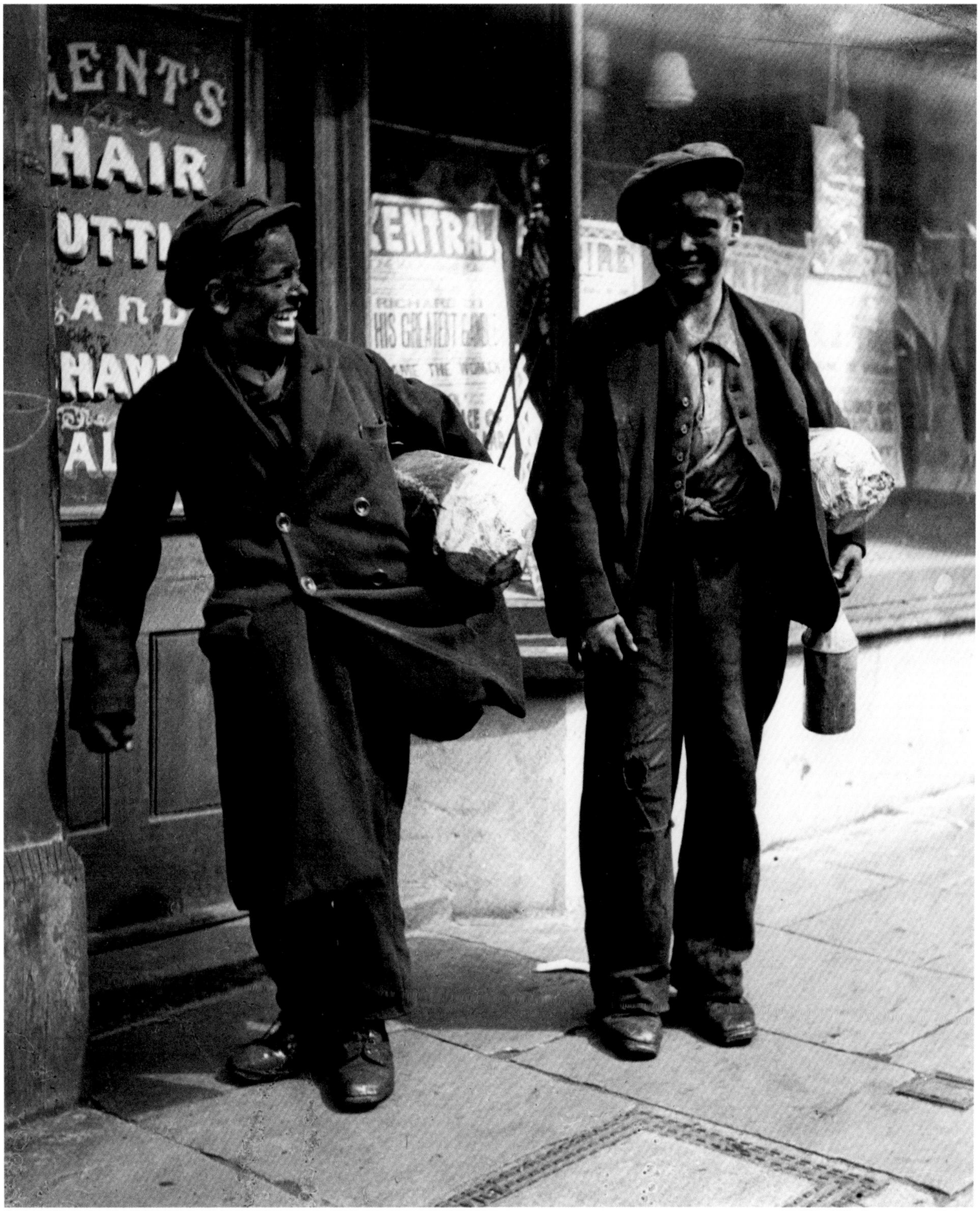

Edith Tudor-Hart
Miners Taking Home Pit Props for Fuel, South Wales, 1935
Silver-gelatin print, 24.4 × 19.6 cm
Wien Museum, 204466

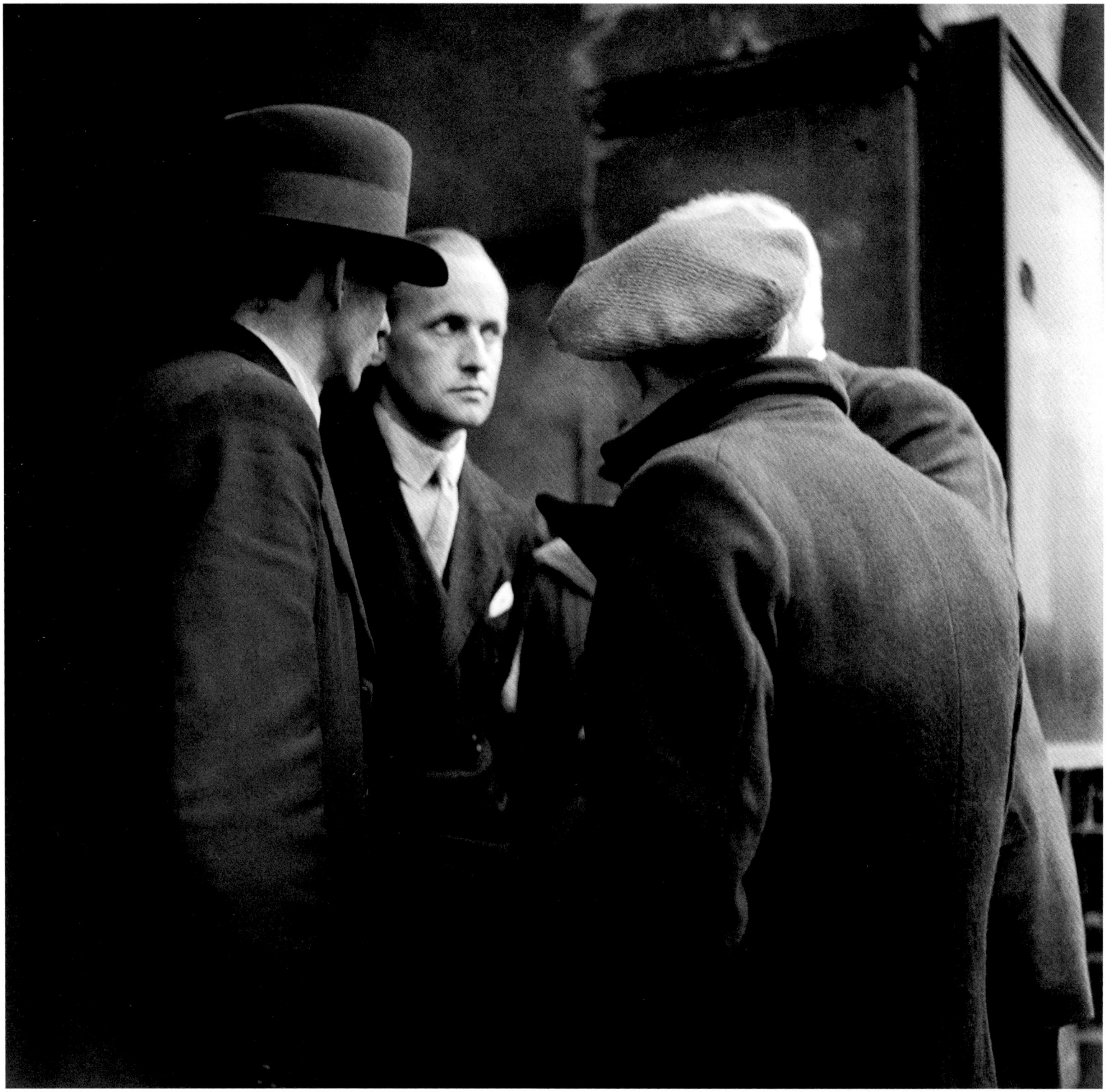

Edith Tudor-Hart
Group of Men, Monmouth Assizes, Wales, 1935
Modern silver-gelatin print, 30.2 × 30.1 cm
National Galleries of Scotland, PGP 279.46

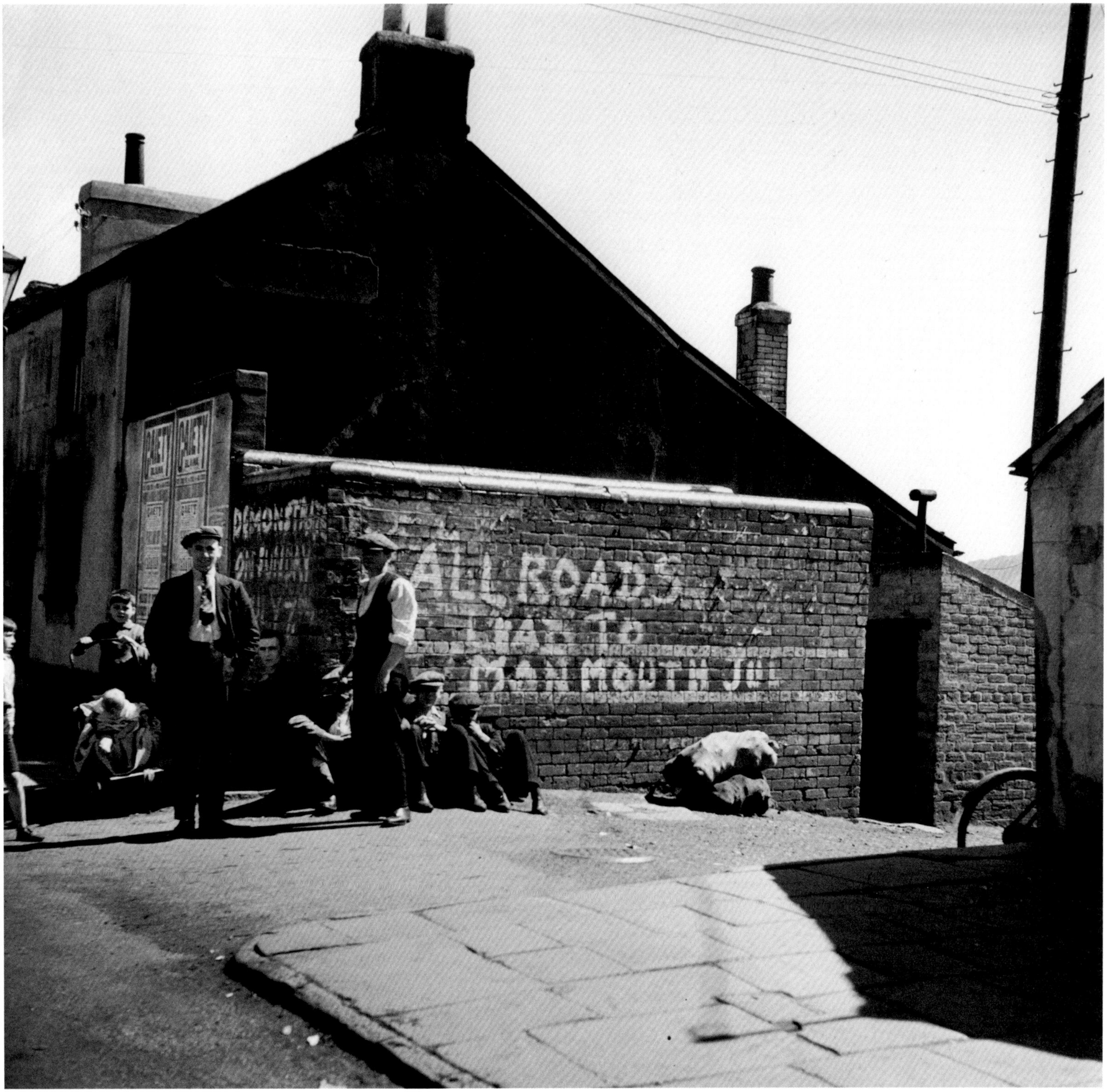

Edith Tudor-Hart
Unemployed Workers, Abertillery, South Wales, 1935
Modern silver-gelatin print, 30.2 × 30 cm
National Galleries of Scotland, PGP 279.45

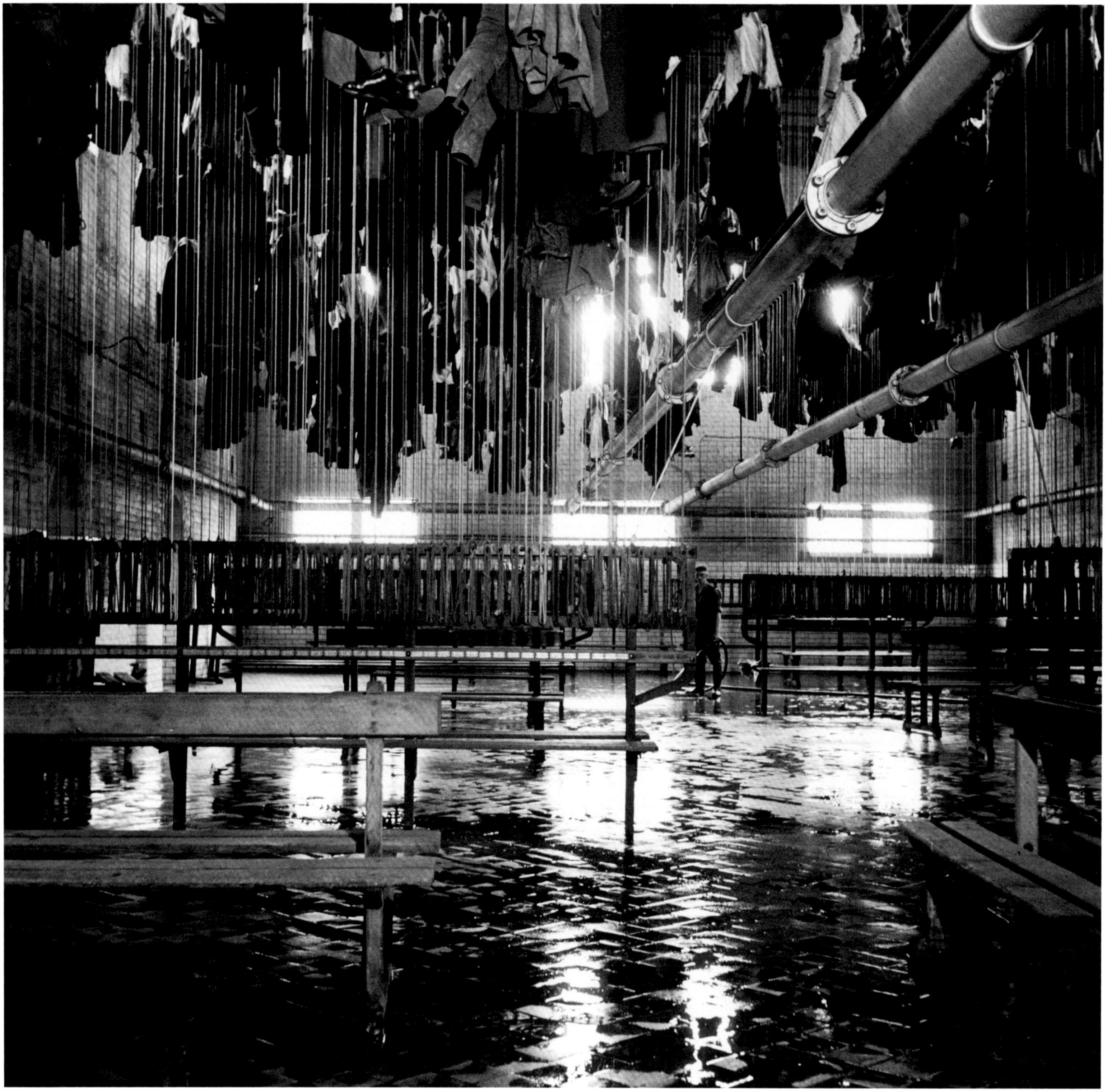

Edith Tudor-Hart
Drying Room, Pit-head Baths, Ashington Colliery, Northumberland, ca. 1937
Modern silver-gelatin print, 30.3 × 30.1 cm
National Galleries of Scotland, PGP 279.48

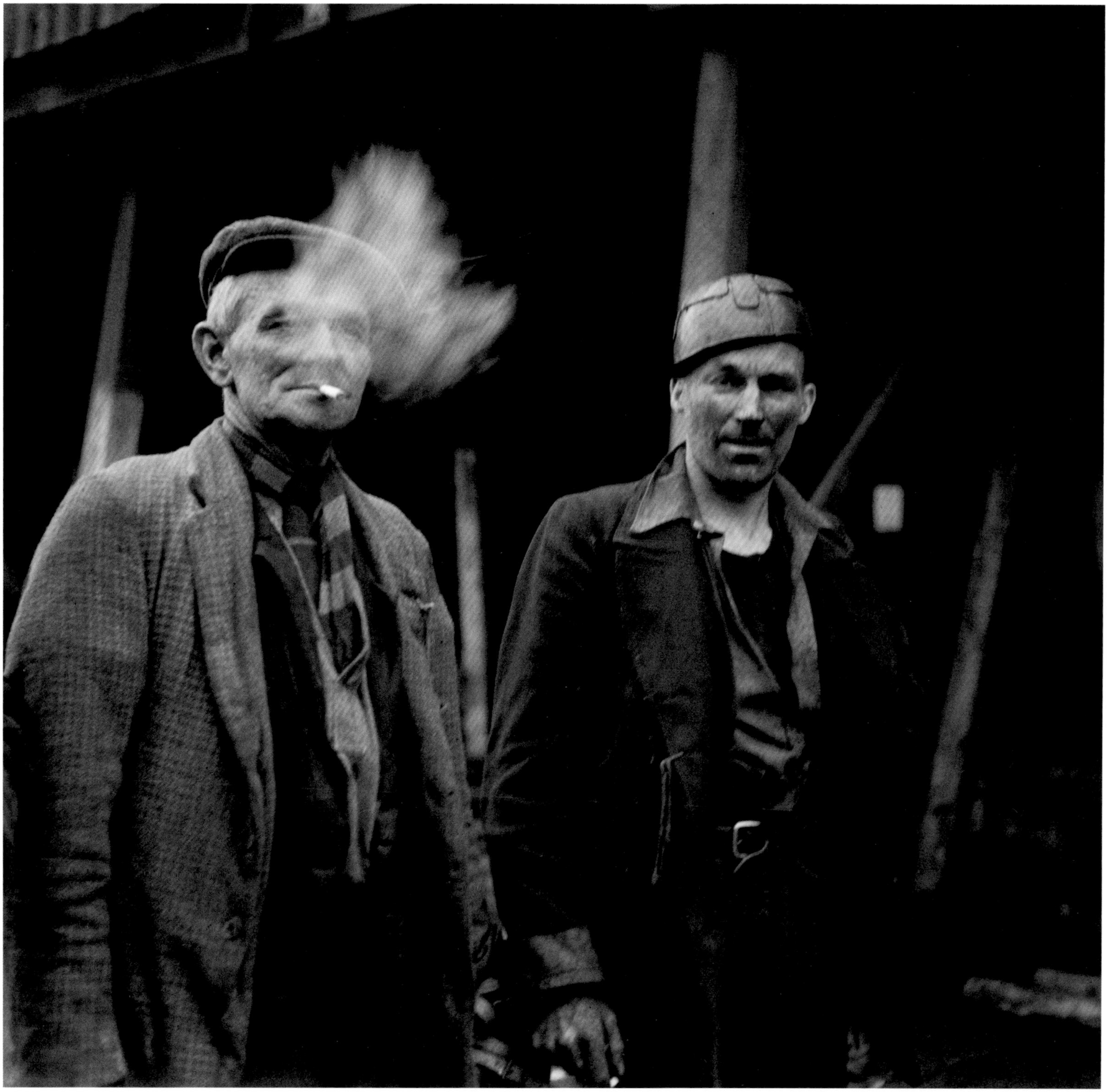

Edith Tudor-Hart
Miners, Tyneside, ca. 1937
Modern silver-gelatin print, 30.2 × 30.1 cm
National Galleries of Scotland, PGP 279.51

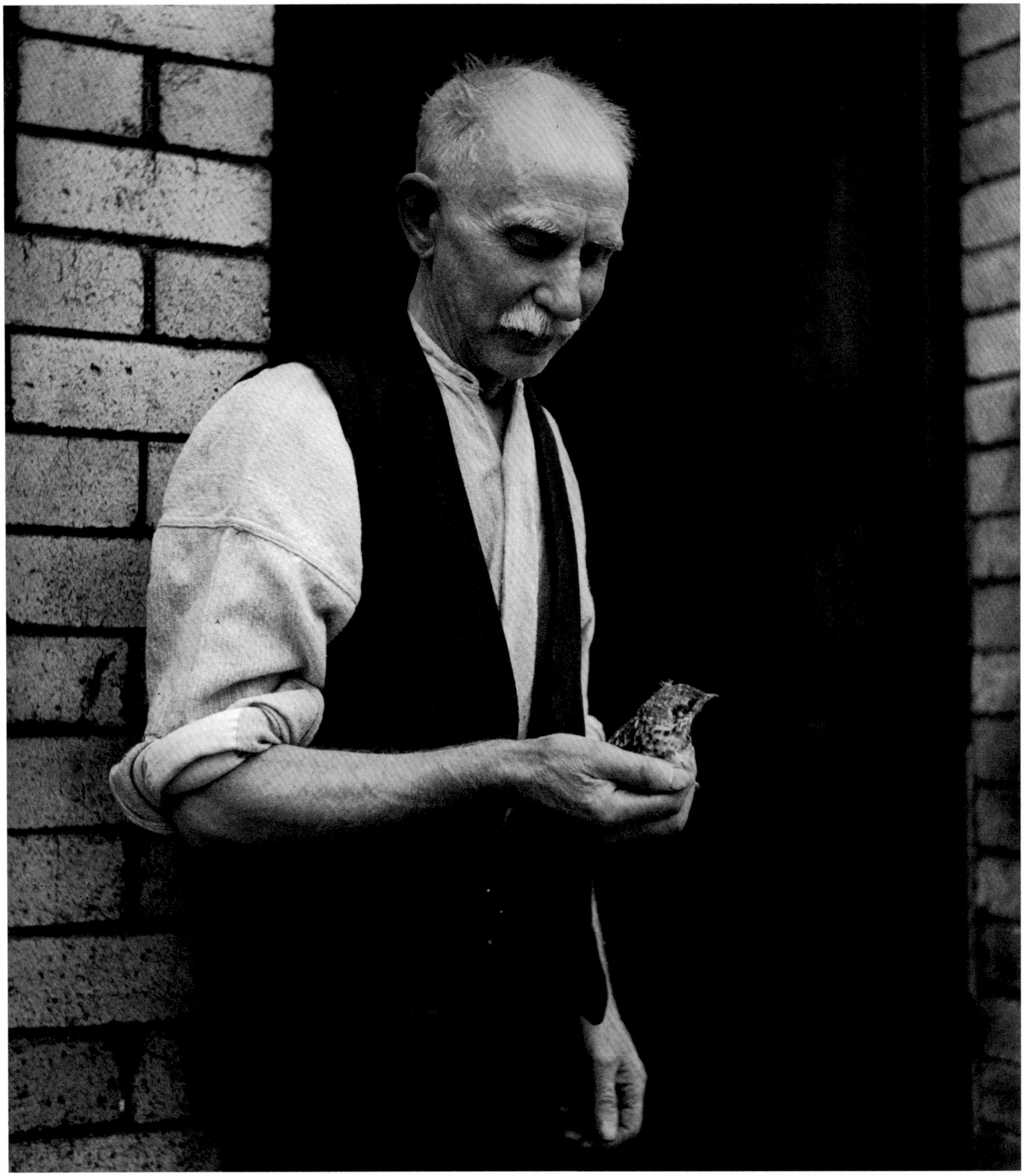

Edith Tudor-Hart
Man with Bird, Tyneside, ca. 1937
Modern silver-gelatin print, 34.2 × 29.1 cm
National Galleries of Scotland, PGP 279.52

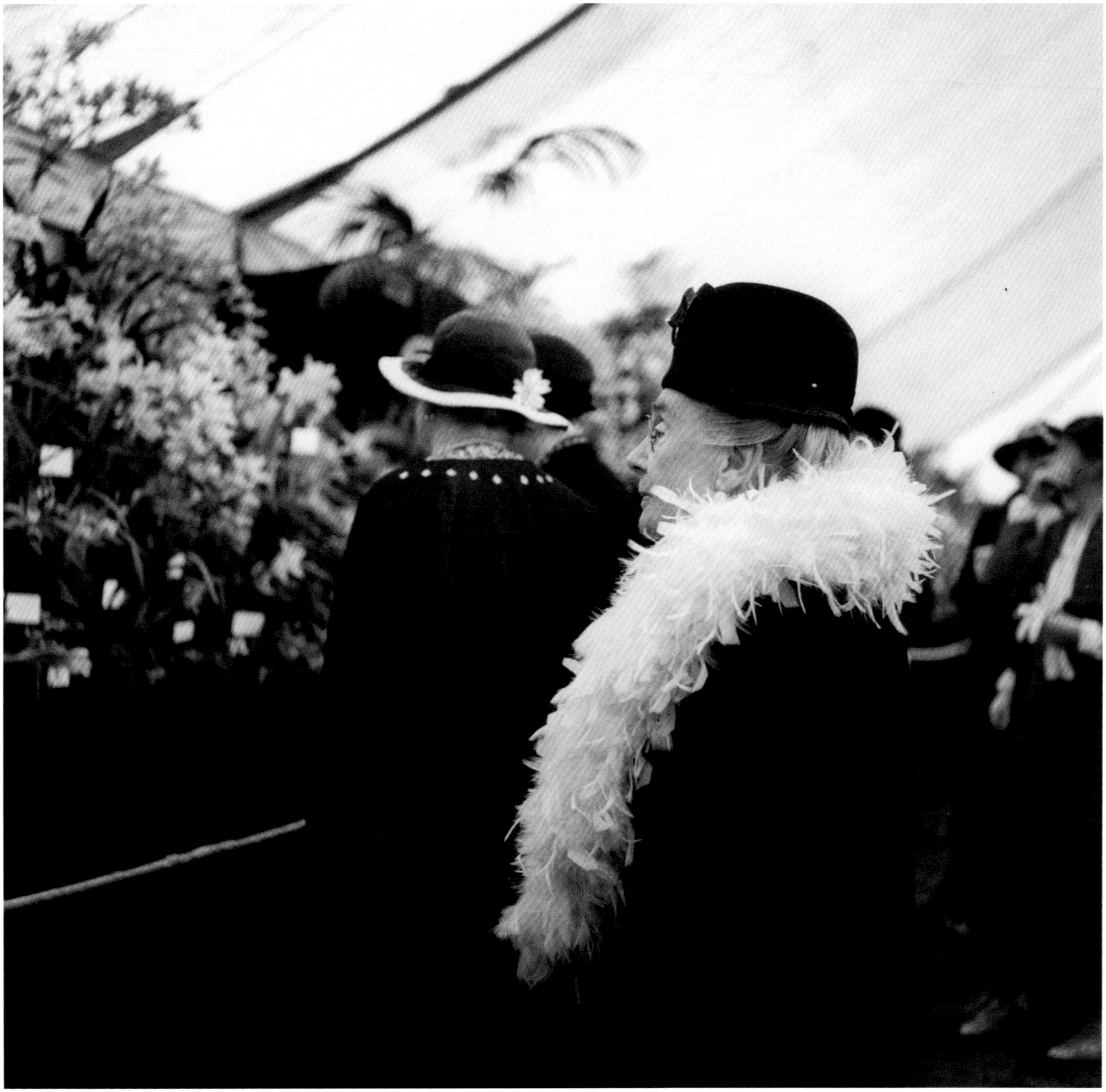

Edith Tudor-Hart
Woman at Chelsea Flower Show, London, ca. 1937
Modern silver-gelatin print, 30.3 × 30 cm
National Galleries of Scotland, PGP 279.30

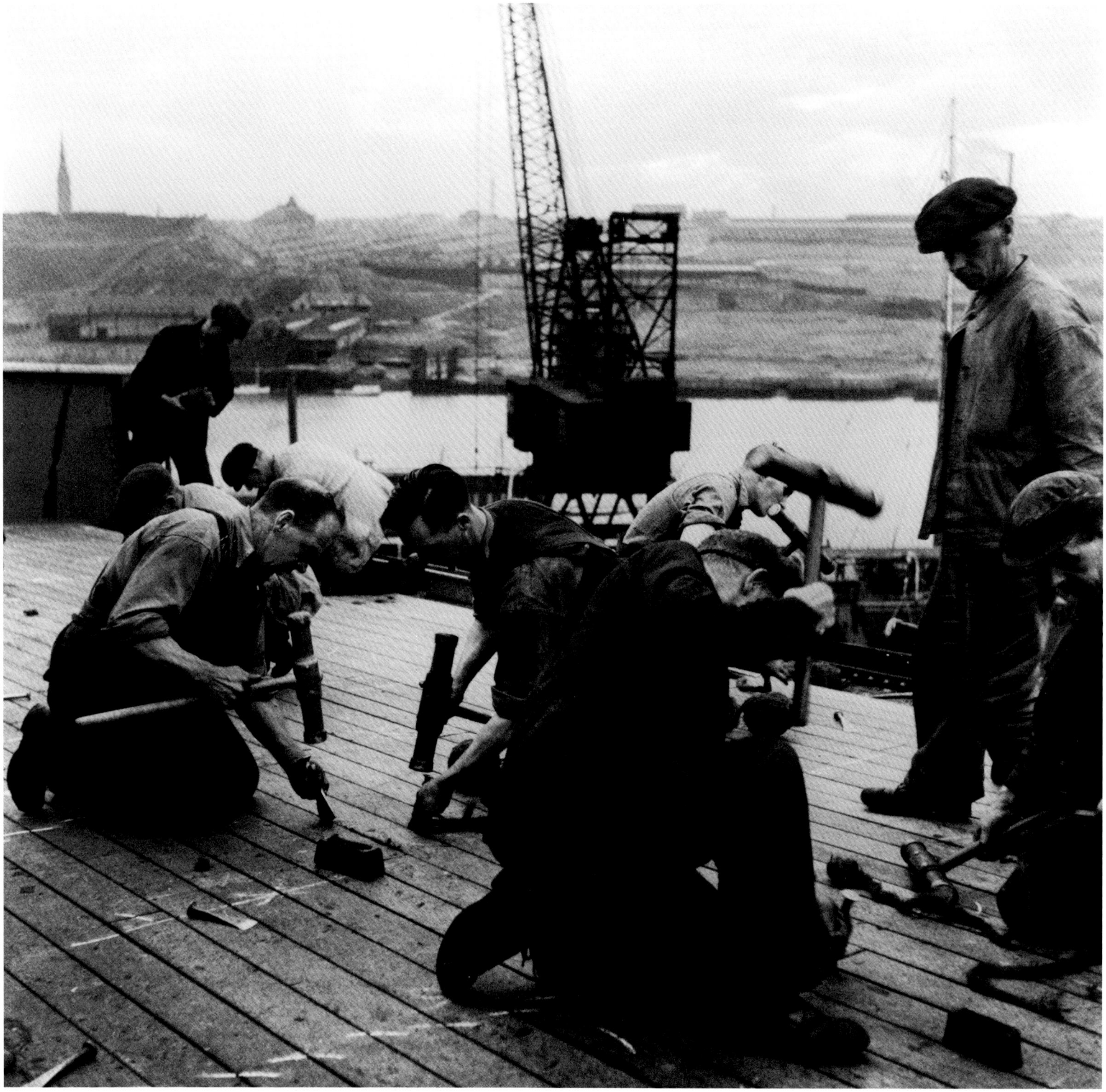

Edith Tudor-Hart
Shipfitters, Tyneside, ca. 1937
Modern silver-gelatin print, 28.3 × 27.7 cm
National Galleries of Scotland, PGP 279.49

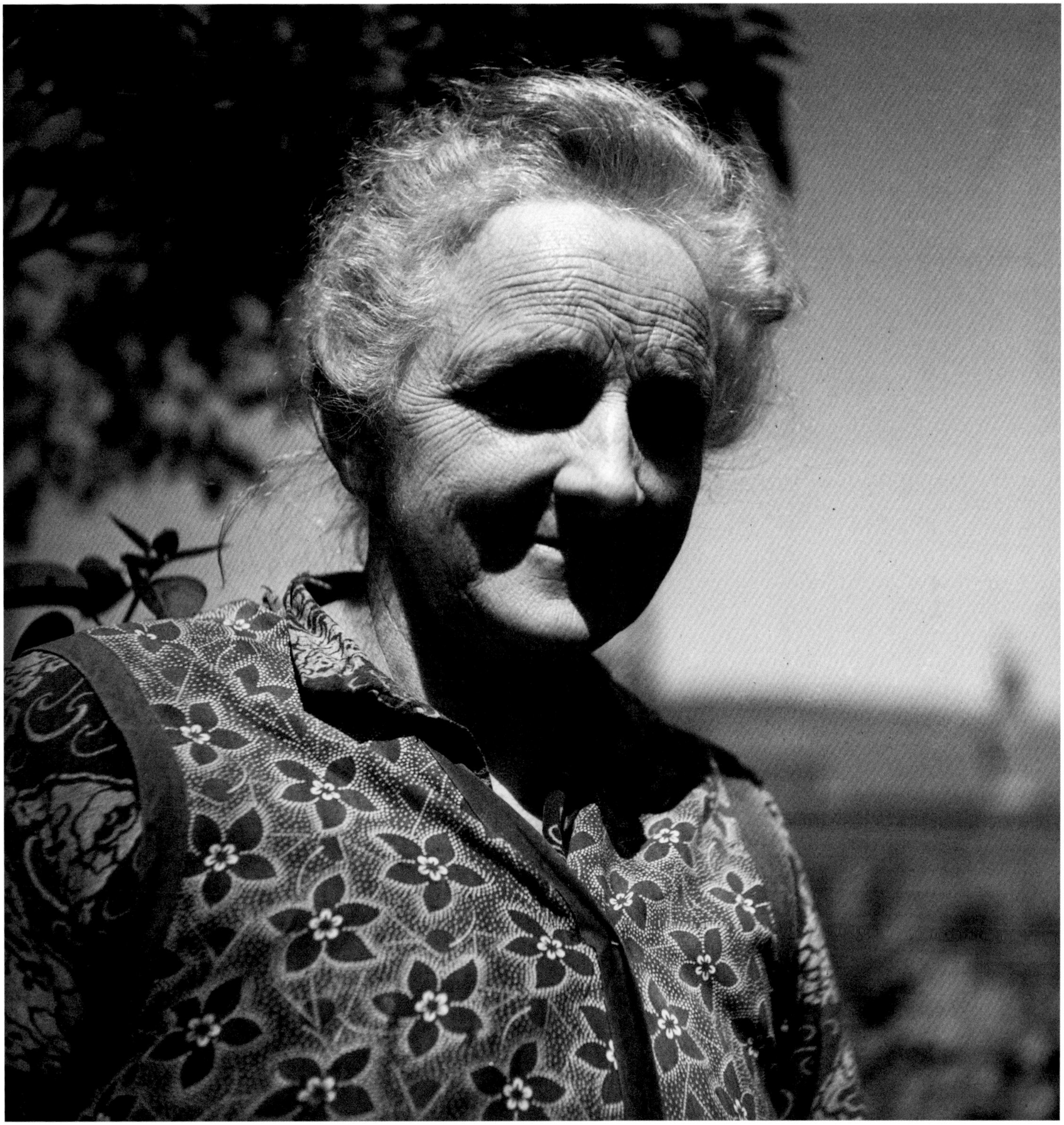

Edith Tudor-Hart
Woman, South Wales, 1935
Digital inkjet print, 32.4 × 29.9 cm
National Galleries of Scotland, PGP 279.90

Passport No. 656336

Roberta McGrath

One suddenly loses the right to live in a land (which after all is necessary for one) like one would lose an umbrella or a purse.[1]

I

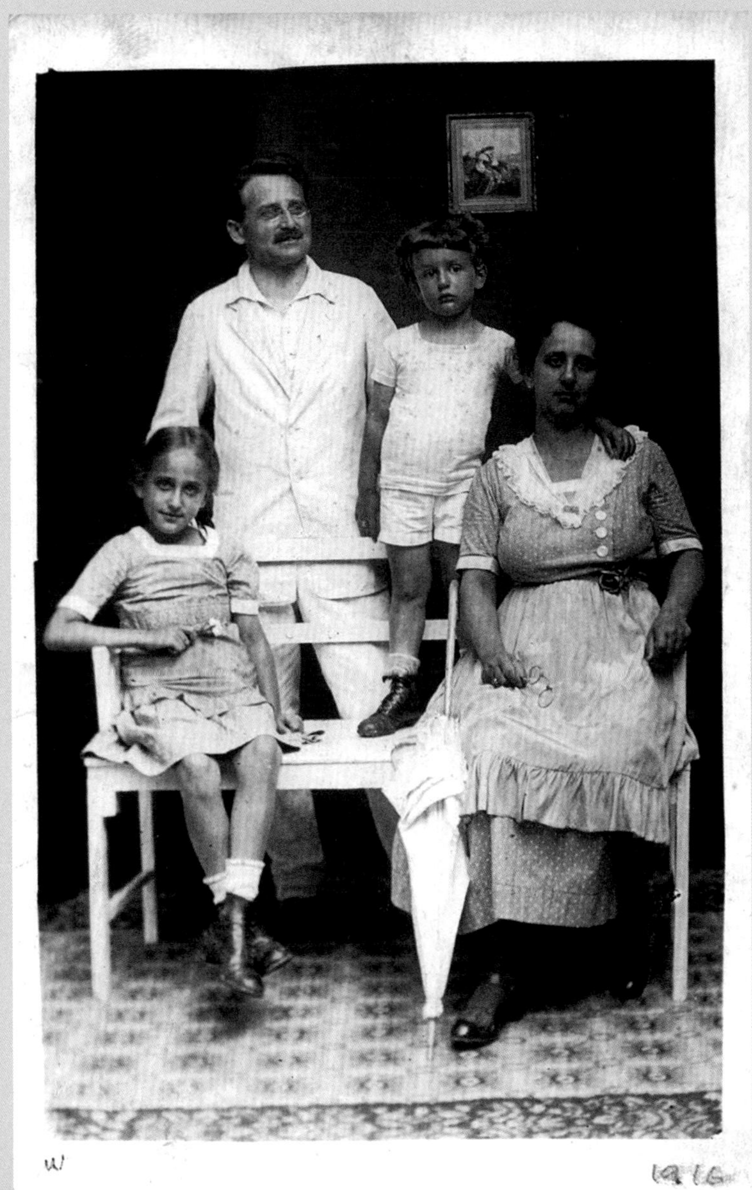

Fig. 33
Photographer unknown, *Wilhelm and Adele Suschitzky with Their Children Edith and Wolfgang, Vienna,* 1916

We first see Edith Suschitzky in 1916 on the other side of the camera as an eight-year-old girl photographed along with her mother, Adele, her father, Wilhelm, and her younger brother, "Wolfi" (fig. 33). Her father and brother stand; she and her mother sit. One reading of this image would be as a beautifully composed, and perfectly exposed, studio photograph of a typical bourgeois Viennese family. However, things are not always as they first appear.

If we look for a little longer, we notice that Edith's head is tilted to one side. She appears thoughtful, perhaps even mischievous. Most of all she seems self-possessed. Seated far apart on a garden bench (although in a studio), she holds a small, single flower. Her younger brother, aged four, stands on the bench between his parents. Now closer to the height of his father, he leans slightly toward his mother. Edith's ankles are crossed and her feet do not quite reach the floor. She and her father seem relaxed; there is a glimmer of a smile. But the mother and son appear serious and stiff, and the mother's legs are awkwardly arranged as if she were ready to pick up her parasol and walk straight out of the frame. Edith now seems isolated in the photograph, set apart on the far left of the image, while the others are linked by their arms. She is independent. In later photographs Edith is the epitome of the New Woman. In one (possibly a self-portrait) she is casually dressed in a man's sweater, smoking, thinking; she appears as a woman who has ideas (p. 97). In another, Edith takes her own picture reflected in a mirror; alongside her is a handsome man who becomes the object of her gaze (p. 105).

In the first quarter of the twentieth century, the radical potential of photography (and its mass distribution through print culture) coalesced with a revolution that was as much technical as it was political and, importantly for the young girl in the photograph, as much sexual as it was social.

Edith Suschitzky was born into a middle-class family, although one that was unconventional: Jewish, but atheist; middle class, but living in a working-class district of Vienna. Her parents belonged to a "loosely woven network of men and women" that "formed the left-liberal, social reformist vanguard of Vienna at the turn of the century."[2] Her father, a Social Democrat, bookseller, and later publisher of radical books and pamphlets, supported the rights of women.

By the nineteen-twenties the Suschitzkys were living in Petzvalgasse in the fourth district of Vienna. Named after Joseph Petzval, the scientist who had revolutionized photography in 1840 by inventing a lens that cut exposure time from minutes to seconds, the street was later remodeled by the Social Democrats, part of a radical city-wide experiment in living with others. Eve Blau describes how the housing blocks built by the municipality included "kindergartens, libraries, medical and dental clinics, laundries, workshops, theaters, cooperative stores, public gardens, sports facilities, and a wide range of other public facilities."[3] This new social order transformed the public and private lives not only of men but also, importantly for Suschitzky, of women and children. For the Social Democrats, culture in all its forms also had a vital role to play. Photography, too, was revolutionized. With the invention of the Leica and the Rolleiflex, the camera was poised to become a weapon in the service of social change.

This historical moment offered a glimpse of a new horizon, one that is made visible in Suschitzky's early photographs. It is there, for example, in the images of a new generation of middle-class women making themselves at home in Viennese public life. In the café, unchaperoned, they take pleasure in their freedom and independence from men (p. 32). Suschitzky contrasts these images with photographs of working-class, destitute women at the margin of society. Housed at the edge of the city, they live in misery; their homes are little more than kennels, which Suschitzky emphasizes by including dogs (p. 34). They are separated by a kind of no-man's-land from the new, solid, public housing which, although it can be seen, remains hopelessly out of reach (p. 35). These photographs are a record of the economic and social misery wrought by capitalism, an example of what Walter Benjamin called "document[s] of barbarism."[4] As unemployment doubled and inflation soared, Suschitzky documented the political crisis that ensued as the long, catastrophic shadow of fascism fell over Vienna.

It is likely that Suschitzky knew of the writings of the Viennese feminists Auguste Fickert and Rosa Mayreder, if only because her father had published their work.[5] Fickert, herself a primary school teacher and leader of the General Austrian Women's Association, believed that the attainment of women's rights should not be the goal of the association. She described it as a petty middle-class point of view, suggesting that it would be a mistake to "imitate men who in the course of history have generally used their attained rights only to oppress those weaker than themselves."[6] As Auguste Fickert knew, rights were all too alienable. The younger Mayreder wrote to Fickert to explain her position:

> It is becoming increasingly impossible for me to see "men" as the enemies of women's concerns; I think more and more that your most serious opponents are "women." . . . I for my part think there are a number of people who belong to us—men and women. One can quarrel about the percentage of participation—according to my subjective experience, however, the male sex would be represented in much larger numbers. That is why I do not believe in the "sisterhood" of women, nor in the task of women uniting against men.[7]

Suschitzky's politics were not liberal, and her understanding of feminism had little to do with prioritizing the interests of women. Understood as a matter of political alignment, sexual equality was tightly interwoven with progressive social and economic struggle. The politics of class was, for Suschitzky, fundamental. The abolition of capitalist exploitation and the overturning of the dominance of men over women and children went hand in hand.

As Harriet Anderson suggests, the Austrian feminist movement left a formidably progressive infrastructure. It included the Heimhof, a housing cooperative specifically built for working women that provided meals, and also legal aid centers established to help impoverished women. However, the feminism that emerged in Austria was not narrowly concerned with institutional change. Sexual reform

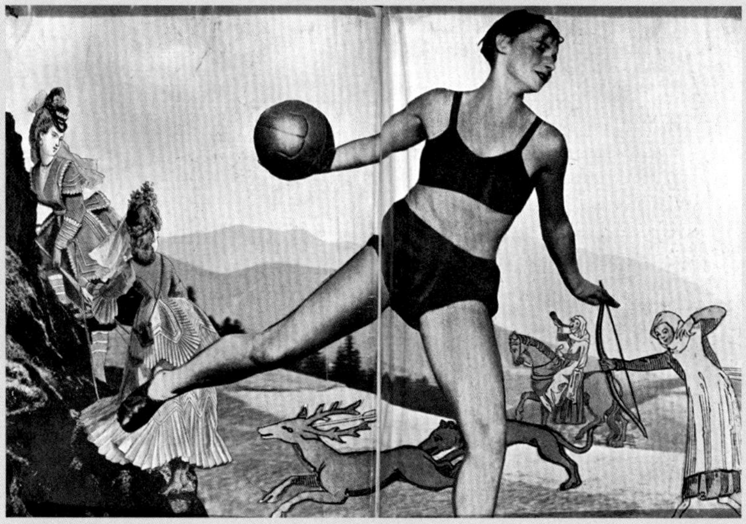

Fig. 34
Edith Suschitzky, *Untitled Montage*, from Edith Tudor-Hart's scrapbook, date unknown

was also seen as vital. Suschitzky might have read Freud, and her father published books not only on the New Woman, but also on the New Man. In Suschitzky's milieu, men and women had been trapped in too narrow definitions—not only of what it meant to be a man or a woman, but of what it meant to be human. Social change was also to come from within, and Red Vienna was, in part, shaped by the psychoanalytic movement whose practitioners, including Freud, often provided free treatment in newly established clinics.[8]

The political themes that would remain with Edith Suschitzky throughout her life emerge here. In Vienna she witnessed first-hand the inequalities of class, gender, and race, and she understood the central importance of access to housing, health care, and education as a means of eradicating such inequalities. It was this that led her to study as a Montessori teacher and to pursue her interest in photography, both professions which had recently been opened up to women.

II

There are no photographs of Edith Suschitzky in The National Archives (TNA) of the United Kingdom. To be found here are only descriptive texts compiled by the security services: intercepted letters, transcriptions of tapped telephone conversations, written accounts of interviews. Suschitzky first appears in the archives of MI5 in 1930. She is identified by her passport number and her appearance: "Height: 5'6". Slim build. Pale complexion. Eyes blue-grey. Blond bobbed hair." In later records she is described variously as "Jewish," "the foreign woman," of "Foreign Jewish appearance," and, bluntly, "Edie the foreigner." She is also described as being "of timid type."[9]

However, Suschitzky was far from timid. She was a Communist activist involved in espionage. She had first arrived in England in April 1925 to attend a workshop with Maria Montessori. At the end of November 1930 she faced deportation as an undesirable alien. We know from the archives that her father did all he could to prevent this. At home he made contact with Karl Seitz, the Mayor of Vienna, "begging" him to take an interest in his daughter's predicament; he also appealed for support to the Austrian Consulate in London. Seitz explained that if Suschitzky's expulsion was for "political reasons," then he could not intervene.[10]

The reasons were, indeed, political. In October 1930, Suschitzky had taken part in a Communist demonstration in Trafalgar Square in support of the Workers' Charter and was noted to "be in conversation with a number of prominent Communists."[11] The Aliens Acts of 1919 and 1920 sought to regulate immigration into Britain, and, in the aftermath of the Russian Revolution, fear of social unrest made it illegal for aliens to promote industrial action. In order to make identification easier, aliens were also prohibited from changing their names: Suschitzky's card was marked. Now identified as "an extremist," she was instructed to leave on December 4, 1930, and after repeated warnings she returned to Vienna on January 15, 1931.[12] She was twenty-two years old.

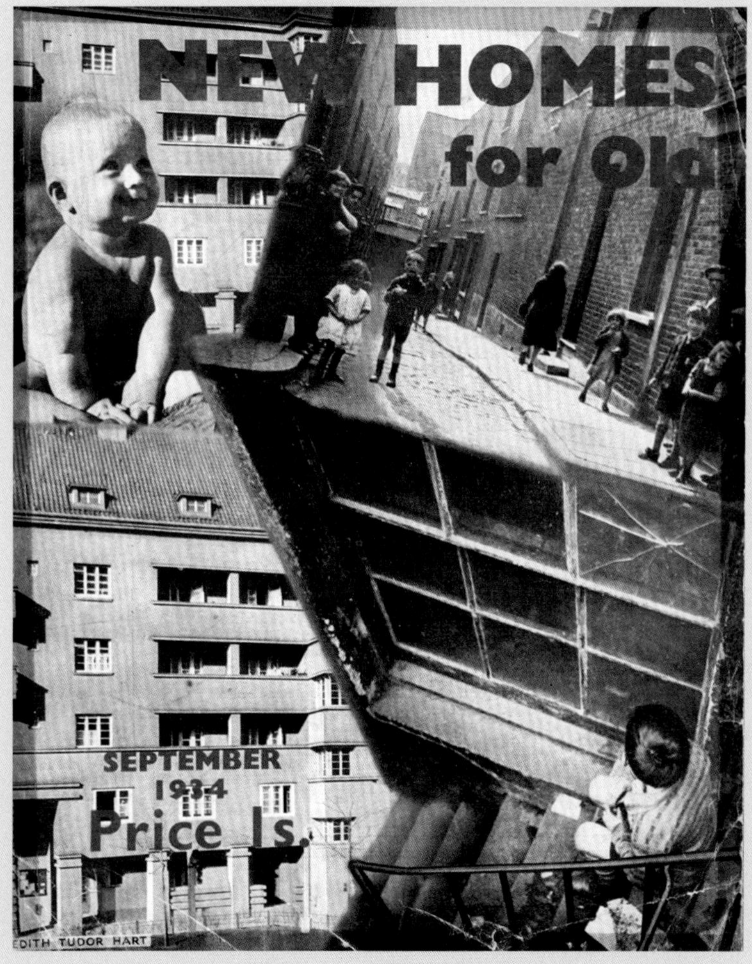

Fig. 35
Edith Tudor-Hart, front cover of *New Homes for Old,* from Edith Tudor-Hart's scrapbook, 1934

In the period between 1925 and 1930, two events—one personal, the other professional—cemented her political and cultural life. Although the exact dates are unclear, we know, firstly, that around 1925 she met, and subsequently lived with, the Cambridge-educated Communist Alexander Tudor-Hart. In a letter written in June 1931, she credits him with having "laid the foundation of my political education."[13] Secondly, she studied photography at the Bauhaus in Dessau.

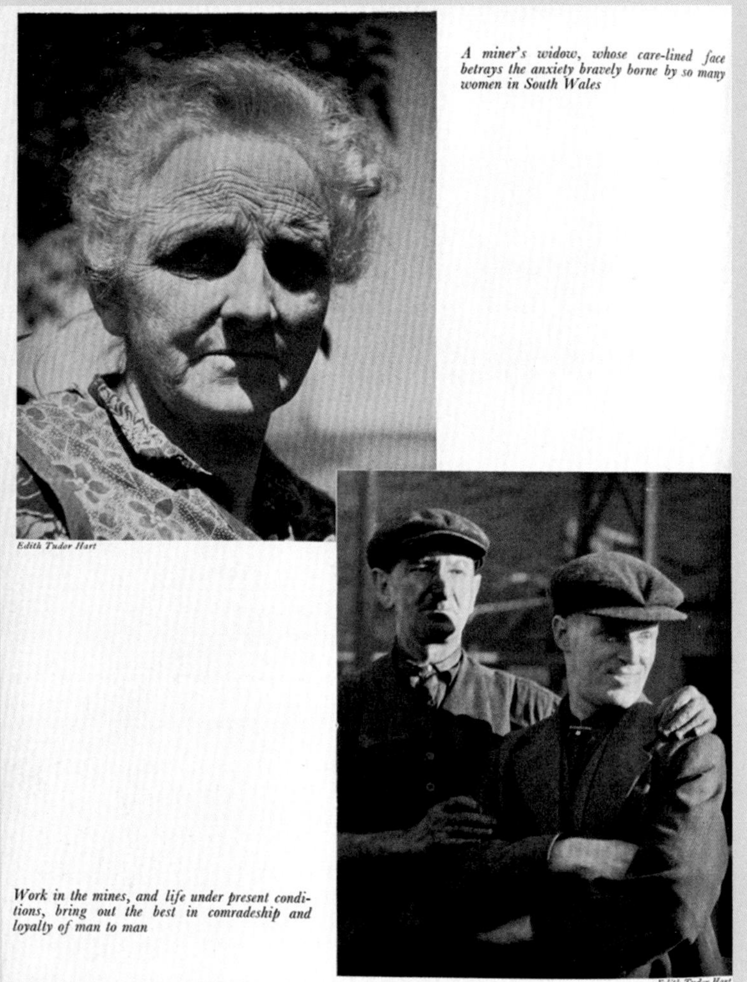

Fig. 36
Edith Tudor-Hart, "The Rhondda Valley," *Geographical Magazine,* March 1936, p. 378

Within two months of her return to Vienna in 1931, Suschitzky had been appointed as the official photographic reporter for the Press Cliché in Moscow. In order to secure her position, she wrote to Tudor-Hart asking him to "get me at once from the Central Committee a statement saying that I, E SUSCHITZKY, as E. WHITE, have worked in the Party and was deported for that reason."[14] This was probably achieved through Sergei Ingulov, who had been a representative of the Soviet news agency TASS in England.[15] The recognition of her work delighted her, for as she put it, "it came all without recommendation—ich bin so froh."[16]

It is also clear that the work she carried out for the party was dangerous. In April 1931 she wrote to Tudor-Hart from Vienna to tell him that she had left her camera in a café and thought she had lost it. In the letter, her anxiety is palpable and she berates herself as an "unreliable comrade" on account of her emotions. She describes her illness as "melancholia," and it is possible that she was suffering from depression.[17] In her letters to Tudor-Hart she discusses the party, comradeship, love, and the impossibility of being with him (he was married when they first met), as well as the deteriorating political situation in Vienna: "[a]t home it has become quite intollerable [*sic*]—my father cries and mother cried the whole day long."[18] Yet by September 1931, Suschitzky had published her first photographic essay on Montessori education titled "Was will der neue Kindergarten?" in the illustrated magazine *Der Kuckuck* (fig. 7).[19]

There is also, however, evidence of a very different form of image-making produced by Suschitzky using montage (fig. 34). This comparatively large (28 × 41.5 cm), undated, and untitled image is preserved in her scrapbook. It is likely to have been made in the late nineteen-twenties and probably before 1931. The montage depicts the New Woman of the future. At the center stands a photograph of a female gymnast about to hurl a medicine ball forward and out of the frame. Occupying a double-page spread, she leaves the past behind. To her right is a reproduced engraving of two women constrained by late nineteenth-century dress, but nonetheless attempting to climb a mountain; to her left is a medieval wood-block print of two women hunting, one on horseback, whilst the other takes aim with a bow and arrow.

This montage, conceptually weak and crudely executed, is a lesson in the role of both women and photography in shaping a future that was yet to come. As Edith Tudor-Hart later put it, photography "ceased to be an instrument for recording events and became a means of stimulating and influencing events. It became a living art, embracing the people."[20] It is an acknowledgment both of women's presence and participation in the past and of their newfound freedom and place at the forefront of the present. Such montages are what Jan Zita Grover calls "subjunctive images—photographs hurled toward the future, cast ahead of us as visual guideposts to what we hope to become."[21] An overtly feminist image (which might be read as a version of Eugène Delacroix's 1830 painting, *Liberty Leading the People*), it could all too easily be dismissed because it does not fit with Tudor-Hart's social and realist photography. However, perhaps it should be valued precisely because it does not fit: the formal experimentation it represents, inspired by revolutionary culture in the Soviet Union and elsewhere, would be largely closed down by 1932.

In May 1933 Victor Gollancz released the Left Book Club's *The Brown Book of the Hitler Terror.*[22] Published in England and France (and with a dust jacket by John Heartfield), it made graphically clear, through its use of photographs, the physical violence unleashed on Jews, Social Democrats, and Communists (including women). The political situation in Austria deteriorated, and, suspected of being a Communist, Edith Suschitzky was arrested and imprisoned in June. In August she finally married Alex Tudor-Hart in Vienna. This enabled her to leave Austria and return to England as a British citizen. She could now legally change her name, and so Edith Suschitzky became Mrs. Edith Tudor-Hart, "specialist in modern photography."[23] For the next twenty years she worked commercially (in order to make a living) and continued her political photographic work both independently and through organizations such as the Artists International, which she joined in 1934.

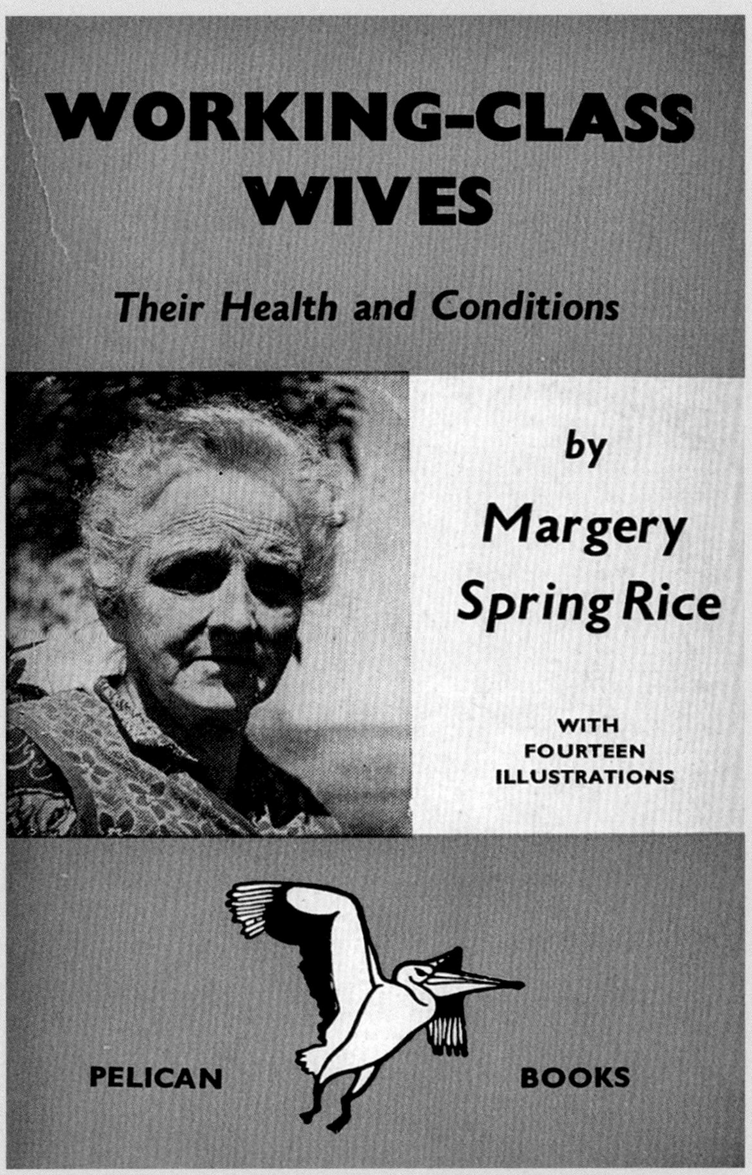

Fig. 37
Edith Tudor-Hart, front cover of *Working-Class Wives: Their Health and Conditions* by Margery Spring Rice (Harmondsworth, 1939)

While Edith Tudor-Hart followed Moscow in her politics, it is a testament to her feminism that she continued to document the ways in which class and racial inequality intersected with gender in Britain and also to show the vital role that new housing, health centers, and better education could play in improving working-class lives (fig. 35). This is evident in the extensive work she produced in the mid-thirties for the architect of Kensal House (with its nursery provision) and for the South London Hospital for Women and Children which, entirely staffed by women, was described as an "Adamless Eden" (pp. 84 and 127). It is also visible in the photographs used in publications such as *The Geographical Magazine* (1936 and 1937) or in Margery Spring Rice's *Working-Class Wives: Their Health and Conditions* (1939), the former considering not only the health of the male miners but also of women in the communities. One photograph published in *The Geographical Magazine* in 1936—with the caption "A miner's widow, whose care-lined face betrays the anxiety bravely borne by so many women in South Wales"—was reemployed as the cover of *Working-Class Wives* (figs. 36 and 37). Inside, it was accompanied by the humanist caption "The abiding maternal personality."[24]

In 1936, Edith Tudor-Hart gave birth to her son Tommy. However, her marriage to Alexander Tudor-Hart was by then effectively over. From 1936, she was a single working mother on a low income and, it appears, no financial support from her estranged husband. With Tommy suffering from what may have been a severe form of autism, these were exceptionally hard times. Tudor-Hart moved home and studio, from Brixton, south of the river, to Haverstock Hill in North London. Implicated as the person who had supplied the camera to the Woolwich spy ring, she was constantly followed and her flat was regularly searched, her mail intercepted, and her phone tapped. Tudor-Hart's bank account was examined (although no evidence of any payments was recorded). Her last studio in Duke Street (off Oxford Street) was bombed in 1942, and thereafter she worked briefly as a housekeeper and then for Studio Sun, a commercial operation.

Although poor, Tudor-Hart was culturally well-connected. One report filed in The National Archives records that while she "disclaimed . . . any connection with the Communist Party" her flat "was the resort of well-known persons connected with extremist propaganda."[25] Another is headed "Tudor Hart Circle."[26] She had by then gathered around her "an interesting circle of intellectuals," including Leo Hornik, Lucia Moholy-Nagy, and the sexologist Norman Haines. Whilst she was "seldom to be seen at the ordinary party functions," she was "much to be met with in German and British Communist circles."[27]

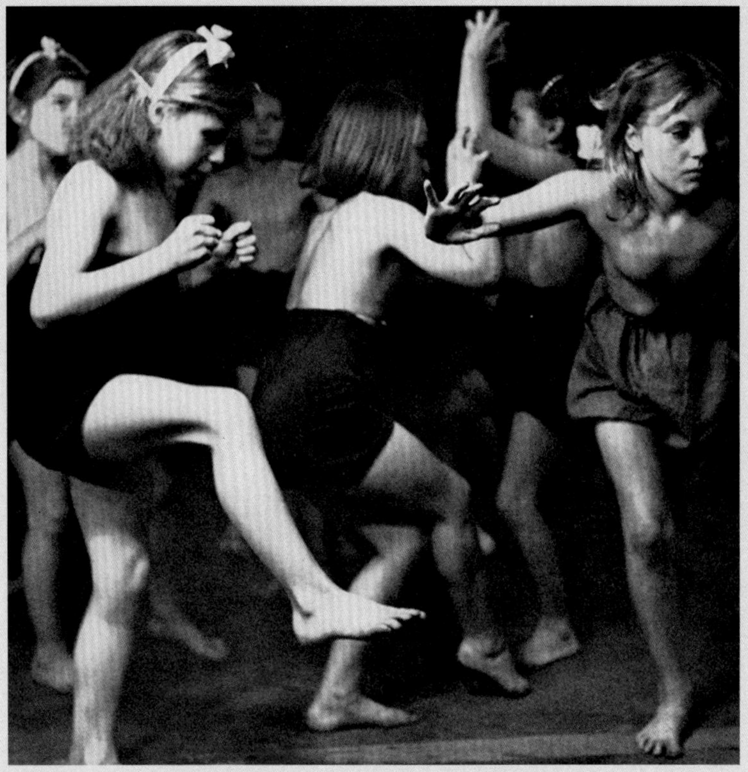

Fig. 38
Edith Tudor-Hart in *Moving and Growing: Physical Education in the Primary School* by the Ministry of Education (London, 1952), p. 96

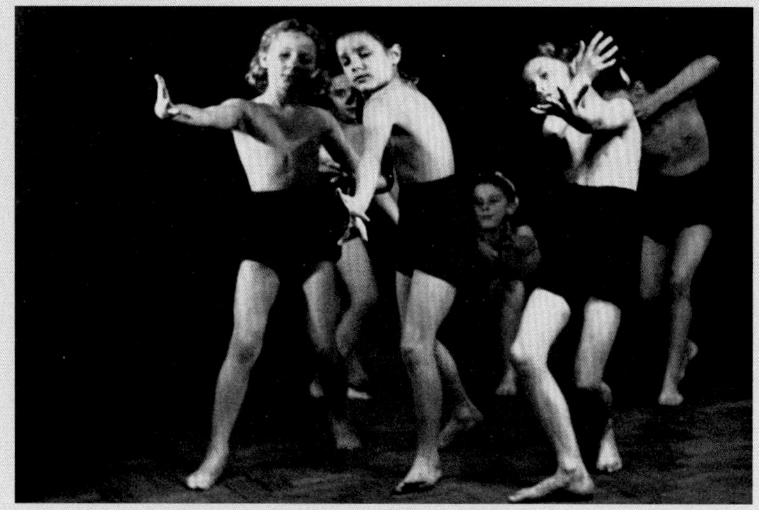

Fig. 39
Edith Tudor-Hart in *Moving and Growing: Physical Education in the Primary School* by the Ministry of Education (London, 1952), p. 97

From 1937, Edith Tudor-Hart produced work for Britain's new illustrated press, including Stefan Lorant's *Lilliput* magazine (where her photographs appeared in issues alongside those of Bill Brandt, John Heartfield, and Cecil Beaton) and *Picture Post.* She also worked for commercial companies such as Boots, Pears, and Glaxo, as well as for government agencies such as the Ministry of Information, contributing photographs to the exhibition *The Two Mrs. Britains,* designed by the exile architect Ernö Goldfinger. Displayed at Boots the Chemist in London's Piccadilly in 1943, its slogans—including "Equal Opportunities and Equal Pay for Victory and Reconstruction"—were aimed at boosting women's wartime productivity and morale.[28] After the war, Tudor-Hart produced photographs for an influential publication titled *Moving and Growing* (1952) for the Ministry of Education (figs. 38 and 39).

In her last essay, "Dancing at School," published in *Amateur Photography* in 1956, Tudor-Hart described her collaborative technique for creating the pictures for *Moving and Growing:*

> When I arrived I would have a short talk with the children, explaining what I was trying to do and letting them have a good look at lights and camera. (I tried to let every child have a look through the viewfinder.) When this was over I switched on my lights and asked them to do their dance for me once, or perhaps twice. Then I proceeded to shoot, and by that time the enthusiasm of the dance had made them forget the camera.

Edith Tudor-Hart knew what it meant to be on the other side of the camera, and she wanted children to understand what it was like to be engaged not just in the taking of a photograph, but also in the making of their own lives. The children in these images are participants in the process, and it is this that creates for the observer a vivid sense of the drama of being a child. These are not children "captured" by the camera, but children who are free to be themselves "dancing to their own tune."[29]

Lost in play or thought—in reading, painting, running, jumping, or in dancing—they inhabit their bodies. These are the longed-for New Children of Tudor-Hart's youth. They reflect her training with Maria Montessori, who believed that the child who was "awake to movement and colour and texture and sky and wind and stars will not be starved of nature even in a city slum."[30] These are lyrical images, beautifully crafted. The children here reach out toward a future that is full of promise, and the photographs stand as an important record of the progressive, democratic vision of health and education that emerged in postwar Britain.

These photographs are also a reminder that free dance was a vital part of the Social Democrats' vision of modernity.[31] They return us to the young girl in the studio photograph who left behind family and home and worked to remake a better world. Photography, too, was part of her vision of modernity. Tudor-Hart suggested that photography should be included in school curricula in order to "encourage young people to use their camera for more than just snap-shotting [*sic*] the family, to go out and observe life around them, to take a more active part in the life of the nation."[32] Her Montessori training had taught her that the purpose of education was to produce "not listless intellectuals, but young men and women filled with constructive hopefulness, conscious that there are great things to be done in the world, and possessed of the skill required for taking their part."[33] Tudor-Hart's archive contains hundreds of images of children playing and working—outdoors, free, often quite independent of adults.

The cultural work that Edith Tudor-Hart had begun in Vienna could not be completed there, or in Britain. Like the project of modernity itself, it remained incomplete, and she made few photographs after the early fifties. Postwar, the fear of communism increased again. By then Tudor-Hart was involved with the Cambridge-based exile nuclear scientist Engelbert Broda, and she was suspected of espionage.[34] Shortly afterward, she was instructed by the British security services to cease her photographic activities.[35] Tudor-Hart destroyed her studio catalogue, as well as a number of negatives and photographs that might have incriminated her or her comrades.[36] The radical political climate of the interwar years was over and the Cold War had begun.

1 Intercepted letter from Karla Suschitzky to Edith Suschitzky, December 5, 1930, The National Archives, United Kingdom, TNA KV 2/1012.

2 Harriet Anderson, *Utopian Feminism: Women's Movements in fin-de-siècle Vienna* (New Haven and London, 1992), p. 17.

3 Eve Blau, *The Architecture of Red Vienna, 1919–1934* (Cambridge, MA, and London, 1999), p. 2.

4 Walter Benjamin, "Theses on the Philosophy of History," in *Illuminations: Essays and Reflections,* ed. Hannah Arendt (London, 1973), p. 258.

5 See http://verlagsgeschichte.murrayhall.com/index.php?option=com_content&view=article&id=141&Itemid=78 (accessed January 23, 2013).

6 "Jahres-Bericht des Allgemeinen Österreichisher Frauenvereines," no. 3 (Vienna, 1895), p. 7.

7 Rosa Mayreder, letter to Auguste Fickert, February 8, 1896, Vienna City Library, Manuscript Collection, HIN 70890/4. Quoted in Harriet Anderson, *Utopian Feminism: Women's Movements in fin-de-siècle Vienna* (New Haven and London, 1992), p. 16.

8 See Harriet Anderson, *Utopian Feminism: Women's Movements in fin-de-siècle Vienna* (New Haven and London, 1992), p. 249, and Elizabeth Ann Danto, *Freud's Free Clinics: Psychoanalysis and Social Justice, 1918–1938* (New York, 2005). Later, in London, Suschitzky sought psychoanalytic support for her son from Anna Freud, and her archive includes negatives of the British psychoanalyst Donald Winnicott.

9 See various reports dated October 31, 1930, August 31, 1935, April 24, 1942, and August 1, 1944, TNA K V2/1012.

10 Intercepted letter from Wilhelm Suschitzky to Edith Suschitzky, November 28, 1930, TNA KV 2/1012.

11 Report dated October 31, 1930, TNA KV 2/1012.

12 Report dated August 16, 1935, TNA KV 2/1012.

13 Intercepted letter from Edith Suschitzky to Alexander Tudor-Hart, June 22, 1931, TNA KV 2/1012.

14 Intercepted letter from Edith Suschitzky to Alexander Tudor-Hart, February 4, 1931, TNA KV 2/1012.

15 See the report dated April 3, 1942, TNA KV 2/1013. Sergei Ingulov was the TASS representative in London in 1930.

16 Intercepted letter from Edith Suschitzky to Alexander Tudor-Hart, undated (probably March 1931), TNA KV 2/1012.

17 Intercepted letter from Edith Suschitzky to Alexander Tudor-Hart, February 27, 1931, TNA KV 2/1012. Later Tudor-Hart had a nervous breakdown. See Wolfgang Suschitzky, *Edith Tudor Hart: The Eye of Conscience* (London, 1987), p. 17.

18 Summary of intercepted letter from Edith Suschitzky to Alexander Tudor-Hart, undated (probably 1931), TNA KV 2/1012.

19 Edith Suschitzky, "Was will der neue Kindergarten?" *Der Kuckuck,* September 27, 1931, p. 10.

20 Edith Tudor-Hart, "Photography as a Profession," *Miniature Camera Magazine,* date unknown [probably 1936].

21 Jan Zita Grover, "Framing the Questions: Positive Imaging and Scarcity in Lesbian Photographs," in *Stolen Glances: Lesbians Take Photographs,* ed. Tessa Boffin and Jean Fraser (London, 1991), p. 184.

22 *The Brown Book of the Hitler Terror and the Burning of the Reichstag,* prepared by the World Committee for the Victims of German Fascisim (London, 1933).

23 It also enabled her to later bring her younger brother and her mother to Britain (her father committed suicide in 1934). Her cousins, Wilhelm and Josef, also came to London after spending time in Buchenwald and Dachau. She is described as a "specialist in modern photography" in *The News Chronicle,* where she is listed with, amongst others, John Grierson, Cecil Beaton, and Dorothy Wilding as a photography competition judge (scrapbook, n.d.).

24 Margery Spring Rice, *Working-Class Wives: Their Health and Conditions* (Harmondsworth, 1939), front cover and facing p. 96. Edith Tudor-Hart produced seven of the fourteen illustrations.

25 Special Branch Report, February 21, 1934, TNA KV 2/1012.

26 Report dated December 31, 1946, TNA KV 2/1014.

27 Report dated May 3, 1942, TNA KV 2/1013.

28 See Nigel Warburton, *Ernö Goldfinger: The Life of an Architect* (London, 2004).

29 "Dancing at School," *Amateur Photographer* (June 27, 1956), pp. 612–14.

30 Maria Montessori quoted in Sheila Radice, *The New Children: Talks with Dr. Maria Montessori* (London, 1920), p. 118.

31 Andrea Amort, "Free Dance in Interwar Vienna," in *Interwar Vienna: Culture between Tradition and Modernity,* ed. Deborah Holmes and Lisa Silverman (Rochester, 2009), pp. 117–42.

32 Edith Tudor-Hart, "Photography as a Profession," *Miniature Camera Magazine,* date unknown [probably 1936].

33 Dora Russell, *The Right to Be Happy* (London, 1927), pp. 31–32.

34 Report dated October 2, 1951, TNA KV 2/1014.

35 Conversation with Wolf Suschitzky, February 4, 2013.

36 According to an unnamed source, these included Paul Robeson, Kim Philby, and the Marxist barrister, D. N. Pritt, October 3, 1951, TNA KV 2/1014. Negatives of Robeson are still to be found in Tudor-Hart's archive.

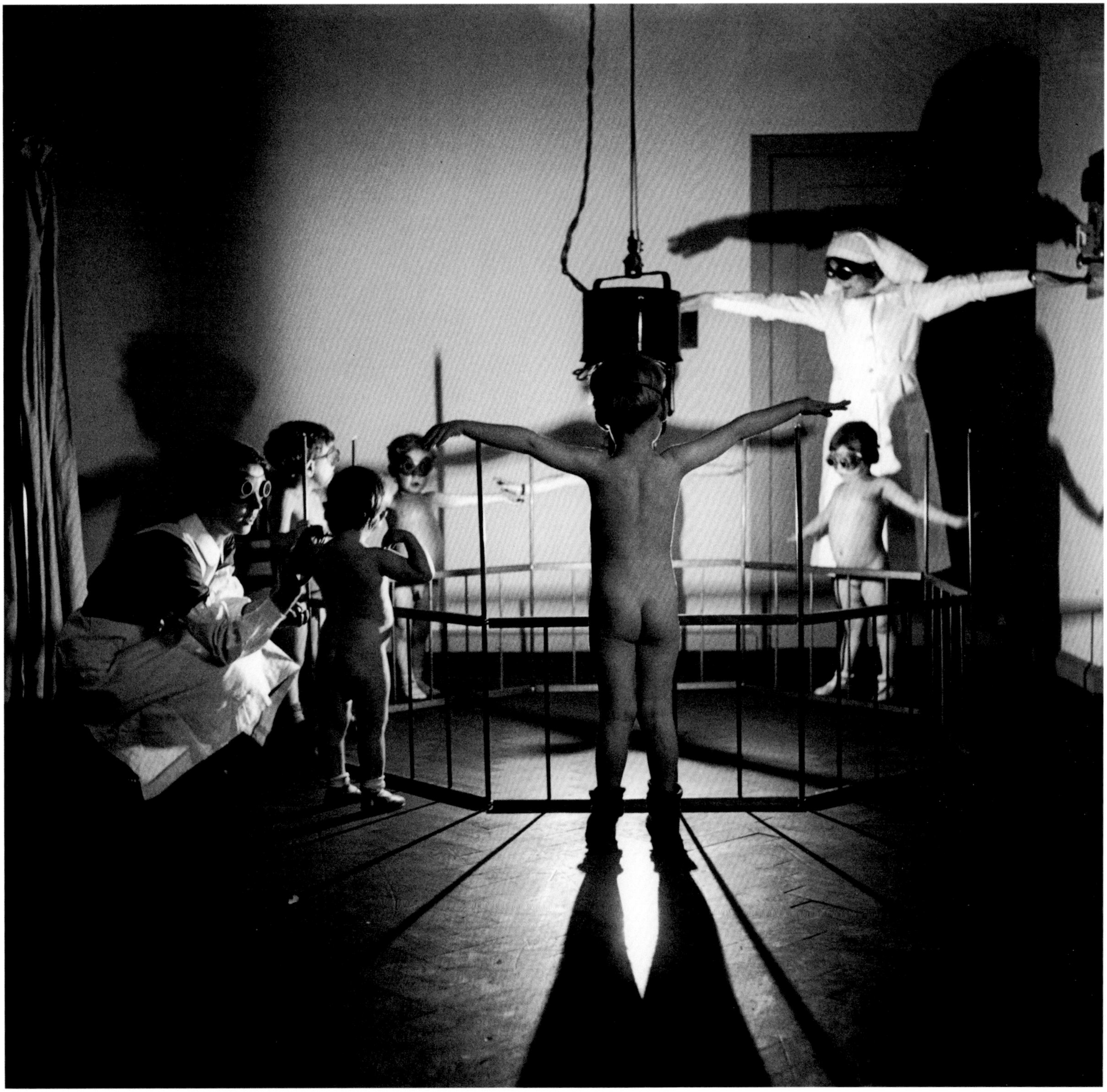

Edith Tudor-Hart
Ultraviolet Light Treatment, South London
Hospital for Women and Children, ca. 1934
Modern silver-gelatin print, 30.3 × 30 cm
National Galleries of Scotland, PGP 279.67

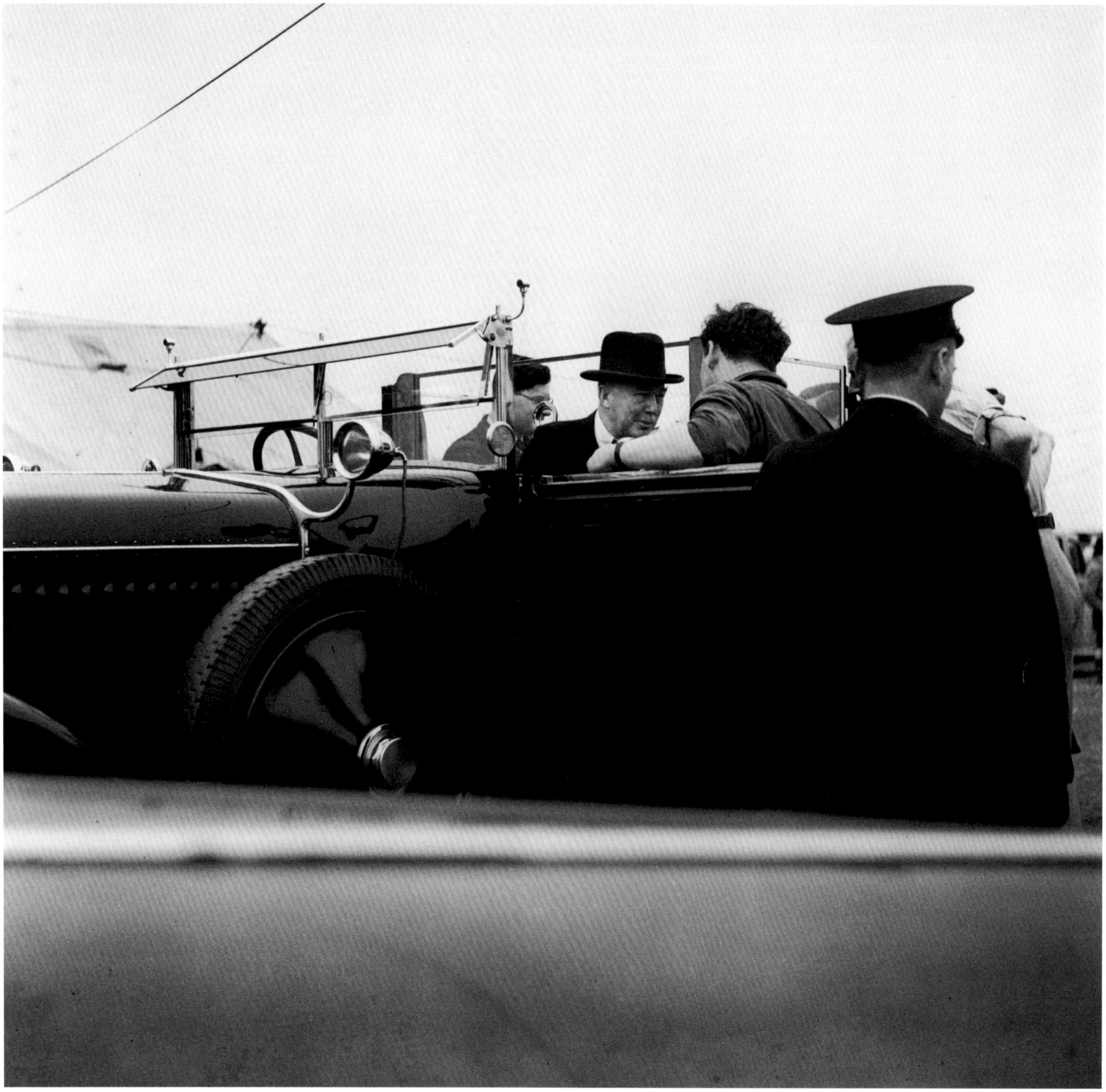

Edith Tudor-Hart
The Duke of Atholl Visiting the Basque Refugee Camp,
North Stoneham, Hampshire, 1937
Modern silver-gelatin print, 30.2 × 29.8 cm
National Galleries of Scotland, PGP 279.34

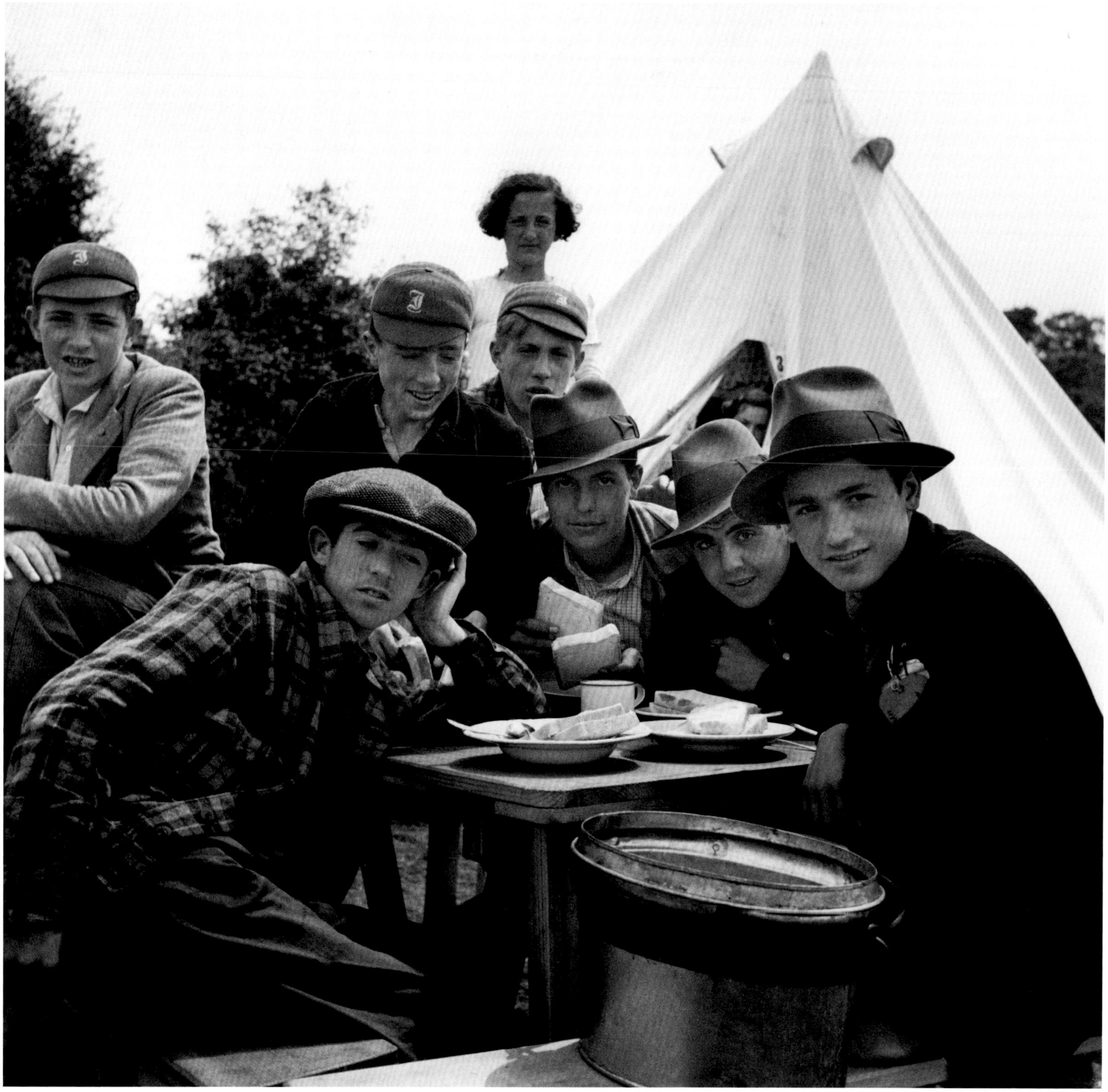

Edith Tudor-Hart
Basque and English School Boys,
North Stoneham Camp, Hampshire, 1937
Modern silver-gelatin print, 30.1 × 30 cm
National Galleries of Scotland, PGP 279.36

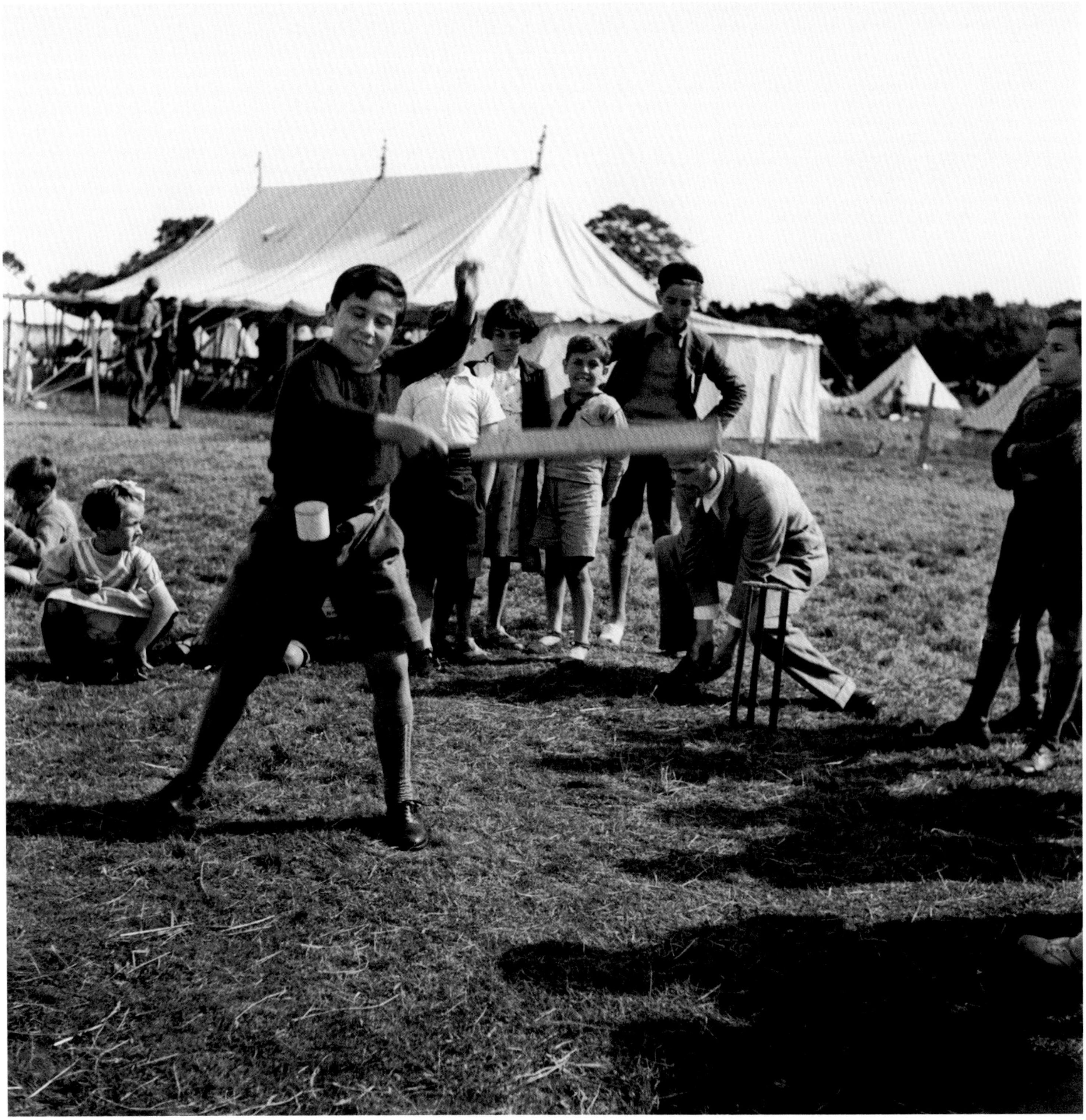

Edith Tudor-Hart
Basque Boy Playing Cricket, North Stoneham Camp, Hampshire, 1937
Modern silver-gelatin print, 30.2 × 30.1 cm
National Galleries of Scotland, PGP 279.35

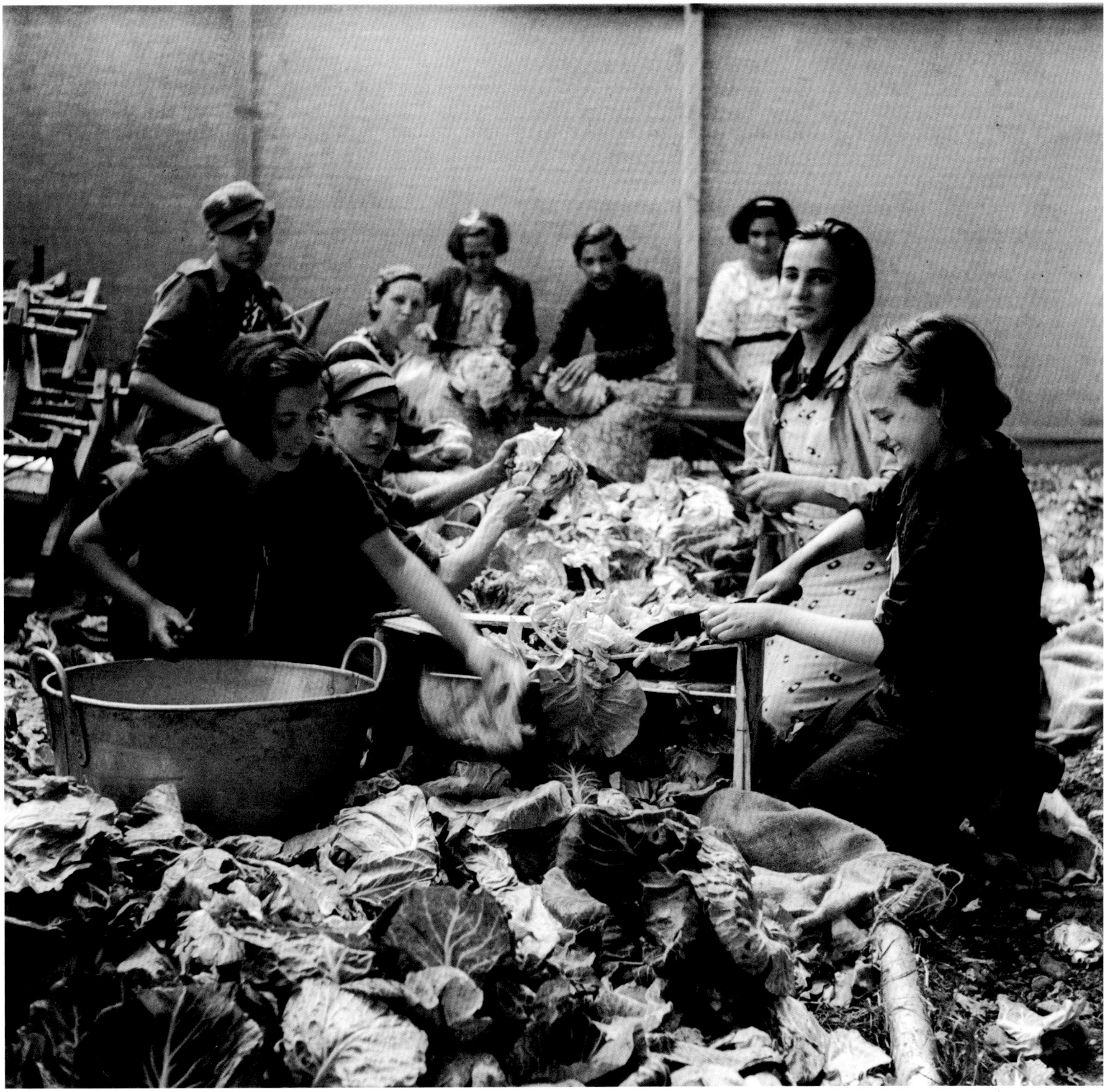

Edith Tudor-Hart
Children Preparing Vegetables, North Stoneham Camp, Hampshire, 1937
Modern silver-gelatin print, 30.2 × 29.8 cm
National Galleries of Scotland, PGP 279.38

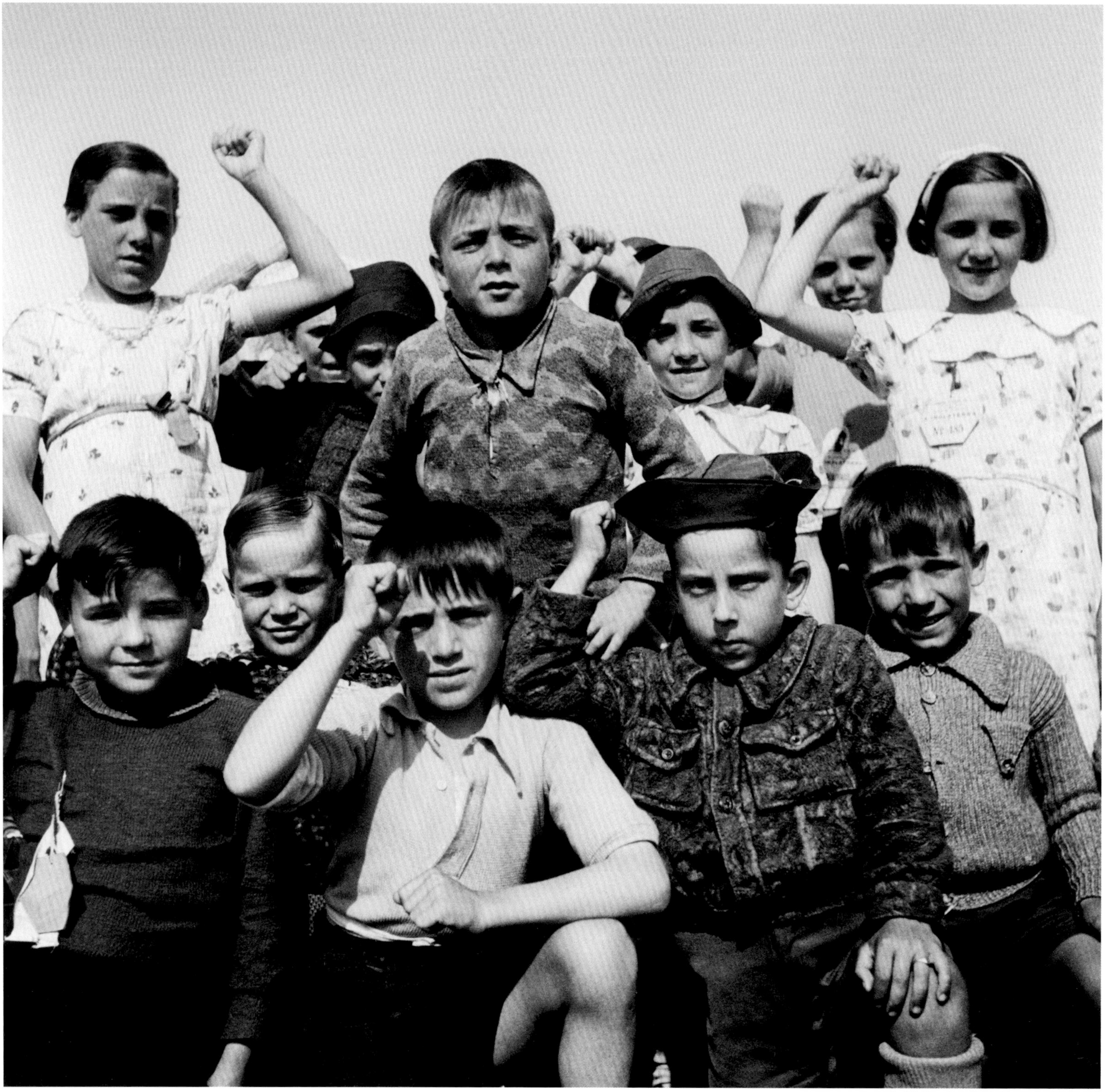

Edith Tudor-Hart
Basque Refugee Children, North Stoneham Camp, Hampshire, 1937
Digital inkjet print, 30.2 × 30 cm
National Galleries of Scotland, PGP 279.39

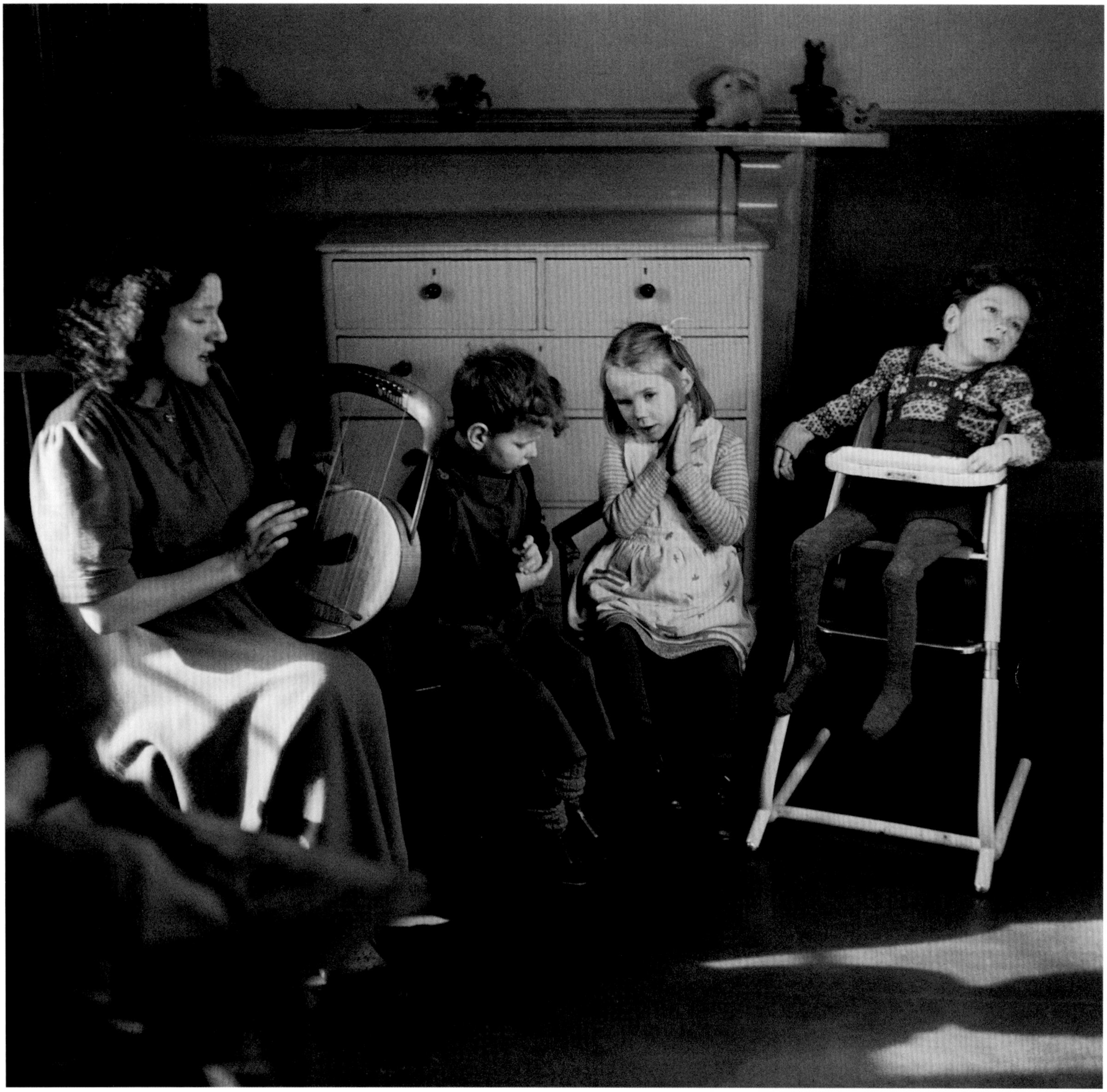

Edith Tudor-Hart
Music Lesson, Camphill School, Bieldside, Aberdeen, 1949
Modern silver-gelatin print, 30.2 × 30 cm
National Galleries of Scotland, PGP 279.44

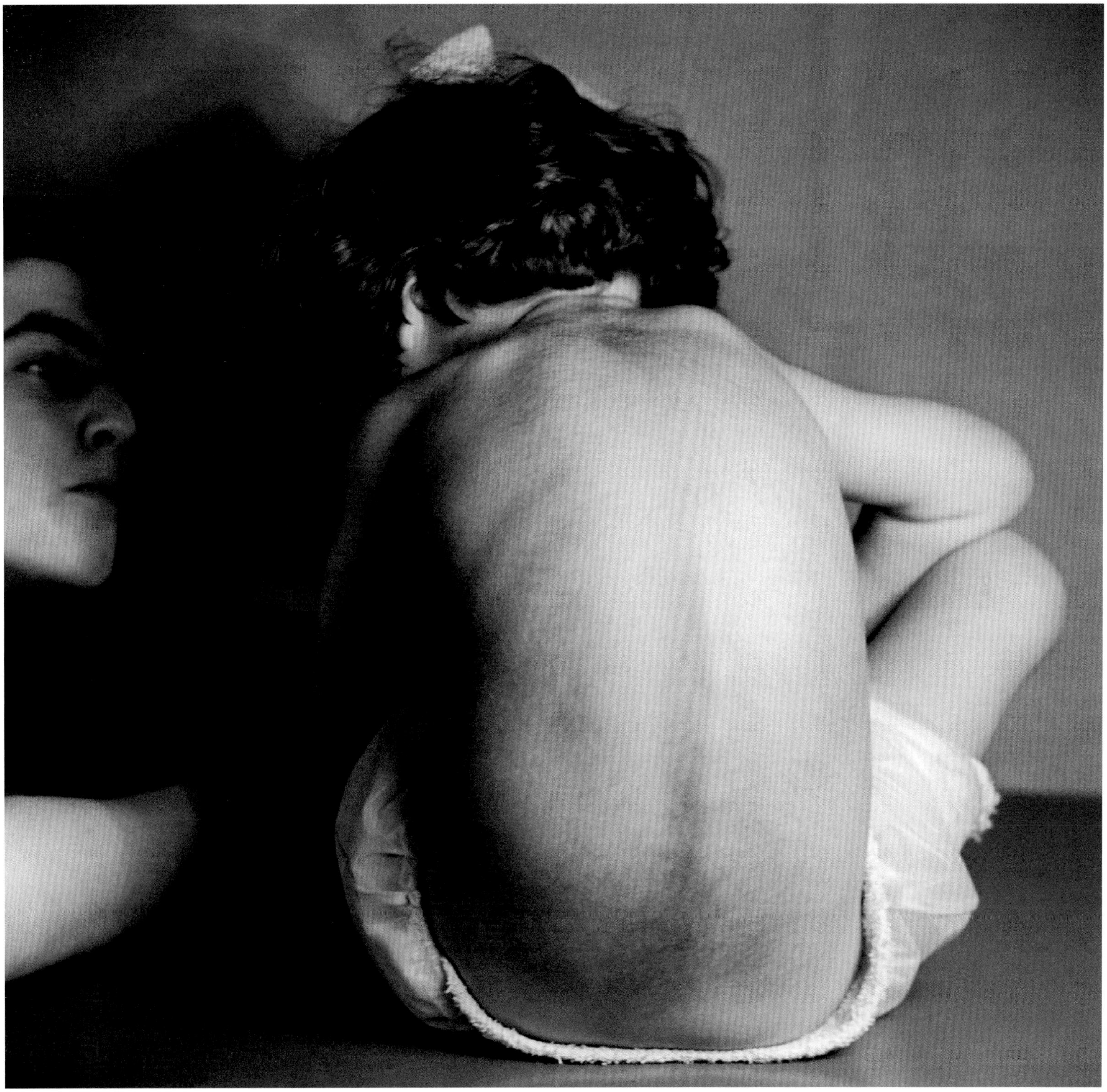

Edith Tudor-Hart
Woman and Child, Camphill School, Bieldside, Aberdeen, 1949
Modern silver-gelatin print, 30.2 × 30 cm
National Galleries of Scotland, PGP 279.43

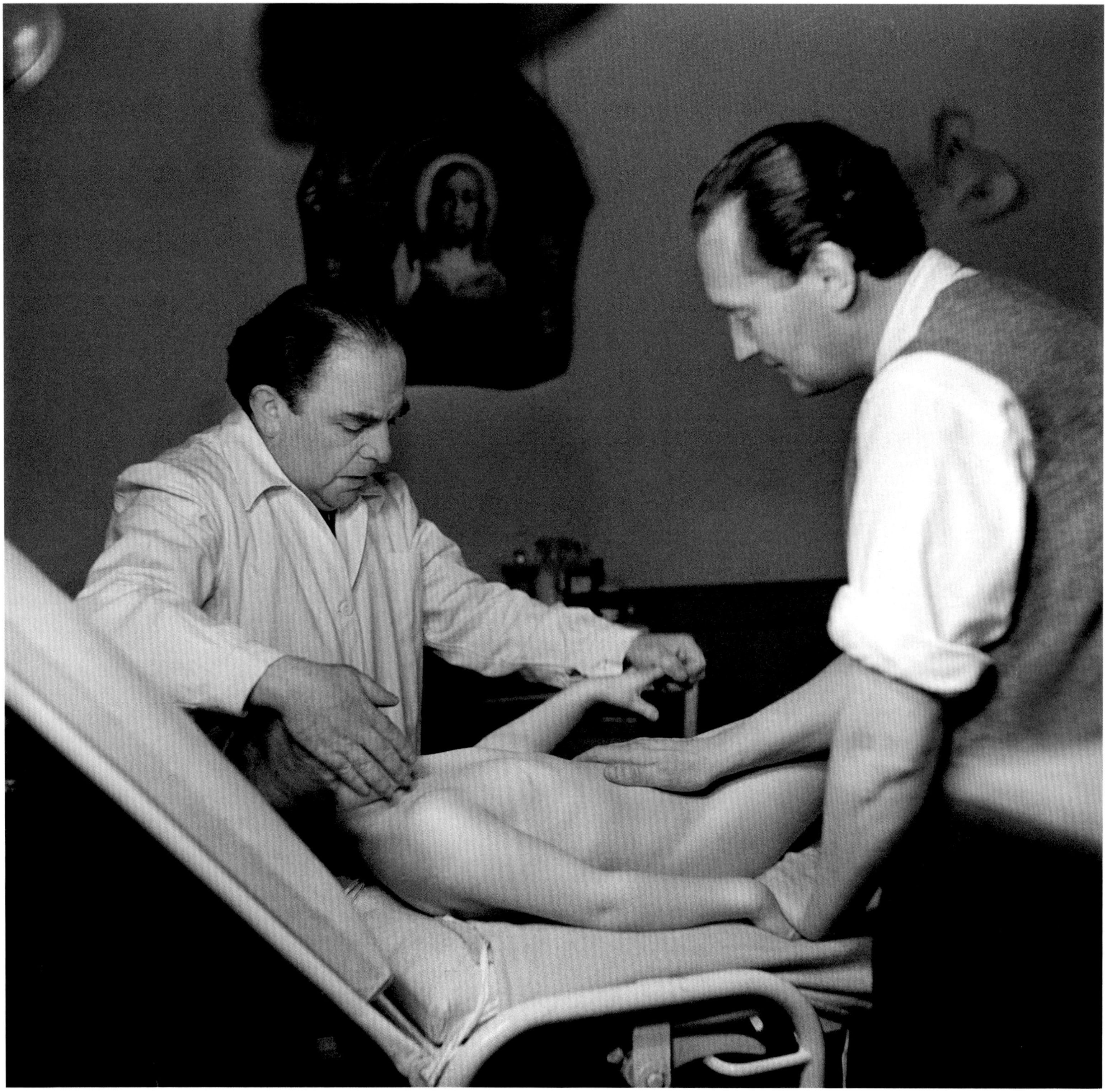

Edith Tudor-Hart
Karl König and Unknown Man, Camphill School, Bieldside, Aberdeen, 1949
Digital inkjet print, 29.9 × 30 cm
National Galleries of Scotland, PGP 279.79

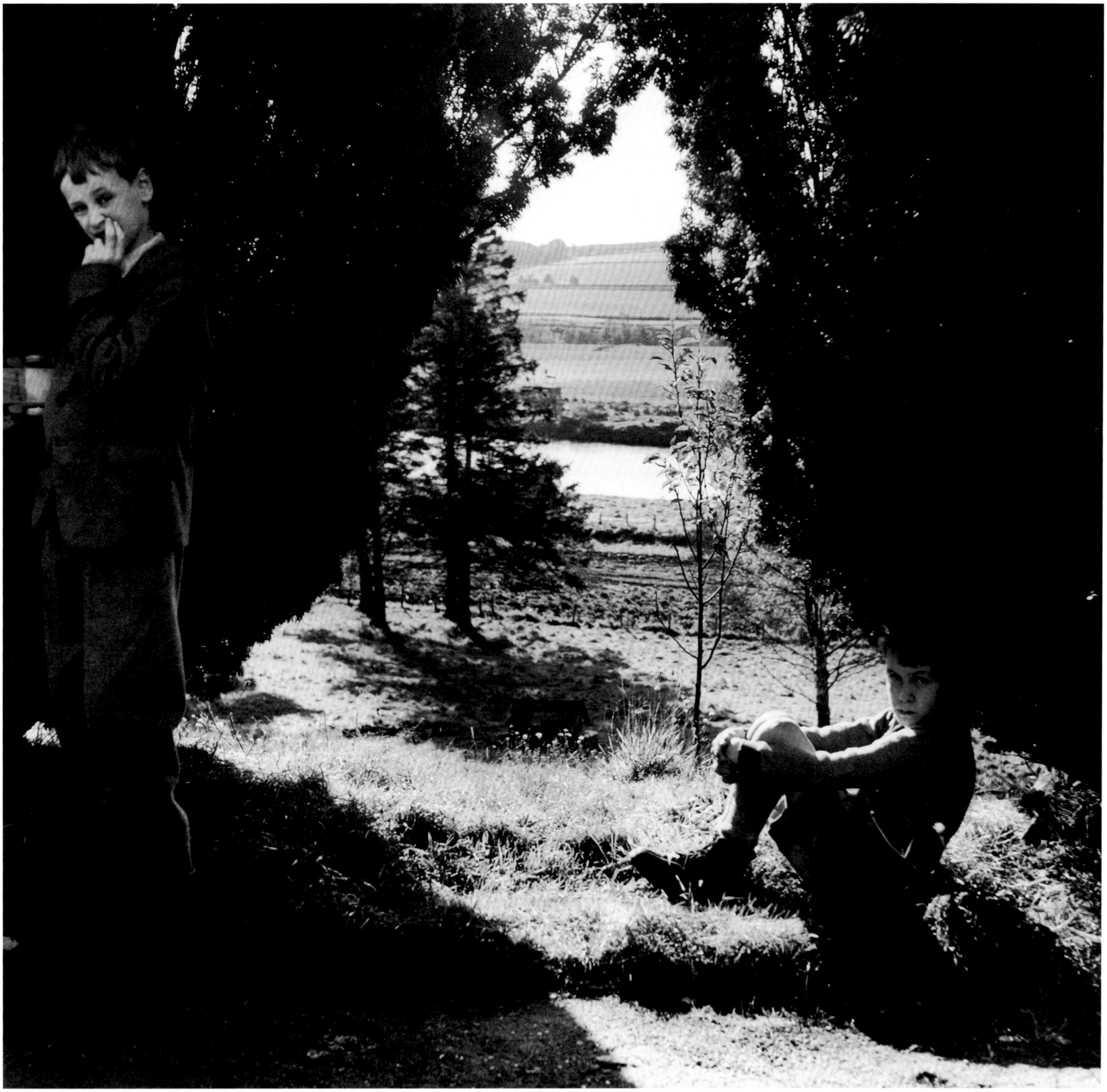

Edith Tudor-Hart
Two Boys, Camphill School, Bieldside, Aberdeen, 1949
Modern silver-gelatin print, 30.2 × 30 cm
National Galleries of Scotland, PGP 279.41

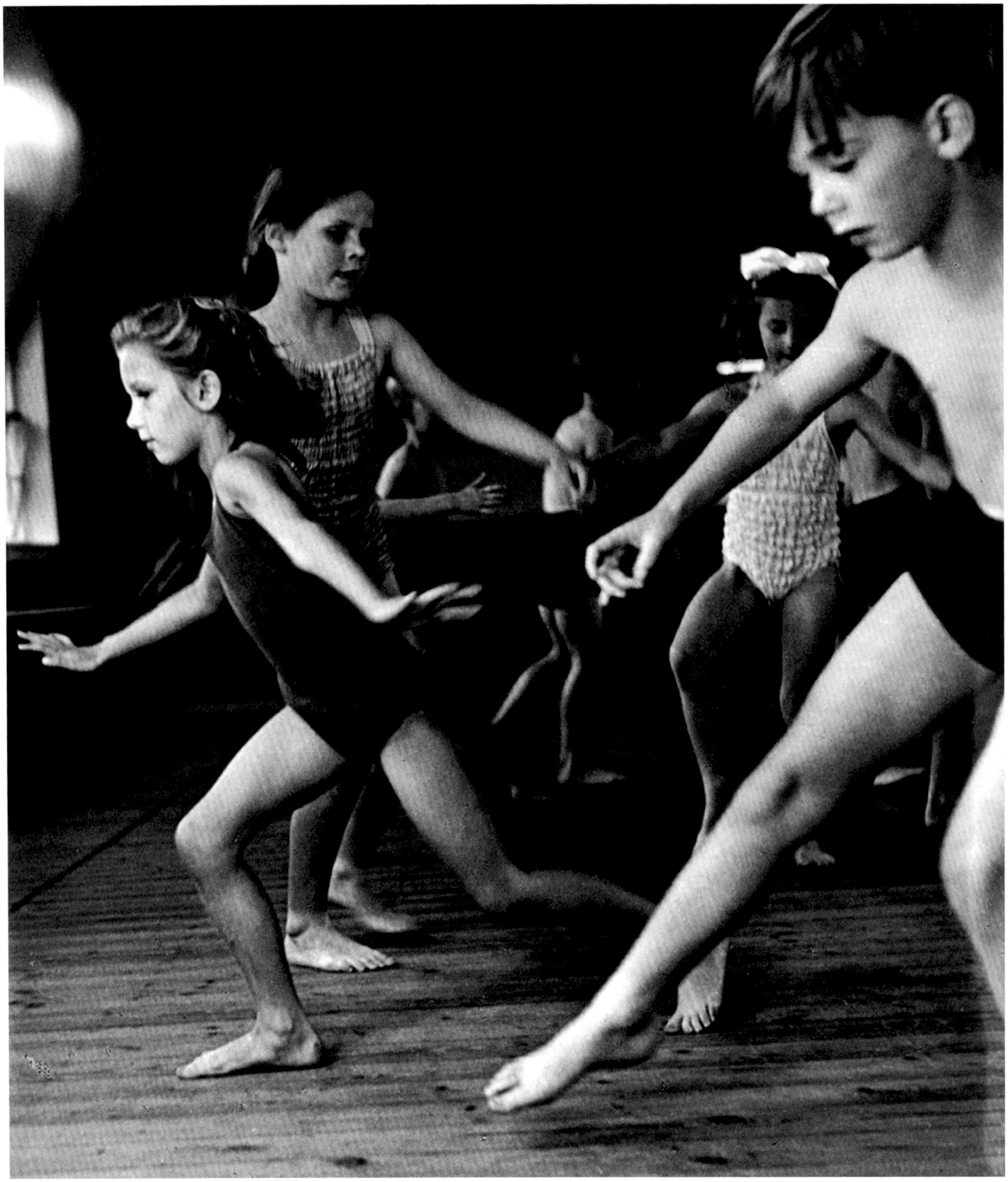

Edith Tudor-Hart
From the Series *Moving and Growing,* 1951
Silver-gelatin print, 28 × 23 cm
Wolfgang Suschitzky

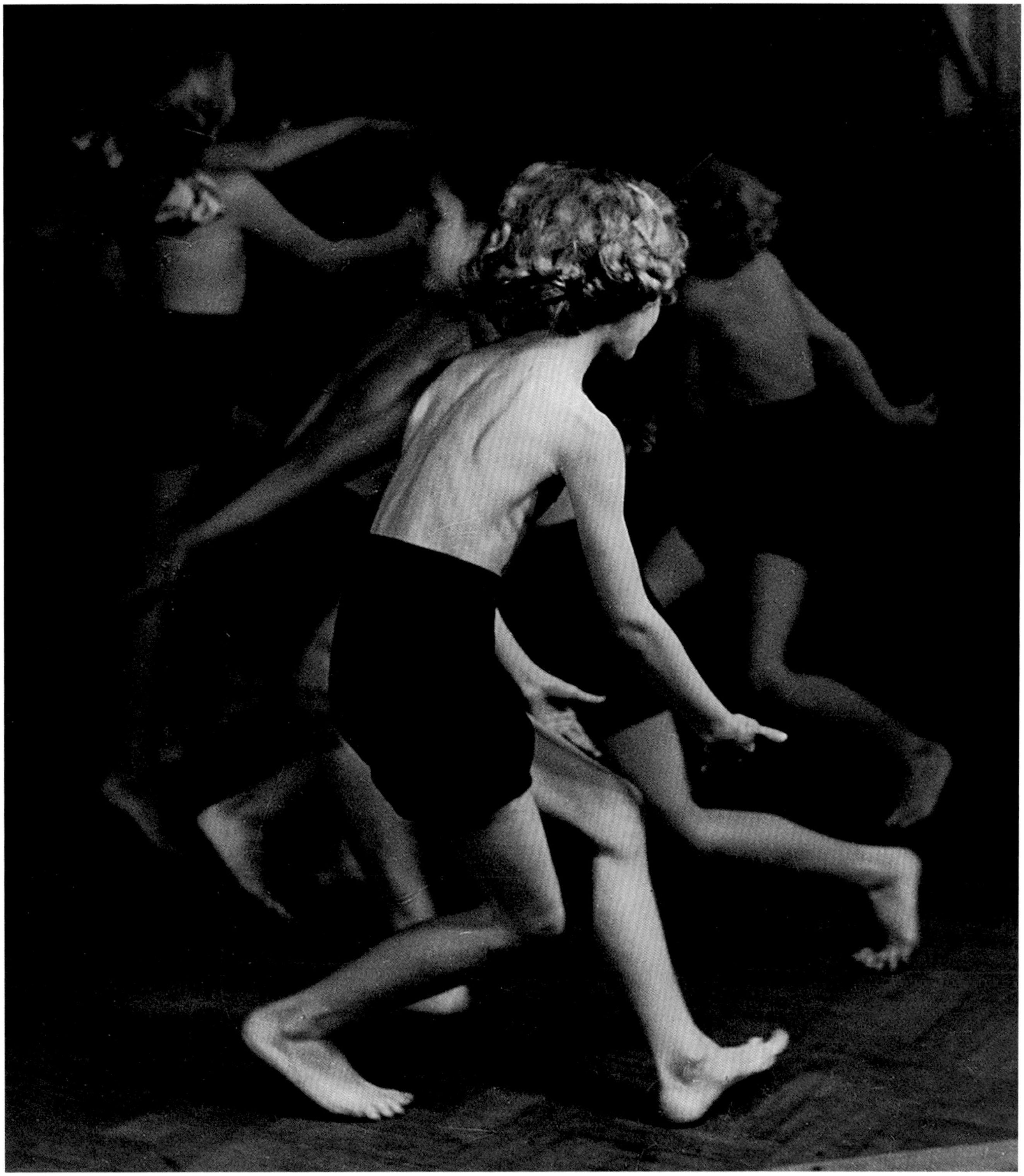

Edith Tudor-Hart
From the Series *Moving and Growing,* 1951
Silver-gelatin print, 23.8 × 20 cm
Wolfgang Suschitzky

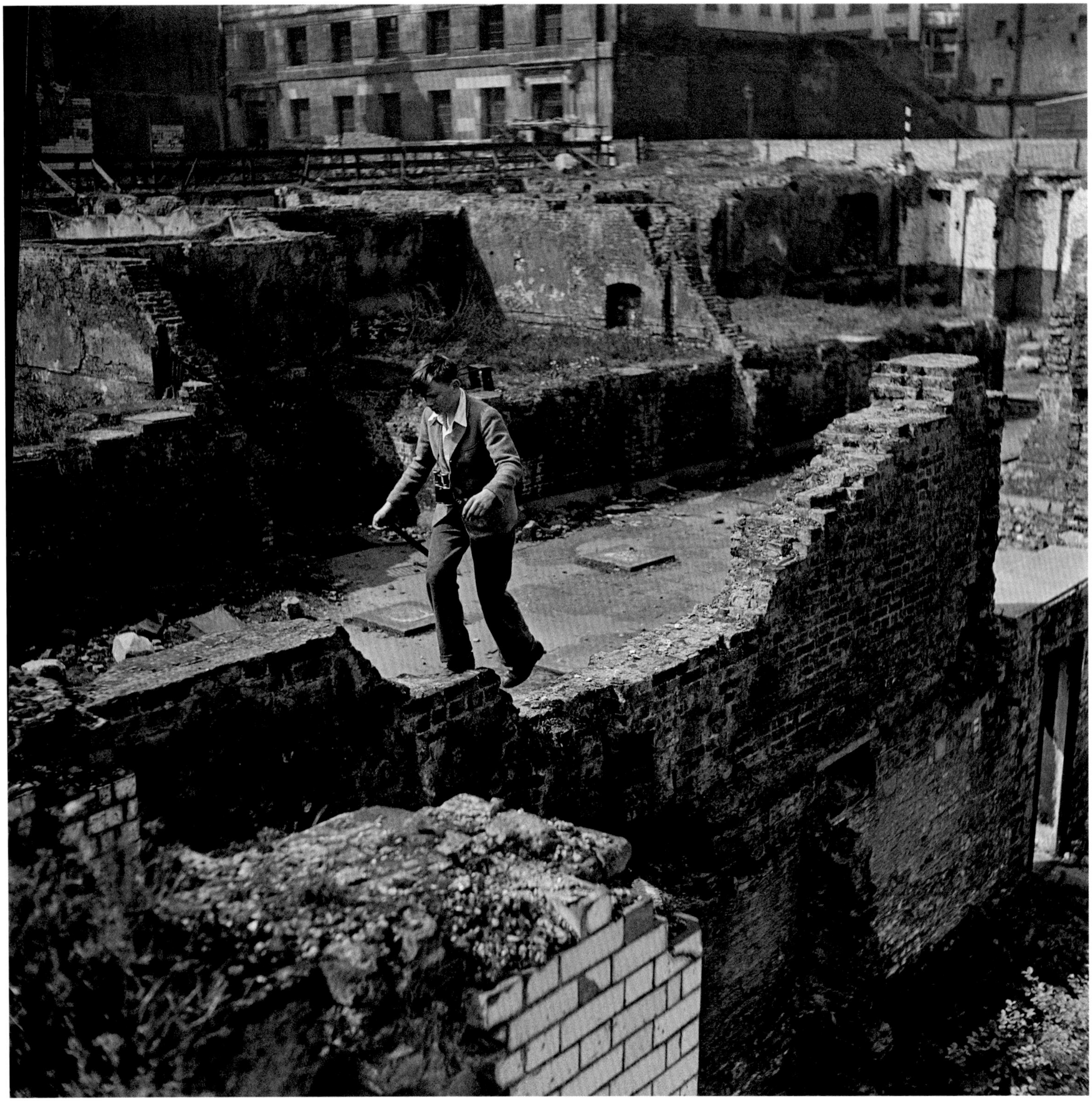

Edith Tudor-Hart
Child Running Across Ruins, Moorgate, London, 1946
Digital inkjet print, 30.2 × 30 cm
National Galleries of Scotland, PGP 279.80

Afterlife

Duncan Forbes

In comparison with film, the political image appeared only fleetingly in British photography during the nineteen-thirties; it would be closed down decisively during the Cold War. A conciliatory liberal humanism diffused the radical engagements of the thirties, and the dialectical image was washed away by the commercial expansion of amateur practice. Rather than vanishing altogether, social realism in photography became subjectified and mythologized within the frame of a formalist aesthetics—in Britain the career of the exile photographer Bill Brandt is paradigmatic. Already in 1948, something of the tenor of Cold War compromise was captured by Wolfgang Suschitzky in an essay he wrote describing his burgeoning career as a documentary filmmaker:

> The photodocument is the reflection of the contemporary scene and represents in its best form subtle photographic comment on social conditions rather than direct social propaganda. The human element dominates, and a photographer who has sympathy with social conditions and has been brought into contact with human suffering has in the photodocument a significant interest for expressing his feelings, and usually takes sides.[61]

There is ambivalence here to be sure, but it is also clear that for documentary a more subjective regime of surface appearances is being asserted.

It was only after her death that Edith Tudor-Hart's photography began to receive critical attention, and it is possible, albeit schematically, to identify three different waves of interest. Robert Radford first "rediscovered" Tudor-Hart in 1973 during research for a thesis on the Artists' International Association (AIA), which subsequently developed into an exhibition in collaboration with Lynda Morris in 1983 and then a full-length book.[62] Working within the context of art history, both Radford and Morris were nonetheless sensitive to the dialogic force of Tudor-Hart's photography, although today their celebration of the AIA appears very unreflective about the politics of the Popular Front. Radford's research was noticed by Shirley Read from the editorial collective at *Camerawork* magazine in London, who began to make contact sheets from Tudor-Hart's archive at the Half Moon Photography Workshop (fig. 40).[63] Read's project never reached exhibition, but in the context of the agitprop politics of the late nineteen-seventies, Tudor-Hart's photography was utilized as a resource for the present, particularly by those involved in the seminal work of history and theory, *Photography/Politics: One,* published in 1979.[64]

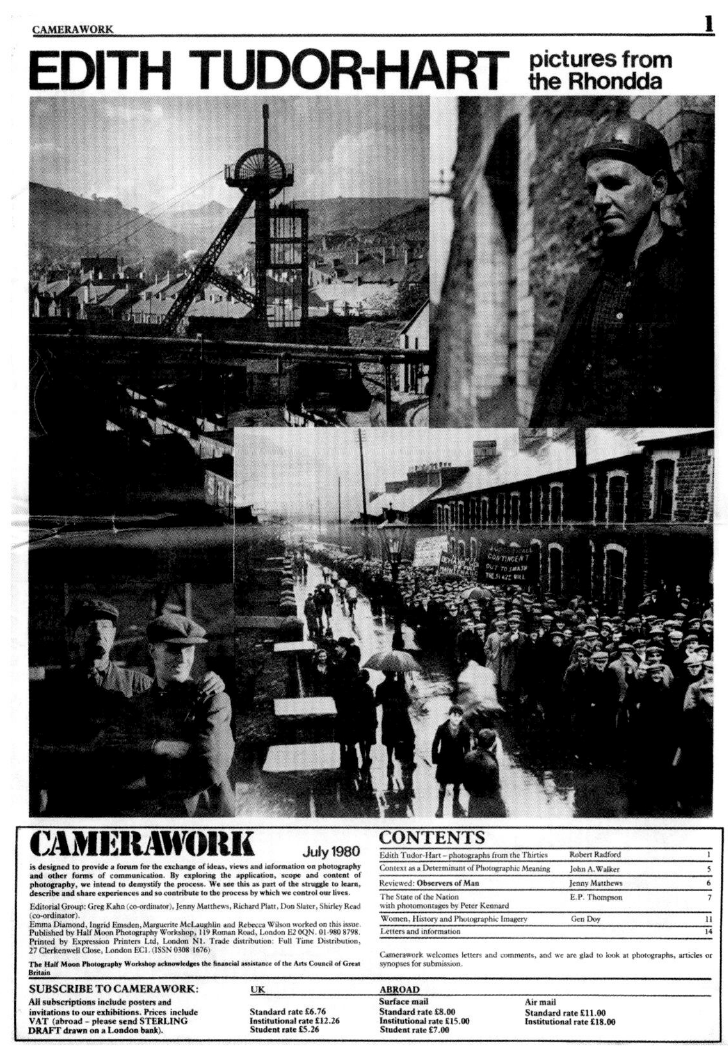

CAMERAWORK 1

EDITH TUDOR-HART pictures from the Rhondda

CAMERAWORK July 1980

is designed to provide a forum for the exchange of ideas, views and information on photography and other forms of communication. By exploring the application, scope and content of photography, we intend to demystify the process. We see this as part of the struggle to learn, describe and share experiences and so contribute to the process by which we control our lives.

Editorial Group: Greg Kahn (co-ordinator), Jenny Matthews, Richard Platt, Don Slater, Shirley Read (co-ordinator).
Emma Diamond, Ingrid Emsden, Marguerite McLaughlin and Rebecca Wilson worked on this issue.
Published by Half Moon Photography Workshop, 119 Roman Road, London E2 0QN. 01-980 8798.
Printed by Expression Printers Ltd, London N1. Trade distribution: Full Time Distribution, 27 Clerkenwell Close, London EC1. (ISSN 0308 1676)

The Half Moon Photography Workshop acknowledges the financial assistance of the Arts Council of Great Britain

CONTENTS

Edith Tudor-Hart – photographs from the Thirties	Robert Radford	1
Context as a Determinant of Photographic Meaning	John A. Walker	5
Reviewed: **Observers of Man**	Jenny Matthews	6
The State of the Nation with photomontages by Peter Kennard	E.P. Thompson	7
Women, History and Photographic Imagery	Gen Doy	11
Letters and information		14

Camerawork welcomes letters and comments, and we are glad to look at photographs, articles or synopses for submission.

SUBSCRIBE TO CAMERAWORK:

All subscriptions include posters and invitations to our exhibitions. Prices include VAT (abroad – please send STERLING DRAFT drawn on a London bank).

UK
Standard rate £6.76
Institutional rate £12.26
Student rate £5.26

ABROAD
Surface mail
Standard rate £8.00
Institutional rate £15.00
Student rate £7.00

Air mail
Standard rate £11.00
Institutional rate £18.00

Fig. 40
Inside pages of *Camerawork,* July 1980

The second wave of interest in Edith Tudor-Hart's photography during the eighties was much more evidently nostalgic. In a series of mainly survey exhibitions, her images were presented as evidence of authentic class experience in which the clichés of working-class iconography were asserted and largely removed from the critique of photographic naturalism that had begun to surface in Britain during the seventies (fig. 41).[65] With the advantage of hindsight, these displays might be considered an assertion of an embattled class identity at precisely the moment of a decisive attack on the British working class during the miners' strike of 1984. But they did serve to entrench Tudor-Hart's photography within a tradition of British documentary in which the voyeuristic treatment of the surface of class relations dominated over any more sophisticated formulation of the politics of class and representation. This served only to obscure vital aspects of her practice.

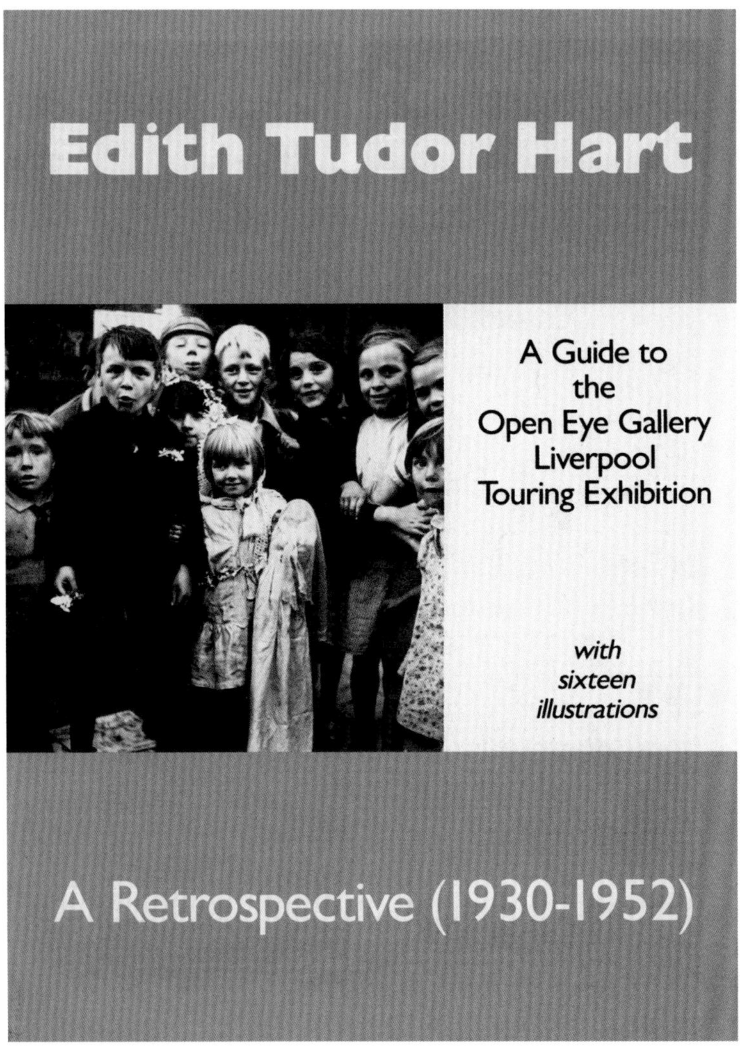

Fig. 41
Front cover of *Edith Tudor Hart: A Retrospective (1930–1952)* (Liverpool, 1987)

Consequently, throughout the nineteen-eighties, Tudor-Hart's photography was presented less as a critical resource and more as a source of empathy and identification. Most significant here was Dirk Nishen's book produced in collaboration with Wolfgang Suschitzky in 1987, the only published volume on Edith Tudor-Hart's photography. Titled *The Eye of Conscience* (a distraction, surely, from its protagonist's politics?), the book made a strong case for Tudor-Hart as a documentary photographer (fig. 42).[66] However, at the same time, it tended to reduce the complexity of her practice in favor of the reader's idealized identification with the figure of the worker. Trained at the more conservative Graphische Lehr- und Versuchsanstalt (Institute for Teaching and Research in the Graphic Arts) in Vienna, and working as a photographer and cameraman in the British documentary movement, Wolfgang Suschitzky presented his sister's photography in a way that (so to speak) Paul Rotha would have approved. Any trace of the active structuring of politics, let alone Bolshevik politics, into the work of representation is reduced here to the poetic elevation of the everyday, embodied by the aesthetically satisfying photograph.

The third context of reception is that of Val Williams's restoration of women photographers to the British photographic canon published as *The Other Observers* in 1986.[67] By now Tudor-Hart's photography was reaching a wider audience, and prints, often produced by her brother, began to find their way into both public and private collections. This activity eventually made an impact in Vienna, where both Wolfgang Suschitzky and Edith Tudor-Hart were included in the exhibition *Übersee* held at the Kunsthalle in 1998, the first acknowledgment of the sheer scale of the flight of Austrian photographers, many of Jewish origin, during the interwar period.[68] There is more to say about both of these projects, but, whatever their evident qualities, they developed a no more thoroughly conceptualized understanding of the problems of class and representation than other curators and writers during the nineteen-eighties. Once again, Tudor-Hart's photography was subsumed into a tradition of photographic naturalism, and she was presented as one of its more colorful exponents.

This is a necessarily schematic summary: the complexities of each different reception context make unitary readings unlikely. However, generally, the British reception has sought to sideline Tudor-Hart's Viennese origins, ignoring her extraordinary formative influences in the fields of photography, pedagogy, and politics. It has sought, too, to obscure the transitions in her practice, above all the transformation wrought by the experience of exile, including competing Germanic and British conceptions of "documentary." These might be characterized as the difference between realism and nat-

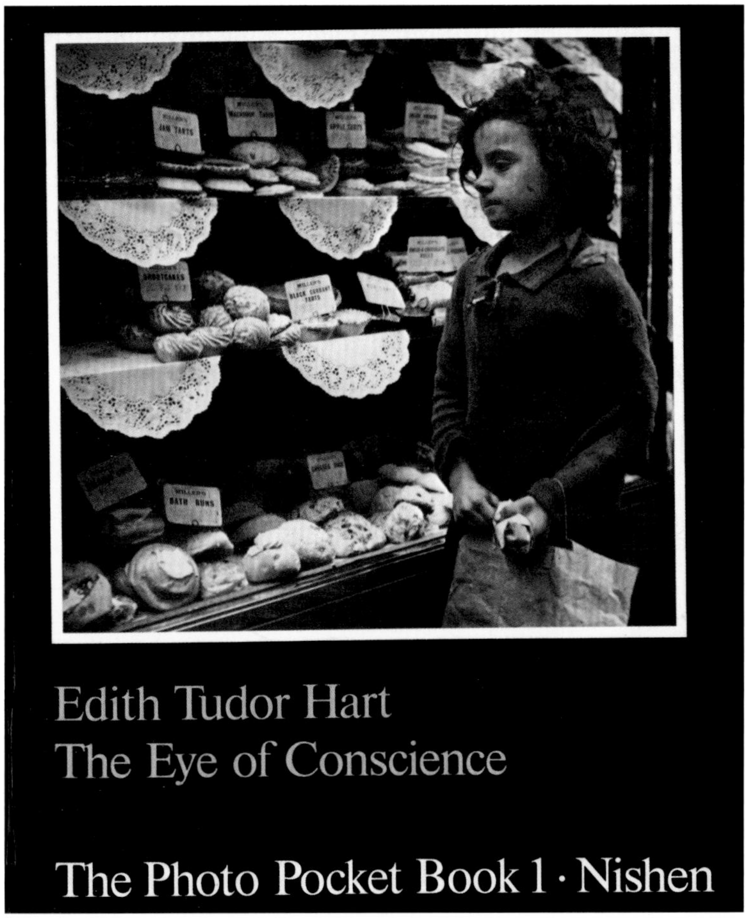

Fig. 42
Front cover of *Edith Tudor-Hart: The Eye of Conscience* by Wolfgang Suschitzky (London, 1987)

uralism, although, as this catalogue reveals, both terms are absurdly abstract when confronted with the contingencies of her practice. Finally, the historical context of Tudor-Hart's photography has been downplayed, a history marked by her complex experience of revolutionary politics, anti-fascist struggle, and fascist and Stalinist counterrevolution. Bearing in mind the sheer scale of these lacunae, it is scarcely surprising that no adequate conceptualization of her photography could be developed. This may reflect a very British intellectual parochialism, but there is also something else at work here: a reaching into the past for images of continuity at a moment of disorientating social change, a grasping for representations of collectivity and working-class identification at the very moment, from the late seventies, that these historic identities came under assault. In short, the reception of Edith Tudor-Hart's photography has become entangled in a dehistoricizing nostalgia.[69]

We are now in a better position to confront that nostalgia, not least since the full international context of the worker photography movement, including Tudor-Hart, has recently been opened up brilliantly to public scrutiny in the Reina Sofia's survey exhibition of 2011, *A Hard, Merciless Light.*[70] It is exciting, too, that this catalogue accompanies the first substantial showing of Tudor-Hart's photography in Vienna, an event that will doubtless generate new insights. There is more research to do on her negative archive, not least exploring her practice as a portrait photographer. And British photography historians need urgently to reconsider the impact of German- and Hungarian-speaking exile photographers, many of them of Jewish origin; arguably, their legacy constitutes the best of twentieth-century British photography. Finally, Tudor-Hart's practice, in both its flashes of success and tragic failure, has much to offer those today keen to investigate the history of the political image. In short, her photography promises to illuminate our own present-day contact with the past, or what—to put it more hopefully—we might describe as the past's utopian transformation of our future. Through half a century of evasion, the remnants of Edith Tudor-Hart's archive survive to remind us, in compromised and fragile form, what is at stake.

Notes continued from page 74.

61 Helmut Gernsheim, ed., *The Man Behind the Camera* (London, 1948), p. 136.
62 Lynda Morris and Robert Radford, *The Story of the Artists' International Association, 1933–1953* (Oxford, 1983) and Robert Radford, *Art for a Purpose: The Artists' International Association, 1933–1953* (Winchester, 1987).
63 See *Camerawork* (July 1980) and especially Robert Radford's article "Edith Tudor-Hart Working in the 30s," p. 4. David Mellor also mentioned Tudor-Hart in a 1980 essay, "British Art in the 1930s: Some Economic, Political and Cultural Structures," in *Class, Culture and Social Change: A New View of the 1930s,* ed. Frank Gloversmith (Sussex, 1980), p. 199.
64 Terry Dennett and Jo Spence, eds., *Photography/Politics: One* (London, 1979).
65 See *The British Worker: Photographs of Working Life 1839–1939,* curated by Colin Osman for the Arts Council of Great Britain (1981), *Valley Visitors,* Ffotogallery in Cardiff (1983), *The Miners' World: Miners in Photography and Literature,* curated by Douglas Gray (1985), and *Edith Tudor Hart: A Retrospective (1930–1952),* Open Eye Gallery, Liverpool (1987).
66 Wolfgang Suschitzky, *Edith Tudor Hart: The Eye of Conscience* (London, 1987).
67 Val Williams, *The Other Observers: Women Photographers in Britain 1900 to the Present* (London, 1986).
68 See Anna Auer, ed., *Übersee: Flucht und Emigration österreichischer Fotografen 1920–1940* (Vienna, 1997). The exhibition was curated by Johannes Faber and ran from January 16 to March 15, 1998.
69 Fredric Jameson is the most sophisticated theorist of this tendency. See his "Postmodernism, or the Cultural Logic of Late Capitalism," *New Left Review* 146 (July–August 1984), pp. 53–92.
70 *A Hard, Merciless Light: The Worker-Photography Movement, 1926–1939,* Museo Nacional Centro de Arte Reina Sofia, Madrid, April 6 to August 22, 2011. The exhibition was curated by Jorge Ribalta.

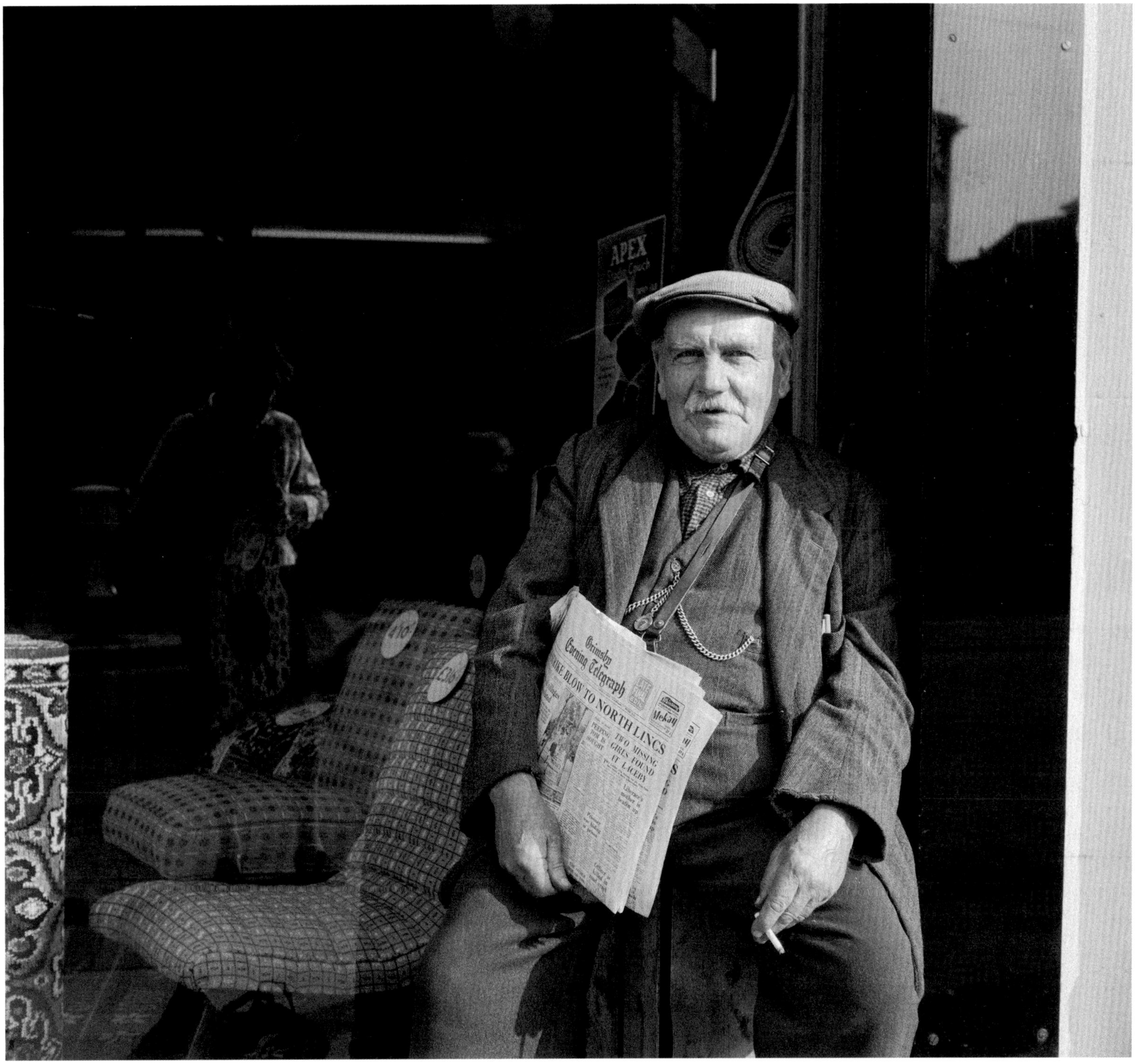

Edith Tudor-Hart
Self-Portrait with Worker, Grimsby, Lincolnshire, ca. 1957
Digital inkjet print, 30.2 × 30 cm
National Galleries of Scotland, PGP 279.82

Acknowledgments and Lenders

Acknowledgments

Heather Anthony, London
Dave Cope, Kendal
Steve Edwards, London
Johannes Faber, Vienna
Monika Faber, Vienna
Joanna Kane, Edinburgh
Owen Logan, Edinburgh
Barry McLoughlin, Vienna
Brigitte Mayr, Vienna
Michael Omasta, Vienna
National Media Museum, Bradford
National Portrait Gallery, London
Open Eye Gallery, Liverpool
Jorge Ribalta, Barcelona
Robert Mapplethorpe Foundation, New York
Wolfgang Suschitzky, London
Jessica Sutcliffe, Swanage

Lenders

Wolfgang Suschitzky, London
Galerie Johannes Faber, Vienna
Filmarchiv Austria, Vienna
Seiter Collection, Vienna
Duncan Forbes, Zurich
Dave Cope, Kendal

Author Biographies

Duncan Forbes

Born 1967 in Paris, lives in Zurich. Forbes studied art history, film history, and history of photography at the University of St. Andrews and Emory University. After earning a doctorate from the University of St. Andrews in 1996, he lectured at the University of Aberdeen before taking up the post of Curator of Photography at the National Galleries of Scotland in 2000. Since 2013 he has served as Director/Curator of the Fotomuseum Winterthur.

Anton Holzer

Born 1964 in San Candido, Italy, lives in Vienna. Holzer studied history, political science, and philosophy in Innsbruck, Bologna, and Vienna. He is a photo historian, author, and exhibition curator. Since 2001 he has been editor of the journal *Fotogeschichte*. He curates exhibitions and edits publications on the history of photography and cultural history.

Roberta McGrath

Born 1956 in Glasgow, lives in Edinburgh. McGrath studied sculpture art at Glasgow School of Art, fine art at Stourbridge College of Art, and social history of art at the University of Leeds. She earned a doctorate from Middlesex University in 2004. She has lectured at Newcastle upon Tyne Polytechnic and the University of Westminster. Currently, she is Reader in photographic history, theory, and criticism at Edinburgh Napier University.

Image Credits

Dave Cope: fig. 17
Helen Muspratt Archive: fig. 18
National Galleries of Scotland: figs. 31, 32
National Media Museum/SSPL: fig. 19
National Portrait Gallery, London: fig. 28
Open Eye Gallery: fig. 41
Österreichische Nationalbibliothek, Vienna: fig. 5
Private collections: figs. 2, 20, 21, 22, 23, 24, 25, 26, 27, 29, 30, 36, 37, 40
Wienbibliothek im Rathaus: figs. 4, 6, 7, 8, 9
Wolfgang Suschitzky: figs. 1, 3, 16, 33, 34, 35, 42

This catalogue is published in conjunction with the exhibition

Edith Tudor-Hart:
In the Shadow of Tyranny

National Galleries of Scotland, Edinburgh
March 2—May 26, 2013
Wien Museum, Vienna
September 26, 2013—January 12, 2014
Das Verborgene Museum, Berlin
March 13—June 29, 2014

Edited by Duncan Forbes on behalf of the National Galleries of Scotland, Edinburgh, and Wien Museum, Vienna

Copyediting
Dawn Michelle d'Atri

Translation
Nathaniel McBride (Holzer essay)

Graphic design and typesetting
Naroska, www.naroska.de

Typeface
Frutiger

Reproduction photography, Edinburgh
John McKenzie

Reproductions
Jan Scheffler, prints professional

Production
Maren Katrin Poppe, Hatje Cantz

Paper
Condat matt Périgord, 150 g/m²

Printing and binding
DZA Druckerei zu Altenburg GmbH, Altenburg

Published by
Hatje Cantz Verlag
Zeppelinstrasse 32
73760 Ostfildern
Germany
Tel. +49 711 4405-200
Fax +49 711 4405-220
www.hatjecantz.com
A Ganske Publishing Group company

You can find information on this exhibition and many others at www.kq-daily.de.

Hatje Cantz books are available internationally at selected bookstores. For more information about our distribution partners, please visit our homepage at www.hatjecantz.com.

ISBN 978-3-7757-3567-4 (English)
ISBN 978-3-7757-3566-7 (German)

Printed in Germany

Cover illustrations
Front: Edith Suschitzky, *Unemployed Workers' Demonstration, Vienna,* 1932

Back: Wolfgang Suschitzky, *Edith Tudor-Hart with Her Son Tommy, London,* ca. 1938

NATIONAL GALLERIES SCOTLAND

WIEN MUSEUM